st in the Financial
Services Industry. What Should We Do About Them?

Geneva Reports on the World Economy 5

International Center for Monetary and Banking Studies (ICMB)

International Center for Monetary and Banking Studies
11 A Avenue de la Paix
1202 Geneva
Switzerland

Tel (41 22) 734 9548
Fax (41 22) 733 3853
Website: www.icmb.ch

This edition reprinted by Pearson Education, Inc., by special permission of CEPR.

Centre for Economic Policy Research (CEPR)

Centre for Economic Policy Research
90-98 Goswell Road
London EC1V 7RR
UK

Tel: +44 (0)20 7878 2900
Fax: +44 (0)20 7878 2999
Email: cepr@cepr.org
Website: www.cepr.org

British Library Cataloguing in Publication Data
A catalogue record for this book is available from the British Library

ISBN: 1 898128 79 0

Conflicts of Interest in the Financial Services Industry: What Should We Do About Them?

Geneva Reports on the World Economy 5

Andrew Crockett
Former General Manager, Bank for International Settlements, Basel

Trevor Harris
Morgan Stanley, New York

Frederic S Mishkin
Graduate School of Business, Columbia University, New York

Eugene N White
Rutgers University, New Jersey

ICMB INTERNATIONAL CENTER
FOR MONETARY
AND BANKING STUDIES

CIMB CENTRE INTERNATIONAL
D'ETUDES MONETAIRES
ET BANCAIRES

International Center for Monetary and Banking Studies (ICMB)

The International Center for Monetary and Banking Studies was created in 1973 as an independent, non-profit foundation. It is associated with Geneva's Graduate Institute of International Studies. Its aim is to foster exchange of views between the financial sector, central banks and academics on issues of common interest. It is financed through grants from banks, financial institutions and central banks.

The Center sponsors international conferences, public lectures, original research and publications. It has earned a solid reputation in the Swiss and international banking community where it is known for its contribution to bridging the gap between theory and practice in the field of international banking and finance.

In association with CEPR, the Center launched a new series of *Geneva Reports on the World Economy* in 1999. The four subsequent volumes have attracted considerable interest among practitioners, policy-makers and scholars working on the reform of international financial architecture.

The ICMB is non-partisan and does not take any view on policy. Its publications, including the present report, reflect the opinions of the authors, not of ICMB or of any of its sponsoring institutions.

President of the Foundation Board   Tommaso Padoa-Schioppa
Director   Charles Wyplosz

Centre for Economic Policy Research (CEPR)

The Centre for Economic Policy Research is a network of over 600 Research Fellows and Affiliates, based primarily in European universities. The Centre coordinates the research activities of its Fellows and Affiliates and communicates the results to the public and private sectors. CEPR is an entrepreneur, developing research initiatives with the producers, consumers and sponsors of research. Established in 1983, CEPR is a European economics research organization with uniquely wide-ranging scope and activities.

CEPR is a registered educational charity. Institutional (core) finance for the Centre is provided by major grants from the Economic and Social Research Council, under which an ESRC Resource Centre operates within CEPR; the Esmée Fairbairn Charitable Trust and the Bank of England. The Centre is also supported by the European Central Bank, the Bank for International Settlements, 22 national central banks and 45 companies. None of these organizations gives prior review to the Centre's publications, nor do they necessarily endorse the views expressed therein.

The Centre is pluralist and non-partisan, bringing economic research to bear on the analysis of medium- and long-run policy questions. CEPR research may include views on policy, but the Executive Committee of the Centre does not give prior review to its publications, and the Centre takes no institutional policy positions. The opinions expressed in this report are those of the authors and not those of the Centre for Economic Policy Research.

Chair of the Board   Guillermo de la Dehesa
President   Richard Portes
Chief Executive Officer   Hilary Beech
Research Director   Mathias Dewatripont

About the Authors

Andrew Crockett was General Manager of the Bank for International Settlements form January 1994 to March 2003, and Chairman of the Financial Stability Forum from April 1999 until March 2003. Prior to joining the BIS, he held positions at the IMF (1972-89) and at the Bank of England (1989-93). He has published widely on issues related to international finance.

Trevor Harris is Managing Director and Head of the Global Valuation and Accounting Team in Equity Research at Morgan Stanley. He is also co-Director of the Center for Excellence in Accounting and Security Analysis (CEASA) at Columbia Business School where he was on the faculty from 1983-2002. He was the Jerome A Chazen Professor of International Business and Chair of the Accounting Department before joining Morgan Stanley in June 2000. He also serves as a member of the User Advisory Council of the FASB, the Standards Advisory Council to the International Accounting Standards Board, and the International Capital Markets Advisory Committee at the New York Stock Exchange. He has published widely in academic journals and in books on valuation and accounting issues.

Frederic S Mishkin is the Alfred Lerner Professor of Banking and Financial Institutions at the Graduate School of Business, Columbia University and a Research Associate at the National Bureau of Economic Research. From 1994 to 1997 he was Executive Vice President and Director of Research at the Federal Reserve Bank of New York and an associate economist of the Federal Open Market Committee of the Federal Reserve System. His research focuses on monetary policy and the impact of financial markets on the aggregate economy, and he is the author of over 100 professional articles and ten books, including The Economics of Money, Banking and Financial Markets, the leading textbook in its field.

Eugene N White is Professor of Economics at Rutgers University and a Research Associate of the National Bureau of Economic Research. His research focuses on asset bubbles, financial architecture, banking crises and deposit insurance. He is author of many articles and books on these topics, and most recently he edited (with M Bordo and C Goldin), *The Defining Moment: The Great Depression and the American Economy in the Twentieth Century*.

Contents

List of Conference Participants

William E Alexander	Senior Advisor, International Capital Markets IMF, Washington DC
Edmond Alphandéry	Chairman of the Supervisory Board, CNP – Assurances, Paris
Ernst Baltensperger	Professor, Department of Economics, University of Bern, Bern
Jean-Pierre Béguelin	Chief Economist, Pictet & Cie, Geneva
Jarle Bergo	Deputy Governor, Norges Bank, Oslo
Franco Bolis	Executive Officer, Ethics and Compliance Market Activities, BNP Paribas (Suisse) SA, Geneva
Antonio Borges	Vice Chairman and Managing Director, Investment Banking, Goldman Sachs International, London
Claudio Borio	Head of Research and Policy Analysis, Bank for International Settlements, Basel
Mark Carney	Managing Director, Investment Banking Division, Goldman Sachs Canada, Toronto
Benoît Coeuré	Deputy Chief Executive, Agency France Trésor, Ministry of Finance, Paris
Andrew Crockett	Chairman, Financial Stability Forum, New York. Formerly, General Manager, Bank for International Settlements
Pierre Darier	Partner, Lombard Odier Darier Hentsch & Cie, Geneva
Jacques Delpa	Director, European Economics, Barclays Capital, Paris
Paul H Dembinski	Director, Observatoire de la Finance, Geneva
Slobodan Djajic	Professor, Graduate Institute of International Studies, Geneva
Robert H Dugger	Managing Director, Tudor Investment Corporation, Washington DC
Klaus Durrer	Head Group Research, UBS AG, Zürich

Charles Freedman	Deputy Governor, Bank of Canada, Ottawa
Stephen Freedman	Senior Economist, Policy & Research, UBS AG, Zürich
Olivier Garnier	Head of Strategy & Economic Research, Société Générale Asset Management, Paris
Vitor Gaspar	Director General, Research, European Central Bank, Frankfurt am Main
Patrice Gautry	Economist, Union Bancaire Privèe, Geneva
Hans Genberg	Professor, International Economics, Graduate Institute of International Studies, Geneva
Yves Genier	Journalist, AGEFI, Geneva
Trevor Harris	Managing Director and Head of Accounting Policy Group, Morgan Stanley, New York
Philipp Hildebrand	Managing Director, Member of the Executive Committee, Union Bancaire Privée, Geneva
Hugo Frey Jensen	Head of Financial Markets, Danmarks Nationalbank, Copenhagen
Karen Johnson	Director, International Finance, Federal Reserve Board, Washington DC
Edward Kane	Professor of Finance, Boston College, Boston
Jean-Pierre Landau	Director, European Bank for Reconstruction and Development, London
Patrick Lane	Finance Editor, *The Economist*, London
Frédéric Lelievre	Journalist, Le Temps, Geneva
John Lipsky	Chief Economist, JP Morgan Chase, New York
David Lipton	Managing Director, Moore Capital Strategy Group, Washington DC
Manijeh Mobasser-Swoboda	Financial Advisor
Carlo Montecelli	Senior Director, International Relations, Ministry of the Economy and Finance, Rome
Dirk Morris	Managing Director, Head of Currencies, Putnam Investments, Boston
Frederic S Mishkin	Professor of Economics, Columbia University, New York
Lars Nyberg	Deputy Governor, Sveriges Riksbank, Stockholm

Tommaso Padoa-Schioppa	Member of the Executive Board, European Central Bank, Frankfurt am Main
Avinash Persaud	Managing Director, Head of Global Research, State Street Bank and Trust Company, London
Michel Peytrignet	Director, Head of Economic Division, Swiss National Bank, Zürich
Charles Pictet	Partner, Banque Pictet & Cie, Geneva
Richard Portes	President, CEPR, London
Cesare Ravara	Vice-President, Head Financial Services Research, Credit Suisse Financial Services, Zürich
Eli Remolona	Head of Financial Markets, Bank for International Settlements, Basel
Jean-Jacques Rey	Honorary Executive Director, National Bank of Belgium, Belgium
Hans-Jörg Rudloff	Chairman of the Executive Committee, Barclays Capital, London
James Sassoon	Managing Director, HM Treasury, London
Claudio Segré	Chairman, Argus Fund, Geneva
Neal Soss	Chief Economist, Economic Research, Crédit Suisse First Boston, New York
Alexander Swoboda	Professor of International Economics, Graduate Institute of International Studies, Geneva
Gertrude Tumpel-Gugerell	Vice Governor, Economics and Financial Markets Department, Oesterreichische Nationalbank, Vienna
Angel Ubide	Director, European Analysis, Tudor Investment Corporation, Washington DC
Ernst-Ludwig von Thadden	Professor of Economics, University of Lausanne, Lausanne
Eugene N White	Professor of Economics, Rutgers University, New Brunswick
Pawel Wyczanski	Deputy Director, Financial System, National Bank of Poland, Warsaw
Charles Wyplosz	Professor of International Economics, Graduate Institute of International Studies, Geneva

List of Figures

Acknowledgements

The authors have benefited from the discussions, both formal and informal, during the ICMB/CEPR Conference in Geneva on 9 May 2003. They also wish to thank participants in seminars at the Federal Reserve Bank of New York and Columbia University's Macro Lunch, for their helpful comments. The views presented in this report are entirely those of the authors and should not be taken to represent those of their employers, past and present.

Foreword

In the last few years, investors have witnessed a sharp fall-off in equity market valuations, the dramatic failures of the Enron Corporation and its auditing firm, Arthur Andersen, and serious manipulation and lack of transparency in the accounts of several large companies. Understandably, they distrust the practices by which firms provide information about companies and financial instruments to market participants. Meanwhile, recent settlements between the State of New York and a number of prominent investment banks have exhibited apparent conflicts of interest in financial services firms. The provision of reliable information is necessary for financial markets to perform their essential function of channelling capital to the most productive investment opportunities. The effects of such conflicts of interest, and possible policy responses to minimize them, are worthy of serious analysis.

In this fifth publication in the series of Geneva Reports on the World Economy, a distinguished team of authors, with extensive experience in capital markets and economics, develops a framework with which to analyze these concerns.The economic theory of information underlies this framework. Conflicts of interest are most evident in firms that provide multiple financial services. The authors single out several cases for closer inspection: conflicts of interest between underwriting and research in investment banks, between auditing and consulting services in accounting firms, between credit assessment and consulting in rating agencies and, finally, between various lines of business in universal banks.

Policy options range from laisser-faire to full socialization of the provision of information to market participants. The trick is to choose policies that do not perversely end up impairing financial markets by reducing the quality of the information available. The authors' information-theory-based approach leads them to recommend supplementing market discipline with a combination of mandatory disclosure and supervisory oversight is the optimal.

This structured approach to analyzing conflicts of interest should provide a robust foundation for debates over policies to limit the potential damage caused by conflicts of interest. ICMB and CEPR are delighted to offer a forum for the authors to contribute their ideas on a topic so important for the healthy functioning of the world's capital markets.

Richard Portes   Tommaso Padoa-Shioppa
CEPR   ICMB

                                                        September 2003

Executive Summary

Recent corporate scandals and the dramatic decline in the stock market since March 2000 have increased concerns about conflicts of interest in which agents who were supposed to provide the investing public with reliable information had incentives to hide the truth in order to further their own goals. This report analyses what conflicts of interest are, explains why we care about them, and develops a framework for evaluating policies to remedy them.

Conflicts of interest occur when a financial service provider, or an agent within such a provider, has multiple interests that create incentives to act in such a way as to misuse or conceal information. Conflicts of interest present a problem for the financial system when they lead to a serious decrease in information flows. Less information makes it harder for the financial system to allocate credit to the most productive investment opportunities, thereby decreasing the efficiency of financial markets and the overall economy.

Four areas of the financial service industry have a high potential for conflicts of interest: underwriting and research in investment banking, auditing and consulting in accounting firms, credit assessment and consulting in rating agencies, and universal banking. Evidence indicates, however, that although conflicts of interest exist, they are difficult to exploit. The market is often able to provide incentives that constrain conflicted agents, discounting the value of services when it perceives a conflict of interest is present. In response, financial service providers frequently institute safeguards to reduce the incentives to exploit conflicts, thereby protecting their reputations. For example, credit rating agencies are paid by issuers of securities to produce ratings, and yet there is little evidence that this leads to more favourable ratings. Similarly, apparent conflicts of interest when commercial banks underwrote securities before the Glass-Steagall Act do not appear to have been generally exploited because the market signalled its distrust of potential conflicts and firms restructured to assuage the concerns of the market. Likewise, the market appears to recognize potential conflicts of interest when evaluating the quality of information about a securities issue provided by research analysts who are employed by the bank that is the lead underwriter. There are fewer empirical studies about auditing, but the limited evidence also suggests that clients who are concerned about conflicts of interest reduce the value they attach to audit opinions and limit non-audit purchases from incumbent auditors.

While conflicts of interest may be constrained, they are more difficult to eliminate. It is easier for the market to identify a potential conflict of interest than it is to observe if it is being exploited because the ability to exploit conflicts depends on the hard-to-monitor internal controls and compensation mechanisms within financial service firms.

In evaluating policy remedies for conflicts of interest, two questions should always be asked: Do markets have the information needed to control conflicts of interest? Even if the incentives to exploit a conflict of interest are strong, would a policy that eliminates the conflict of interest destroy economies of scope, thereby reducing information flows? If the answer is yes to either question, then policy remedies that would reduce overall information in financial markets are more likely to do harm than good. We examine five generic approaches to remedying conflicts of interest going from least intrusive to most intrusive: (1) market discipline, (2) mandatory disclosure for increased transparency, (3) supervisory oversight, (4) separation by functions, and (5) socialization of information.

The information-oriented framework developed in this study leads us to find that the combination of market discipline, supplemented by mandatory disclosure of conflicts, and supervisory oversight are generally sufficient to contain the exploitation of conflicts of interest and the consequent damage to the efficiency of the financial system. Specifically, we make nine recommendations to remedy the conflicts of interest in the financial services industry:

1. Increase disclosure for investment analysts, credit rating analysts and auditors to reveal any interests they have in the firms they analyse.
2. Improve corporate governance to control conflicts of interest, ensuring that auditors are responsible to shareholders not managers.
3. Increase supervisory oversight over conflicts of interest.
4. Provide adequate resources to supervisors to monitor conflicts of interest.
5. Establish best practice codes of conduct to control conflicts of interest, devised by industry and supervisors in cooperation.
6. Enhance competitiveness in the rating agency industry.
7. Prevent co-option of private information producing agents by regulators and supervisors.
8. Avoid the forced separation of financial service activities except in unusual circumstances.
9. Avoid the socialization of information in the financial service industry in most circumstances.

Radical solutions to conflict of interest problems that socialize information or stringently separate financial service activities are likely to do far more harm than good. We believe that with increased disclosure of information and supervisory oversight plus additional reforms of the rules governing audit opinions and official use and sanction of ratings, the problems created by conflicts of interest can be minimized. More radical approaches have the potential to reduce, rather than increase, the quality of information in financial markets, with the result that channelling funds to productive investments, which is so crucial to strong economic growth, could be severely compromised.

1 What Are the Issues?

1.1 Introduction

This year, 2003, is the 70th anniversary of the Glass-Steagall Act, passed in the depths of the depression in 1933. The stock market crash of 1929 initiated a long decline in the market, which fell over 80% from its peak.

Those who had bought into the exuberant bull market of 1928-9 were confident that the long expansion of the 1920s represented a new era of permanent growth and eagerly bought up new issues of what were then high tech companies. When the market collapsed, shareholders felt cheated by the bankers, or as the pundits called them 'banksters', who had sold them the stocks and bonds that were now worthless or nearly so. The most aggressive promoters of securities were the newly formed universal banks. Their ability to shift intermediation from one part of the bank to another offered considerable synergies but also had the potential for exploiting conflicts of interest.

The crash revealed stories of the extraordinary greed of some of the formerly esteemed leaders of the financial industry, who profited at the expense of their customers and sometimes their own firms. Problems were not confined to banking and a young reforming accountant, by the name of Arthur Andersen, denounced the slipshod and deceptive practices that had enabled companies to fool the investing public.

Bankers' exploitation of conflicts of interest became part of the popular legend of the excesses of the era. The response from Congress was the Glass-Steagall Act, which completely separated commercial and investment banking, reaffirming the US regulatory tendency to separate financial institutions forcibly by function. Decades later, financial journalists cited these prominent cases as evidence of the dangers of universal banking, and they were used as justification for the continued existence of the Glass-Steagall Act.

For the second time in a century, a stock market bubble, fuelled by a belief in a 'new economy' and 'new tech' companies, has ended in an extraordinary crash. Although the European 'tech' bubble was not as large as in the United States, European economies shared much of the run-up and subsequent collapse in share prices. Moreover, just as occurred 70 years ago, financial markets have been jolted by one corporate scandal after another. The cycle began with the spectacular bankruptcy of Enron Corporation in December 2001, once valued as the seventh largest corporation in the United States, and the indictment of Enron's auditor, Arthur Andersen, one of the big five accounting firms. Subsequently, there have been revelations of misleading accounting statements at numerous other corporations, including WorldCom, Tyco Industries and more recently Ahold, which have added to doubts about the quality of accounting information in the corporate sector. Legal settlements have imposed fines on investment banks for encouraging their stock analysts to hype stocks that they had serious doubts about and which turned out to be disastrous investments.

These scandals have received tremendous public attention, not only because resulting bankruptcies have cost the employees of these firms their jobs and even their pensions, but also because of the accompanying stock market declines – measured at 43% for the S&P500, 72% for Nasdaq, and 61% for the EuroSTOXX50 from March 2000 to March 2003.

A contributory factor in these scandals may have been conflicts of interest in which agents who were supposed to provide the investing public with reliable information had incentives to hide the truth in order to further their own goals. What are these conflicts of interest and how serious are they? What role have they played in the financial markets' recent woes? What should be done about them?

This report seeks to provide some answers to these questions. This introductory chapter provides a framework for answering these questions by first discussing the crucial role of information in financial markets. This analysis will then enable us to define the conflicts of interest that concern us here, explain why we should care about them, and develop a framework for thinking about policies to remedy them. The chapter then briefly outlines the types of conflicts of interest that will be analysed later in the report.

1.2 Information and financial markets

In order to understand why conflicts of interest are important, we need to step back a bit and think about the function of financial markets in the economy. Well-functioning financial markets perform the essential economic function of channelling funds from individuals and firms who lack productive investment opportunities to those who have such opportunities. By so doing, financial markets contribute to higher production and efficiency in the overall economy. Reliable information is the key to financial markets performing this function.

A crucial impediment to the efficient functioning of the financial system is asymmetric information, a situation in which one party to a financial contract has much less accurate information than the other party. For example, managers of a corporation usually have much better information about the potential returns and risk associated with the investment projects they plan to undertake than do potential purchasers of the corporation's stock. Asymmetric information leads to two basic problems in the financial system: adverse selection and moral hazard.

Adverse selection is an asymmetric information problem that arises before a transaction occurs, when parties who are the most likely to produce an undesirable (adverse) outcome for a financial contract are most likely to try to enter the contract and thus be selected. The concept originally arose in connection with insurance, where those most likely to benefit from an insurance contract (for example, those at risk of contracting a disease or likely to have an accident), are most liable to seek coverage. Adverse selection is a problem for most types of financial contracts. For example, managers of businesses who want to divert funds to less productive uses (e.g. enlarging their own pay and perquisites) are likely to be the most eager to raise external funds. Since adverse selection makes it more likely that investments in firms will turn out badly, investors may decide not to invest even if there are attractive investments in the market-place, thus penalizing those with good projects. This outcome is a feature of the classic 'lemons problem' first described by Akerlof (1970). Clearly, minimizing the adverse selection problem so that capital flows to productive uses requires that investors have the information to screen out good from bad investments.

Moral hazard is also a concept from insurance, where it applies to the risk that those with insurance coverage take less care to avoid risks against which they carry insurance. In financial contracts, moral hazard occurs after the transaction takes place because the provider of funds is subjected to the hazard that the receiver of funds has incentives to engage in activities that are undesirable from the lender's point of view (i.e., activities that will produce a higher return for the borrower but incur a higher risk). Moral hazard occurs because the receiver of funds has incentives to misallocate funds for personal use, or to undertake investment in unprofitable projects that increase the firm's or the individual's power and stature. As a result many investors will decide that they would rather not provide firms with funds, so that investment will be at sub-optimal levels. In order to minimize the moral hazard problem, investors must have information so that they can monitor managers' activities and make sure that the managers use the funds to maximize the value of the firm.

As this discussion of the asymmetric information problems of adverse selection and moral hazard illustrates, the provision of reliable information is crucial to the ability of financial markets to perform their essential function of chanelling funds to those with productive investment opportunities. In order for investors to be willing to provide funds for investment projects, they need to be able to screen out good from bad credit risks in order to get around the adverse selection problem; and they also need to monitor those to whom they provide funds in order to minimize the moral hazard problem. But how is the information that enables investors to both screen and monitor to be provided?

1.3 The role of financial institutions in financial markets

One answer to the question above is that private investors could collect the necessary information themselves to screen and monitor their investments. There are two barriers to their doing so, however:

1. the free-rider problem;
2. the cost of information production due to lack of diversity and/or scale of cooperations of investors.

The free-rider problem occurs because people who do not spend resources on collecting information can still take advantage of (free-ride off) the information that other people have collected. The free-rider problem is particularly important in securities markets. If well-informed investors are able to buy a security in advance of others on the basis of their superior research, then they can capture the value of their superior information. If other investors who have not paid for this information quickly obtain it, however, they may be able to capture some of the value. If enough free-riding investors can do this, investors who have acquired information will no longer be able to earn the increase in the value of the security arising from this additional information. The weakened ability of private investors to profit from producing information will mean that less information is produced in securities markets, so that the adverse selection problem, in which overvalued securities are those most often offered for sale, is more likely to be an impediment to a well-functioning securities market.

Possibly even more important, the free-rider problem makes it less likely that there will be sufficient monitoring to reduce incentives to commit moral hazard. By monitoring borrowers' activities to see whether they are complying with restrictive covenants and enforcing the covenants if they are not, lenders can prevent borrowers from taking on risk at their expense. Similarly, monitoring of managers can help to ensure that they do not divert funds to their personal use or make expenditures that bring them prestige or perquisites rather than raise shareholder value. Since monitoring is costly, however, the free-rider problem discourages this kind of activity in securities markets. If some investors know that other securities holders are monitoring and enforcing restrictive covenants, then they can free ride on the other securities holders' monitoring and enforcement. Once the monitoring securities holders realize that they can do the same thing, they may also stop their activities, with the result that insufficient resources are devoted to monitoring and enforcement. The outcome is that moral hazard is likely to be a severe problem in financial markets.

Financial institutions can help mitigate the free-rider problem by acquiring funds from the public and then using them to buy and hold assets in a diversified portfolio based on the specialized information they collect. As financial intermediaries, they can act as delegated monitors (Leland and Pyle, 1977). They are not as subject to the free-rider problem and profit from the information they produce because they can make investments such as bank loans. Even if other investors can obtain or infer intermediaries' collected information, they cannot get a free ride and profit at the banks' expense because these investments are often non-traded. Similarly, it is hard to free-ride off the monitoring activities of financial intermediaries when they make bank loans. Financial institutions making private investments thus receive the benefits of monitoring and so are better equipped to prevent moral hazard on the part of borrowers or managers.

While this strategy works for non-depository intermediaries if their shareholders participate in the information discovery or are given signals by the managers, depository intermediaries would be subject to the same challenge as businesses in signalling the value of the portfolio of assets in which they have invested. Rather than signal by their managers' ownership of substantial deposits, the solution for depository intermediaries is the issue of demandable deposits. Deposits that are quickly redeemable enable depositors to discipline managers by withdrawing their funds if they believe that risk has increased (Calomiris and Kahn, 1991).

A second barrier to private production of information is that investors may not be able to diversify sufficiently or operate on a sufficient scale so that information production is too costly. Financial institutions can attain a size large enough so that they can diversify and reduce average screening and monitoring costs (Diamond, 1984, and Ramakrishnan and Thakor, 1984). A financial institution must, however, convince primary investors that it is adequately monitoring the business it is funding. To do this, it must conduct internal monitoring of its employees so that they engage in the appropriate level of screening and monitoring of investments.

In the literature described thus far, financial institutions are treated as though each type of financial institution focuses on only one kind of informational asymmetry. Thus, one could rationalize many different types of financial institutions on the grounds that each type addresses a different informational asymmetry. The information that any one institution possesses may be useful, however, beyond the provision of one narrow type of service. For instance, banks, owing to their established long-term customer relationships, obtain reusable private information about firms' resources, cash flows and other characteristics.

For individual customers, they gather information, often confidential, beyond what is publicly available, which is obtained by the provision of services over time. The closeness of a long-term relationship may induce the customer to reveal more confidential information and thereby gain some advantage with the financial firm (Boot, 2000).

Financial institutions gain a cost advantage in the production of information because they develop special skills to interpret signals and exploit cross-sectional information across customers. Furthermore, the reusability of information gives them another advantage as the initial information producer specializing in its production and distribution (See Chan *et al.*, 1986; and Greenbaum and Thakor, 1995). Thus, not only are they lower cost producers of information for one type of financial service, but they can also be lower cost producers of information for multiple financial services, which become complementary activities. It is also often conjectured that institutions that combine several financial services have advantages over specialized ones. By providing a broader set of financial products, an institution may develop wider and longer-term relationships with firms that may be the source of further economies of scope (Santos, 1998). A financial institution may learn more about a firm by the provision of a diverse portfolio of financial services from which it can collect more varied information and which may give it more monitoring and disciplinary power.

1.4 What are conflicts of interest?

While the presence of the synergies or economies of scope described above may offer substantial benefits, they also create potential costs in the form of conflict of interests. These conflicts exist 'whenever one is serving two or more interests and can put one person in a better position at the expense of another' (Edwards, 1979). Because conflicts of interest are present in almost all aspects of our lives, we need to be more precise about the conflicts of interest that concern us here. Given our concern about the role of information in financial markets, we use the following definition for the conflicts of interest:

> Conflicts of interest arise when a financial service provider, or an agent within such a service provider, has multiple interests which create incentives to act in such a way as to misuse or conceal information needed for the effective functioning of financial markets.

Conflicts of interest may occur within specialized financial institutions. Conflicts of interest stand out most sharply, however, when an institution provides multiple financial services, thereby creating an opportunity for exploiting the synergies or economies of scope by inappropriately diverting some of their benefits. Combinations of services that bring together any group of depository intermediaries, non-depository intermediaries, and brokers or allow any of these to directly invest in business have attracted the greatest criticism for putative conflicts of interest.

1.5 Why conflicts of interest are important

We care about these conflicts of interest because if they reduce the amount of information in financial markets sufficiently, they increase asymmetric information and keep financial markets from chanelling funds to those with productive investment opportunities. There are clearly broader definitions of conflicts of interest than the one we have stated above, and many of these broader conflicts of interest are important. In this report, however, we restrict ourselves to a narrower view because we take the position that conflicts of interest require pubic policy interventions only if they make financial markets less efficient.

1.6 A framework for evaluating policies to remedy conflicts of interest

The information view of conflicts of interest we have proposed here also provides a framework for evaluating whether they require public policy actions to eliminate or reduce them. Some combinations of financial service activities may result in incentives for agents to conceal information, but they may also result in synergies that make it easier to produce information. Thus, preventing the combination of activities to eliminate the conflicts of interest may actually make financial markets less efficient. This reasoning suggests that there are two propositions that are critical for evaluating what should be done about conflicts of interest:

1. The fact that a conflict of interest exists does not mean that the conflict will have serious adverse consequences. Even though a conflict of interest exists, the incentives to exploit the conflict of interest may not be very high. Exploitation of a conflict of interest which is visible to the market will typically result in a decrease in the reputation of the financial firm where it takes place. Given the importance of maintaining and enhancing reputation, exploiting the conflict of interest would then decrease the future profitability of the firm because it will have greater difficulty selling its services in the future, thus creating incentives for the firm to prevent exploitation of the conflict of interest. Hence, the market-place may be able to control conflicts of interest because there is a high value to financial firms' reputations. When evaluating the need for remedies, this proposition raises the issue whether the market has the information and incentives to control conflicts of interest.
2. Even if incentives to exploit conflicts of interest remain strong, eliminating the conflict of interest may be harmful, if doing so destroys economies of scope, thereby reducing information flows. Thus in evaluating possible remedies, we also need to examine the issue of whether imposing the remedy will do more harm than good by reducing the flow of information in financial markets.

Specific remedies for conflicts of interest can be grouped into five generic approaches:

1. Market discipline.
2. Mandatory disclosure of increased transparency.
3. Supervisory oversight.
4. Separation of functions.
5. Socialization of information production.

1.6.1 Market discipline

This approach has a powerful appeal to many economists, and this may be a sufficient response in many cases. Market forces can work through two mechanisms. They can penalize the service provider if they exploit conflicts of interest. For example, a penalty may be imposed by the market in the form of higher funding costs or lower demand for its services, even to the point of forcing demise of the firm. Second, market forces can promote new institutional means to contain conflicts of interest, for example, by generating a demand for information from organizations structured to reduce conflicts.

The advantages of market-driven solutions include the fact that they can hit where it hurts most, through pecuniary penalties. Moreover, they may help avoid the risk of over reaction. In the face of public outrage to perceived conflicts of interest, it may be hard to resist the temptation to adopt non-market solutions that may reduce information production in financial markets. On the other hand, market-based solutions may not always work if the market cannot obtain sufficient information to appropriately punish financial firms that are exploiting conflicts of interest. Memories may be short in financial markets; once a triggering event has faded from memory, conflicts may creep back in unless reforms have been 'hard-wired'.

1.6.2 Mandatory disclosure for increased transparency

A competitive market structure usually develops mechanisms to provide information that is needed by market participants. This information should include financial data and disclosure of the existence of any relationship that may give rise to conflicts of interest that induce agents to distort or conceal data.

The gathering of information is costly, and any individual economic agent will only gather information if the private benefit outweighs the cost. When the information collected immediately becomes available to the market, the free-rider problem may become serious. Information thus has the attribute of a public good, which may be undersupplied in the absence of some public intervention. Mandatory disclosure of conflicted relationships increases investors' ability to judge how much weight to place on information provided by an agent. Although mandatory information disclosure can alleviate information asymmetries it can also create problems if it reveals so much proprietary information that the financial institution is unable to profitably engage in the information production business. The result could then be less information production rather than more and an intensification of the informational asymmetry between insiders and other market participants.

1.6.3 Supervisory oversight

If mandatory disclosure does not work because firms are still able to hide relevant information, the free-rider problem remains severe or mandatory disclosure would reveal proprietary information, supervisors can intervene and contain conflicts of interest. Supervisors can observe whether a conflict of interest is being exploited without revealing confidential information to a financial firm's competitors so that the firm can continue to engage profitably in information production activities. Supplied with this information, the supervisor can take actions to prevent financial firms from exploiting conflicts of interest. As part of this supervisory oversight, standards of practice can be developed by the supervisor and the firms engaged in a specific information-production activity. Enforcement of these standards would then be in the hands of the supervisor.

Supervisory oversight of this type is very common in the banking industry. In recent years, bank supervisors have increased their focus on risk management. They examine banks' risk management procedures to ensure that the appropriate internal controls on risk-taking are in place at the bank. In a similar fashion, supervisors can examine the internal procedures and controls to restrict conflicts of interest. When they find weak internal controls, they can require the financial institution to modify them so that incentives to engage in conflicts of interest are eliminated.

Although supervisory oversight has been successful in improving internal controls in financial firms in recent years, if the incentives to engage in conflicts of interest are sufficiently strong, financial institutions may be able to hide conflicts of interest from the supervisors. Furthermore, as seen in recent banking crises, supervisors sometimes have engaged in regulatory forbearance in which they do not sufficiently enforce penalties on financial firms engaged in undesirable behaviour. There is always the issue of whether supervisors can be adequately insulated from short-term political pressures to let financial institutions off the hook, avoid regulatory capture, and be made sufficiently accountable to prevent conflicts of interest from getting out of control. On the other side, supervisors could become overbearing and interfere with the efficient function of financial firms in order to avoid having a scandal occur on their watch.

1.6.4 Separation of functions

When the market cannot obtain sufficient information to constrain conflicts of interest because there is no satisfactory way of inducing information disclosure by market discipline or supervisory oversight, the incentives to exploit conflicts of interest may be reduced or eliminated by regulations enforcing separation of functions. There are several degrees of separation. First, is the separation of activities into different in-house departments with firewalls between them. Second, is the organization of different activities into separately capitalized affiliates. Third, is the prohibition of a combination of activities in any organizational form.

Separation by function has the goal of ensuring that 'agents' are not placed in the position of responding to multiple 'principals'. Moving from less to more stringent separation of functions, conflicts of interest are reduced. More stringent separation of functions weakens synergies of information collection, however, thereby preventing financial firms from taking advantage of economies of scope in information production. Deciding on the appropriate degree of separation thus involves a trade-off between the benefits of reducing conflicts of interest and the cost of lowering economies of scope in producing information.

1.6.5 Socialization of information production

The most radical response to conflicts of interest generated by asymmetric information is to socialize the provision or the funding source of the relevant information. For example, much macroeconomic information is provided by publicly funded agencies, recognizing the argument that this particular public good is likely to be undersupplied if left to private provision. It is conceivable that other information-providing functions, for example credit ratings and auditing, could also be publicly supplied. Alternatively, if the information-generating services are left to the private sector, they could be funded by public sources or by a publicly mandated levy to ensure that information production is not tainted by obligations to fee-paying entities with special interests.

Of course, the problem with this approach is that a government agency or publicly funded entity, not operating in a competitive market, may not have the same incentives as private financial institutions to produce high quality information. Forcing information production to be conducted by a government or quasi-government entity may reduce conflicts of interest, but it may lower the flow of information to financial markets. Furthermore, as a practical matter, there is a compensation problem in government agencies because they may be constrained from paying market wages to attract the best people.

1.7 The types of conflicts of interest studied in this Report

There are four areas of financial service activities that we believe have the greatest potential for conflicts of interest which reduce information in financial markets. They are as follows:

1.7.1 Underwriting and research in investment banking

The information synergies from underwriting, research and market making provide a rationale for combining these distinct financial services. This combination of activities leads to conflicts of interest, however. The conflict of interest that raises the greatest concern occurs between underwriting and brokerage, where investment banks are serving two client groups – issuing firms and investors. Issuers benefit from optimistic research while investors desire unbiased research. If the incentives for these two activities are not appropriately aligned, there will be a temptation for employees on one side of the firm to distort information to the advantage of their clients and the profit of their department. When the potential revenues from underwriting greatly exceed brokerage commissions, there will be a strong incentive to favour issuers over investors or risk losing the former to competitors. As a result analysts in investment banks may distort their research to please issuers, and the information they produce on securities will not be as reliable, thereby diminishing the efficiency of securities markets.

1.7.2 Auditing and consulting in accounting firms

The traditional role of an auditor has been to act as an efficient monitor of the quality of information produced by firms so as to reduce the inevitable information asymmetry between the firm's managers and other stakeholders, especially its suppliers of capital. In auditing, threats to truthful reporting arise from several potential conflicts of interest. The conflict that has received the most attention lately occurs when an accounting firm, as well as providing audit services, also provides non-audit consulting services – tax advice, accounting, management information systems, and strategic advice, commonly referred to as management advisory services (MAS). These multiple services enjoy economies of scale and scope, but create two potential sources of conflict of interest. The most commonly discussed conflict is the potential to pressure auditors to bias their judgements and opinions to limit any loss of fees in the 'other' services. The second more subtle conflict is that auditors often evaluate systems or tax and financial structures that were put in place by their non-audit counterparts within the firm. Both conflicts may lead to biased audits, with the result that less information is available in financial markets, which will make it harder for them to efficiently allocate capital.

1.7.3 Credit assessment and consulting in rating agencies

Ratings are widely used by investors as a guide to the creditworthiness of the issuers of debt. As such, they play a major role in the pricing of debt securities and in the regulatory process. Conflicts of interest can arise from the fact that there are multiple users of ratings; and, at least in the short term, their interests can diverge. Investors and regulators are interested in a well-researched, impartial assessment of credit quality; the issuers in a favourable rating. Because issuers pay to have their securities rated, there is a fear that credit agencies may bias their ratings upwards in order to get more business. A further concern is that rating agencies have begun to provide ancillary consulting services. Rating agencies are increasingly asked to advise on the structuring of debt issues, usually to help secure a favourable rating. In this case, the credit-rating agency would be in the position of 'auditing its own work' raising conflicts of interest similar to those in accounting firms when they provide both auditing and consulting services. Furthermore, providing consulting services creates additional incentives for the rating agencies to deliver more favourable ratings in order to further their consulting business. The possible reduction in the quality of credit assessment by rating agencies could then increase asymmetric information in financial markets, thereby reducing their ability to allocate credit.

1.7.4 Universal banking

Although commercial banks, investment banks and insurance companies originally arose as distinct financial institutions, there were economies of scope that could be attained by their combination, thus leading to the development of universal banking in which all of these activities are combined in one organization. Yet, given that activities within a universal bank serve multiple clients, there are many potential conflicts of interest. If the potential revenues from one department surge, there will be an incentive for employees in that department to distort information to the advantage of their clients and the profit of their department. For example, issuers served by the underwriting department will benefit from aggressive sales to customers of the bank, while these customers are hoping to get unbiased investment advice. A bank manager may push the affiliate's products to the disadvantage of the customer or limit losses from a poor public offering by placing them in the bank's managed trust accounts. A bank with a loan to a firm whose credit or bankruptcy risk has increased, has private knowledge that may encourage it to use the bank's underwriting department to sell bonds to the unsuspecting public, thereby paying off the loan and earning a fee. A bank may make loans on overly favourable terms in order to obtain fees from activities like underwriting securities. To sell its insurance products, a bank may try to influence or coerce a borrowing or investing customer. All of these conflicts of interest may lead to a decrease in accurate information production by the universal bank, thereby hindering its ability to promote efficient credit allocation.

<u>1.8</u> Plan of the study

The next four chapters discuss the conflicts of interest in each of the four types of financial service activities discussed above. These discussions are followed by a final chapter which provides an overview of our analysis of conflicts of interest and the policy remedies that may help to reduce these conflicts of interest, making the financial system more efficient.

2 Investment Banking: Conflicts of Interest in Underwriting and Research

2.1 Information synergies and conflicts of interest

Investment banks provide a varied array of financial services that bridge informational asymmetries in the primary and secondary capital markets. In the primary market, they float new and seasoned securities and advise on mergers and acquisitions; in the secondary markets, they act as brokers or dealers, providing research for both markets (Bloch, 1986). Joined with market making and proprietary trading, these services have important complementarities in the collection and use of information that encourage their joint provision. Taken altogether, investment banks, as intermediaries, play a central role in the formation of capital and provision of liquidity to the markets.

When a new issue is floated by a syndicate of investment banks, the bank that serves as the lead underwriter engages in intense information collection. The bank needs to provide information to build a book of committed investors, set the price of the initial public offering (IPO) and create a secondary market. The lead underwriter of an IPO syndicate is the delegated monitor not only for individual investors who are considering purchasing newly issued equities but also for the other members of the syndicate. This underwriter incurs quasi-fiduciary responsibilities to other members of the syndicate and risk from holding the largest share of the issue. Moving a firm 'from the closet to the goldfish bowl' gains the lead underwriter an information advantage, which is greatest at the beginning when there is relatively little public information. This advantage can form the basis for a long-term relationship with the issuing firm. In addition, to promote transparency, the Securities Act of 1933 imposes legal sanctions to ensure that the lead bank energetically pursues all material information in a process called due diligence.[1]

The investment bank's research analysts who have been part of this discovery process should be able to offer better buy/sell recommendations and superior forecasts of the firm's performance. Market making in the secondary markets for brokerage customers, provides investment banks with skills to manage the sale of IPOs. The lead underwriter is the dominant market maker, taking a substantial inventory, while co-managers play a negligible role (Ellis *et al.*, 2000). Even if there are other market makers, many lead underwriters act as market makers after the offering is completed and the syndicate is dissolved because it takes time for the market to deepen. The information gained will be additionally valuable if the firm issues more securities.

The information synergies from underwriting, research and market making thus provide a rationale for combining these distinct financial services.[2] The success of an investment bank's combination of these activities will contribute to its reputation, thereby enhancing its future business in this information intensive industry.

There are potential conflicts of interest between these activities, however. For example, proprietary trading may conflict with the fiduciary responsibility of an investment bank to its brokerage clients for the best execution of trades. While this is a potential problem, the greatest focus of public concern has centred on the perceived conflicts between underwriting and brokerage, where investment banks are serving two clients, the issuing firm and investors. Issuers may benefit from optimistic research while investors should desire and seek unbiased research. If the incentives for these two activities are not appropriately aligned, there will be a temptation for employees on one side of the firm to distort information to the advantage of their clients and the profit of their department. When the potential revenues from underwriting greatly exceed brokerage commissions, there will be a strong incentive to favour issuers over investors or risk losing the former to competitors. Yet, these conflicts may not be exploited because investment banking is an information intensive industry, where reputation is a key element in a firm's long-term success, and conflicts of interest are potentially damaging to reputation.

Given the multiple services that are provided, informational advantages and conflicts of interest will be present to some degree in an investment bank. The concern is whether costly conflicts of interest may dominate the benefits from the informational synergies. Conflicts of interest may be minimized either by a firm's desire to maintain and build its reputation or by legal sanctions. An investment bank's reputation is vital to attract and retain customers. If it is concerned about the discipline of the market, it will devise various structures and incentives to prevent the exploitation of conflicts that would alienate customers. In the United States, the law recognizes the potential for conflicts and attempts to discourage corporate finance departments from exerting inappropriate influence on analysts. Although the Investment Advisers Act of 1940 does not require a firewall to prevent information transmission between departments, the idea was endorsed by the Securities and Exchange Commission (SEC) in its rules promulgated under the Securities Act of 1933 and the Securities Exchange Act of 1934. The 1940 Act and the Codes of Ethics and the Standards of Professional Conduct of the Financial Analysts Federation required that if a firm provides corporate finance services to a company, the analysts must disclose this information in research reports (Dugar and Nathan, 1995). In spite of these sanctions and the threat of market discipline, conflicts of interest were not suppressed in the late 1990s, imposing costs on many individual customers. Furthermore, damage appears to have been done to the capital markets and economy by the diminished reputation and confidence in investment banks as intermediaries.

2.2 The problem of analysts' compensation

The difficulty in setting appropriate compensation for analysts is a key factor contributing to the conflict of interest between research and underwriting. An underlying problem is the appropriateness of the analysts' information. The information generated by analysts for a bank's investing customers is not a purely private good. Like the information produced by the ratings agencies, it is to some degree a public good. As the disseminated information cannot be confined to the firm's clients, it is difficult to set a price and charge them for the information. Typically, brokerages do not charge clients for research, and research reports are usually provided free to institutional investor clients (Dugar and Nathan, 1995). A further problem arises in the evaluation of analysts' performance when there are divergences between their success at picking stocks and at correctly forecasting earnings and other fundamentals. During the recent boom, some stock prices appeared to move far away from fundamentals, burnishing the reputation of those who successfully picked stocks at the expense of those who were more focused on fundamentals.

Analysts' research is thus often treated as an overhead and generates little direct profit. If analysts operated only to advise investors, it might be desirable to tie their compensation to the trading they help to generate. Michaely and Womack (1999) caution, however, that many customers use the research information and trade at firms that offer the best bids and offers independent of the source of information; and external reputation is often more important for analysts' compensation.[3] External reputation is influenced by the annual Institutional Investor's All-American Research Team poll (Stickel, 1992).[4] The poll is based on a questionnaire sent to money managers and institutions that asks them to rank analysts on buy/sell recommendations, earnings forecasts, reports and overall service. By industry, analysts are ranked one, two and three, and runner-ups.[5] Providing external certification, directors of equity research often use these results to help set compensation levels. Yet, there remains considerable variation among banks because of their differing emphasis on stock picking and earnings forecasts. Because of these varied problems, it is difficult to set the compensation for the analysts and there is considerable variation in compensation and promotion schemes among firms, creating potential incentive problems.

Analysts' reputation is important not just for attracting and retaining brokerage customers.[6] Well-known analysts are considered to be an essential marketing tool for investment banks in the IPO market. For example, when bankers do not have an established relationship with a potential issuer, they often use the Institutional Investor polls to promote their firm. In surveys of CEOs and CFOs whose firms issued IPOs in the 1990s, approximately 75% indicated that the reputation of the research department and the analysts in their industry were key factors in selecting a lead underwriter (Galant, 1992).[7] Analysts' support is often considered part of an implicit understanding between underwriter and issuer. Positive recommendations after an IPO may also ensure that an underwriter will be chosen to lead the firm's next issue. As a result, by helping to attract issuers, analysts make important contributions to a bank's revenue; and thus their compensation may be linked to the bank's underwriting activity.

Analysts' specialized knowledge also leads them to facilitate meetings between institutional investors and companies. In addition, some analysts provide an additional service to underwriters by screening companies that are coming to market. By watching specific industries, analysts observe and gather information about firms, sometimes long before they are ready to issue securities. This activity puts them in a position to encourage or discourage investment bankers to assist these firms with corporate financing.

If they are compensated by both the brokerage and underwriting departments, there is a strong conflict of interest potential for analysts. Analysts may offer excessively bullish opinions about stocks to attract new corporate issuers, at the expense of investing customers. Even if incentives are correctly aligned, there may be pressure to bias their reports from corporate finance departments that desire analysts to follow issues and maintain positive recommendations of a current or potential issuer. The conflict of interest will be most acute if the IPO market is highly profitable relative to brokerage. Thus, the short-term payoff for an analyst may outweigh the benefits of investing in a long-term reputation in a soaring market. The temptation would be to seize the reputational rents with a short-term guaranteed contract while promoting 'hot' issues.

Given the important role and booming IPO markets of the 1990s, it is not surprising that a huge amount of attention in the financial media was devoted to analysts' pronouncements. When prices appeared to deviate from their historic relationship with fundamentals, meeting earnings expectations or changes in ratings or price targets had dramatic effects on investor sentiment. Whereas analysts were little known in the past, some became media stars in the 1990s, reaching out to millions of investors via television and the internet and attaining celebrity status. The financial press dubbed the 1990s, the 'Age of the Analysts' (Hong and Kubik, 2003). There appears to have been rising pressure on analysts as the market began to soar. Some who did not join in the optimistic promotion of stocks were dumped by banks in favour of more bullish analysts. One often cited example is the rise of Henry Blogdet. In late 1998, most analysts held that Amazon.com was overvalued at $240; Jonathan Cole of Merrill Lynch believed $50 to be a reasonable price. Henry Blodget at Oppenheimer and Co. set a price target of $400. When Amazon.com surpassed it, he was hailed as a guru; Cole departed and Merrill Lynch hired Blodget.

The multiple uses of research creates a potential problem if analysts' compensation is not set appropriately. Unfortunately, information on the compensation of analysts is not easy to obtain. Hong and Kubik (2003) were, however, able to compile data on the movement of analysts from job to job to higher or to lower status brokerage houses, enabling them to study the determinants of upward and downward mobility. Examining the brokerage house employment and earnings forecasts of 12,000 analysts working for 600 brokerages between 1983 and 2000, they found that accuracy of earnings forecasts was important, and relatively accurate forecasters were more likely to move up to higher status and presumably higher compensation brokerage houses. But, controlling for accuracy, analysts who were more optimistic than the consensus were also more likely to experience favourable job separations. Furthermore, when analysts covered stocks underwritten by their firms, the outcome of job separations depended less on accuracy and more on optimism. Breaking their sample into 1983-95 and 1996-2000, they found that job separation outcomes became more sensitive to optimism and less to accuracy in the stock market boom of the late 1990s.

2.3 The IPO boom of the 1990s

If there was potential to exploit conflicts of interest between research and underwriting, the 1990s was an ideal decade because of huge opportunities for profit from IPOs. When the stock market boomed in the 1980s, there was a wave of IPO activity, averaging $8 billion per year in new issues. The rise and fall of the US stock market as measured by the Dow Jones, S&P500 and Nasdaq Composite indexes is depicted in Figure 2.1, and the surge in IPOs is shown in Figure 2.2. In the first half of the 1990s, the average value of IPOs rose to $20 billion per year and then $35 billion for 1995-98. In a last spurt it doubled to $65 billion per year for 1999-2000 before falling to $34 billion in 2001 (Ritter and Welch, 2002). A notable feature of the market was the tilt in the composition of IPOs towards technology firms, reflected in the rise of the technology heavy Nasdaq index.[8] In the 1980s and early 1990s technology firms comprised only 26 and 23% of IPOs respectively. By 1995-98, this rose to 37%, before hitting 72% in 1999-2000.

The market devoured the new issues, and the first day returns on IPOs climbed from 7.4% in the 1980s to 18.1% in the late 1990s before hitting 65% at the peak. Also shown in Figure 2.2 is how this apparent underpricing left more and more 'money on the table', reaching a total of $65 billion out of gross sales proceeds of $129 billion for 1999-2000. While IPOs sold each year earned significant returns from three-year buy and hold strategies, they underperformed relative to the market for all of the last two decades save those purchased in 1997 and 1998.

The change in the prima facie quality of the companies going public was remarkable. According to Ritter and Welch (2002), top drawer investment banks rarely took a firm public in the 1960s and 1970s if it did not have four years of positive earnings. This benchmark was still the standard in the 1980s with only 19% of IPOs having prior negative earnings. The share of firms with negative earnings rose to 37% in 1995-98 and finally 79% in 1999-2000. While they may have had long-term potential, few new IPOs had any immediate prospect of profitability. Furthermore, the age of the firms at the time of their IPO also dropped. These seemingly poorer prospects did not reduce the first day returns. In fact, during 1999-2000, firms with negative earnings experienced mean first day returns of 72%, compared to 44% of those with positive earnings.

The underpricing of IPOs is an important anomaly in the finance literature.[9] One explanation for underpricing relates to the potential conflict of interest between underwriting banks and issuing firms. Loughran and Ritter (2002) argue that if underwriters are given discretion in share allocation, they may underprice the issue and allocate shares to favoured buy-side clients. They point to evidence that underpriced share allocations have been used for 'spinning', that is, the practice of currying favour of the executives of other prospective IPOs firms. Spinning also implies a personal conflict of interest for the executives who receive shares in return for their companies' future business with the investment bank. It is costly for their firms as underpricing raises the cost of capital.

While investment bankers and analysts have been blamed for exploiting the conflicts of interest, it is important to point out that they have not been held primarily responsible for the bubble in the market. Whereas many rode the rising market and some may have exploited it, the rising tide of stock prices took most people on Wall Street by surprise. By most measures, many stock prices had moved far away from their conventional relationships with fundamentals. The number of companies not paying dividends rose sharply, as did price-earnings ratios. Investors appear to have ignored these standard signals, giving more attention to target prices and other information, thus raising the reputation of the most optimistic analysts.[10] Outside of investment banking, there were great enthusiasts who claimed that the economy had entered a new epoch of higher growth and stability. They saw stock prices as justified by future higher earnings growth or a decline in the equity premium (Glassman and Hassett, 1999; Heaton and Lucas, 1999). This optimism echoes the optimism during the stock market boom of the 1920s. Bankers then as now may have exploited some conflicts of interest, but no serious scholarship today suggests that the boom was driven by the behaviour of investment bankers.

2.4 Analysts' 'excessive' optimism

In most popular accounts of the stock market boom of the late 1990s, analysts played an important role, promoting stocks of technology, media and telecommunications companies, helping the firms to raise capital. Stories after the crash of the stock market suggest that pressures on analysts and misaligned

Figure 2.1 The boom and crash, 1995-2003

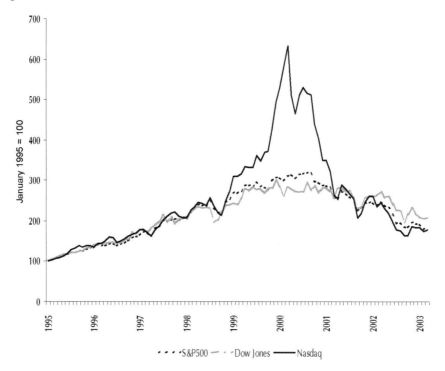

Figure 2.2 Initial public offerings, 1980-2001

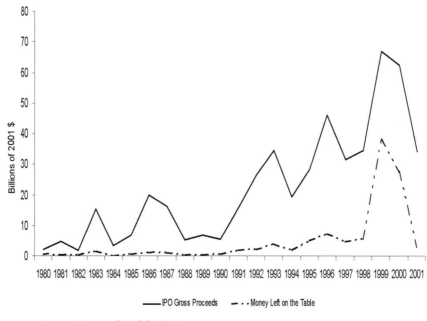

Source: Ritter and Welch (2002).

incentives were greatest in the last few years of the boom. Even with the decline in the market, some analysts appeared to be cheerleading, giving very positive reports and recommendations to investors. Complaints by investors prompted New York State's Attorney General Eliot Spitzer to use his powers under the 1921 Martin Act to investigate and bring charges against any individual or firm involved in the fraudulent purchase or sale of securities. As a result of his investigation, a sweeping settlement of the leading investment banks with the SEC, the New York Attorney General, NASD, NASAA, NYSE, and state regulators was announced on 20 December 2002 whose purpose was to reform the abusive practices that had been uncovered.

One of the common complaints was that analysts made far more buy than sell recommendations. For example, Shiller (2000) viewed the predominance of buy recommendations and the optimistic forecast bias as obvious evidence for conflicts of interest. At the peak of the market in March 2000, 73% of recommendations were to buy, 27% advised holding, and only 1% counselled sale. A year later, these shares had changed little: 69, 30 and 1% respectively. In spite of the bear market, by May 2002, they still stood at 62, 35 and 3% (Anderson and Schack, 2002). Research directors at investment banks are known to dislike offering negative judgements; many prefer to drop coverage of companies rather than continue to follow them with a sell recommendation. This aversion arises in part because they do not want to anger investor clients, especially institutional investors and their internal analysts. These analysts also make recommendations, help to direct trading, and vote for the Institutional Investor polls. Similarly, changing a recommendation to a sell may risk angering issuing companies and losing their business (Pratt, 1993).

The high percentage of buy recommendations looks like obvious evidence for excessive optimism. Yet, many research-only houses also have far more buy than sell recommendations. Furthermore, the predominance of buy recommendations and positive earnings forecasts may not be the result of over-optimism but of censoring. If analysts censor by discontinuing coverage of a stock or failing to update their forecasts, then the observed average buy recommendations and earnings forecasts will be higher than the unobserved means. This censoring behaviour, rather than some bias in their true beliefs, may explain some of the observed over-optimism in analysts' forecasts and recommendations (McNichols *et al.*, 1997). This does not explain, however, the differences in optimism between analysts working for underwriting and non-underwriting banks and the optimistic trend in the stock market boom (Hong and Kubik, 2003).

The perception of conflicts between research and underwriting in investment banks is longstanding. There is considerable anecdotal evidence suggesting that investment banks have not sought to separate the activities of their analysts and investment bankers if only to present a consistent face to the public. The *Wall Street Journal* (14 July 1992, quoted in Michaely and Womack, 1999, p. 654) reported an internal Morgan Stanley memo: 'Our objective…is to adopt a policy, fully understood by the entire firm, including the Research Department, that we do not make negative or controversial comments about our clients as a matter of sound business practice'. While the conflicts may have existed before, there is a general belief among observers that during the stock market boom of the late 1990s, research departments were co-opted and induced to provide overoptimistic reports.[11] The scandals emerging from the collapse of stock market give the impression that conflicts appeared at most major investment banks.

A trio of bullish technology analysts who gained enormous investor followings – Henry Blodget at Merrill Lynch, Mary Meeker at Morgan Stanley and Jack Grubman at Salomon Smith Barney (Citigroup) – were dubbed the King, Queen, and Jack of the internet. Although they all came under scrutiny, only Blodget and Grubman currently face charges. Differences in how they operated and the environment of their banks reveal a considerable divergence in how potential conflicts were and were not exploited.

The New York Attorney General's investigation found that Blodget often issued very positive reports on internet stocks, while he privately derided them in emails (*New York Times*, 22 November 2002, p. C1). It is alleged that he issued bullish research reports for InfoSpace, even though its price had fallen to a tenth of its peak, because the firm was planning to buy Go2Net which was one of Merrill Lynch's investment bank clients. In spite of continuing complaints from brokers with unhappy clients, Blodget only downgraded InfoSpace after it had completed its purchase of Go2Net. Similarly, while Merrill Lynch was seeking to manage a new stock issue for GoTo.com, Blodget maintained a positive recommendation for this troubled company, only to immediately downgrade it when the firm chose Credit Suisse First Boston (Cassidy, 2003).

Grubman's behaviour at Salomon Smith Barney appears to have been similar to Blodget's at Merrill Lynch. Spitzer accused Grubman of being wildly bullish on telecom companies, including WorldCom Inc., Global Crossing Ltd and Winstar Communications, even when these now bankrupt companies began to get into serious trouble and he dismissed them in private (*Wall Street Journal*, 3 September 2002, p. C1). In 1999, Grubman upgraded his rating on the stock of AT&T, a surprising move given that he had criticized the company for years. At the time, AT&T was planning to spin off its cellular division in a huge stock offering. Salomon Smith Barney was competing for this new issue, and its chances of winning AT&T business would have been poor if its analysts offered negative assessments. Six months after the bank won the contract with Goldman Sachs and Merrill Lynch, Grubman downgraded AT&T (Cassidy, 2003).

At Morgan Stanley, Meeker was the star internet analyst. Like others, she kept her ratings high after stocks plummeted. Morgan Stanley's research department was criticized by the Attorney General and regulators for issuing faulty reports that misled investors and for keeping track of analysts' work on investment banking deals when conducting reviews of analysts' performance to set compensation. Unlike Blodget and Grubman, however, there was no evidence that she did not believe in her ratings and recommendations; and she discouraged many internet issues when she did not believe that the companies would fare well. Morgan Stanley argued that 'research analysts helped screen out IPO candidates such that Morgan Stanley rejected five internet IPOs for every one the firm underwrote. Mary Meeker was an integral part of this screening process, which benefited the firm's investor clients' (Gasparino and Craig, 2003; Cassidy, 2003). While Meeker might be accused of undue enthusiasm for internet stocks, there was no evident exploitation of conflicts, and there may have been some benefit to investors from the screening that was provided.

Complaints were not limited to these three banks. At Donaldson, Lufkin & Jenrette, analyst Kevin A McCarthy complained to the head of equity research that investment bankers had pressured him to write positively about Lantronix Inc, a network device server company, even though its IPO had done extremely poorly, and its price was plummeting. In an email McCarthy stated that the bankers had acted as a proxy for the management of Lantronix and had blocked his attempts to do an in-depth analysis of the financial statements. He wrote 'I put my reputation on the line to sell this piece' of junk 'calling favors from very important clients' (*New York Times*, 12 September 2002, pp. C5 and 12).

In another important case, Frank Quattrone of Credit Suisse First Boston, a formerly highly regarded investment banker specializing in technology companies, had a complaint filed against him by NASD for improperly pressuring his analysts (Thomas, 2003). He was accused of soliciting banking business by promising favourable coverage, breaking the 'firewall' barrier between research and investment banking. He engaged his analysts by linking their bonuses to their investment banking work and apparently permitted executives of companies whose stock he handled to make changes in his staff's draft research reports. NASD also alleged that Quattrone was heavily involved in spinning, maintaining more than 300 'Friends of Frank' accounts of executives at technology companies that were active or prospective clients of the bank. These 'friends' were allocated hot shares at his discretion (Thomas, 2003). Salomon Smith Barney also allocated hard-to-get IPO shares to executives like Bernard Ebbers of WorldCom, Philip Anshutz and Joe Nacchio of Qwest, Stephen Garfalo of Metromedia and Clark McLeod of McLeodUSA (*The Economist*, 5 October 2002). The bank claimed that they were issued shares because they were among the firm's best individual customers not because Salomon Smith Barney wanted investment banking business.

It is generally conceded that while this alleged exploitation of conflicts had been practised for a long time, it has only received much attention since the collapse of the stock market. Michaely and Womack (1999) find some indications, however, that the potential conflicts of interest increased during the 1990s. Previously an investment bank's corporate finance department typically used its own staff to perform due diligence for an issue it was underwriting. After the offering was completed, the bank assigned an equity research analyst to cover the stock. More recently, equity research analysts have been used directly for due diligence process and marketing issues. While duplication of expertise may have been reduced, the 'wall' between the two departments potentially became much thinner (McLauglin, 1994 and Dickey, 1995). The SEC reported that research analysts were heavily involved with start-up companies well before they had established an investment banking relationship. They often established the initial relationship with the company, reviewed its operations and provided strategic advice. It also found that banks even allowed analysts to invest privately in firms before shares were available to the public. Furthermore, after an IPO the management of companies often applied pressure on analysts for favourable reports and recommendations. Analyst ownership of stocks that they cover creates a personal conflict of interest. Although current regulations do not prohibit this practice, some firms limit or prohibit it (Boni and Womack, 2002).

Analysts' 'excessive' optimism and spinning became lightening rods for angry investors after the collapse of the stock market.[12] While the individual cases highlighted in the media reveal some exploitation of conflicts for considerable gain, they also show that there were differences in how firms and analysts grappled with the problem. Whether these practices were characteristic of the industry and whether the market acted to discount biased information is important for determining what specific remedies are required.

2.5 Evidence of increasing conflicts in the 1990s

While individual cases of conflict of interest have recently figured prominently, some empirical studies find support for their presence, even years before the stock market boom. To identify how a potential conflict of interest was exploited it is necessary to examine how the actual information was transmitted by analysts and used by investors.

The idea that investors could be 'fooled' seemed unlikely to many researchers in academic finance, given the strong prior that analysts' reports and recommendations contain little new information because the market are governed by rational expectations. Beginning with Cowles (1933), it was long believed that recommendations of equity analysts did not influence the market, producing abnormal returns. In a seminal article, however, Grossman and Stiglitz (1980) argued against a naïve informational efficiency in markets. They pointed out that market prices would not reflect all available information, otherwise there would be no return on the millions of dollars spent every year by investment banks on research. Accumulated recent evidence based on very detailed data bears out this insight and reveals that analysts' reports do move the markets. One prominent example (Womack, 1996) examined 150,000 analysts' comments for the period 1989-91 and found that buy recommendations produced a 3% price increase and sell recommendations a 4.7% drop in a three-day event window. In addition to this notable asymmetric response, which indicated more news came from the less frequent sell recommendations, there was also considerable drift in prices in subsequent months, suggesting that full adjustment was not immediate.

Furthermore, given that they can influence the market, what is even more striking is analysts' tendency to be overoptimistic. Studying IPOs during an earlier, relatively quiet period, 1975-87, Rajan and Servaes (1997) found a strongly optimistic bias in analysts' behaviour. The more underpriced an IPO, the larger following of analysts it attracted. Analysts then systematically over-estimated the earnings of these companies, with their longer-term forecasts being more (excessively) optimistic. Rajan and Servaes also found that more firms complete IPOs when analysts are especially optimistic about growth prospects, consistent with their finding that more firms conduct IPOs when seasoned firms in their industries are trading at historically high multiples.

If analysts do influence the market and their information is biased, is the new information they provide aimed at exploiting a conflict of interest? The answer to this question should be found in the differential behaviour of analysts at under-writing and non-underwriting banks. If conflicts of interest are minor and the informational advantages gained by combining underwriting and brokerage are dominant, then there are implications for the reception of analysts' information. Owing to their key position, lead underwriters' analysts' reports should carry extra weight and their predictions should be unbiased and more accurate than those of other equity analysts. Consequently, the market should react more to their announcements than to reports of other analysts. Their recommendations should have more predictive power of future prices and give investors better investment results. If conflicts of interest dominate informational advantages, however, lead underwriter analysts will issue recommendations that are biased toward being overly optimistic. Underwriter analysts will also issue relatively more positive recommendations for firms that trade poorly in the IPO aftermarket. In a rational market, participants should then discount underwriter analysts' recommendations relative to non-underwriter analysts.[13]

Examining data for seasoned equities between 1983 and 1988, Dugar and Nathan (1995) find that while underwriters' analysts are optimistically biased, their earnings forecasts are just as accurate on average as those of non-underwriter analysts. They uncover some limited evidence that investors rely relatively less on underwriters' analysts since market reaction around the report dates of non-underwriter analysts was greater than the reaction for underwriter analysts, although the difference was not statistically significant. This finding offers some support for the contention that investors are not 'fooled' by the optimism of underwriter analysts.

Michaely and Womack (1999) examined 'buy' recommendations of lead underwriter and other analysts after the SEC's 25 day post-IPO 'quiet period' for 391 IPOs in 1990 and 1991. They found that in the month after the quiet period, lead underwriters' analysts made 50% more buy recommendations than other firms' analysts for the same securities, suggesting some conflict of interest. One striking feature was that stock prices of firms recommended by lead underwriting banks declined during the quiet period, while other banks' picks rose. The market appears to recognize this difference in the quality of information, and the excess return at the recommendation date is 2.7% for underwriters' analysts and 4.4% for other analysts. Considering a two year holding period from the IPO date, the performance of other analysts' recommended issues was 50% better than the performance of underwriters' recommendations. Finally, the same investment banks made better recommendations on IPOs when they were not the lead underwriter, implying that it was not a difference in analysts' ability but an underwriter bias.

While Michaely and Womack's findings are consistent with the presence of conflicts of interest, one cannot rule out two alternative explanations. It is possible that underwriters' analysts exhibit cognitive bias (Kahneman and Lovallo, 1993), where they have very strong prior beliefs that the firms they underwrite are better and additional research will not alter this view. Non-underwriters' analysts do not have strong prior beliefs and allow their judgement to evolve. There may also be some selection bias if underwriters are chosen by issuers because they hold favourable views of the firm and interpret new information differently than other analysts.[14] These alternative interpretations may explain some of the considerable heterogeneity in the industry. One interpretation is that conflicts of interest may have dominated Merrill Lynch, Salomon Smith Barney and Credit Suisse First Boston's research departments, while cognitive bias may have been the leading force at Morgan Stanley.

It is popularly believed that investors' attention to earnings performance increased in recent years. This increased sensitivity of the market to earnings forecasts seems to have influenced management behaviour with companies under heavy pressure to prevent earnings from falling short of targets – including analysts' forecasts. Managers have some discretion in reporting the timing and magnitude of revenue and expenses and can manipulate earnings through accruals and other devices (Chan *et al.*, 2003). Missing earnings targets is regarded as extremely bad news. Managers may thus have an incentive to ensure that analysts keep down their forecasts – permitting analysts to exceed their forecasts and thereby gain a boost to the firms' stock prices. There is some empirical evidence for this increased focus of the markets on companies' earnings. Francis *et al.* (2002) and Landsman and Maydew (2002) find that the magnitude of abnormal returns and abnormal volume increased around earnings announcements from the 1980s to the 1990s. In addition, the Francis *et al.* (2002a) study also produced evidence that market reaction to analysts' earnings announcements has increased.

Again, anecdotal evidence in the popular press implies that analysts manipulate their forecasts. These beliefs find some support in recent academic research. Chan *et al.* (2003) examined whether analysts bias their opinions in favour of a company by adjusting earnings estimates to help managers match or exceed expectations. They found that for the period 1984-2001 there was a pronounced shift in the cross-sectional distribution of earnings surprises for the United States. The share of non-negative surprises rose from 49% in the late 1980s to 76% in 1999-2001. Furthermore, there is evidence that the higher incidence of non-negative surprises arose from analysts' strategic adjustments. When earnings fell short of the consensus three months before the announcements, analysts revised the estimates downward by enough to yield a non-negative surprise upon announcement. This pattern was more pronounced for growth firms compared to value firms, which Chan *et al.* (2003) attribute to analysts' disposition to deliver a positive surprise for firms with relatively high valuations. In addition, more firms initially meet or surpass expectations for consecutive quarters, than would be expected statistically, suggesting manipulation. In the late 1990s, growth firms with four consecutive quarters of non-negative surprises occurred 35% more often than predicted. Non-negative surprises became increasingly predictable based on whether it was a growth or value firm and the sign on past surprises.

It should be noted, however, that managers have significant incentives to ensure they limit the 'surprise' on an earnings announcement especially if it is negative. The price effects of a negative surprise are positively correlated with the price-earnings ratio, and in the late 1990s these multiples were very high by any standard. Any shock was met with a sharp price reaction and some class action suits against the management. The result was that managers started informing the market giving guidance through various sources including favoured analysts.

Compared to the United States, foreign markets typically do not show this increased disposition to positive earnings surprises. Overall, they display a median negative surprise and a stable distribution of surprises over time. While European markets certainly experienced a boom in technology and telecommunication industries, only in the United Kingdom was there a pattern similar to the US one. The proportion of positive surprises rose from 45% in the late 1980s to 59% in 1998-99. For the European Continent, over half of the surprises were negative. The relatively depressed Japanese market of the 1990s did not have a wave of IPO activity and there is no trend in earnings surprises. Chan *et al.* (2003) argue that the incentives for firms and managers to control earnings surprises are weaker in foreign equity markets. Only in the United Kingdom, which shares similar investment bank features with the United States, does it appear that analysts were managing earnings surprises. Elsewhere, conflicts of interest due to investment banking business were seemingly less severe because IPO activity was lower and competition among investment banks weaker, while compensation for analysts was lower.

2.6 Remedies for the underwriter/analyst conflict of interest

The extraordinary disclosures about the exploitation of conflicts of interest have elicited a wide range of proposed remedies. Proposals fall into one of five categories discussed in the first chapter: let the market resolve conflicts of interest; require increased disclosure; increase supervisory oversight; separate activities; and socialize information production.

Having removed much of the New Deal banking regulation in the past decade, there was initially little interest in broad new regulations. In September 2001, SEC Chairman, Harvey Pitt stated that he would prefer that the securities industry set its own rules for dealing with analysts' conflicts rather than have the SEC create more regulations. In fact, after the crash of the market, some firms with damaged reputations responded with internal reforms and some 'overly' optimistic analysts departed.

For the market to solve the conflicts of interest, investors need to be able to identify and respond to inaccurate, biased information.[15] Boni and Womack (2002) conducted a survey and found that 86% of the professional money managers and buy-side analysts said that they discount the recommendations and reports of analysts when there is an investment banking relationship between the bank and the company analysed. Looking at data for 1990-91, Michaely and Womack (1999) found that the market slightly discounted post-IPO recommendations of underwriting analysts, but their recommendations were not entirely discounted, perhaps reflecting some value to their information advantage. Boni and Womack conjecture that this result arises because institutional investors and money managers understand the bias, but less sophisticated individuals do not. Institutional investors are aware of the conflicts of interest, but they make adjustments to the biases of analysts' reports because they have their own in-house research staffs and buy independent research. To the degree that they focus on fundamentals, the individual investors, who lack the funds or skills to judge brokerage research analysts, would be the most affected.

If the market does not provide sufficient disclosure, regulation may be necessary to coerce firms to permit investors to observe whether there are any conflicts of interest behind the information provided by analysts. Mandatory disclosure of the relationship between the bank and its employees and the issuing firms is the minimum information required. Such information would include whether the firm was a client of the bank's underwriting or other departments, and any conflicts of interest for individual analysts. Disclosure is more difficult when banks are assisting mergers and acquisitions. Disclosure of a relationship with corporate clients or a change in ownership stakes would provide private information about impending mergers and acquisitions to the market (Anderson and Schack, 2002). The problem here is that there is a trade-off between disclosure and the loss of proprietary information. The appropriate solution to this problem is to substitute disclosure with supervisory oversight by regulators when appropriate.[16]

Another solution is to increase the distance between analysis and underwriting by either strengthening firewalls within investment banks or forcing a complete separation.[17] The difficulty here is that although the potential conflicts of interest are reduced by this approach, the greater the degree of separation, the more potential synergies in information collection and use are lost. There is no simple guide to striking the right balance of costs and benefits. The SIA Best Practices for Research 2001 report recommended a reinforcement of the firewalls by ensuring the following: that analysts do not report to investment banking; that analysts' pay is not directly linked to specific investment banking transactions; and that their reports are not submitted to corporate finance or company management for approval (Securities Industry Association, 2001). Having separate analysts – analysts in underwriting and in brokerage – could lead to the embarrassing and probably intolerable situation where they issue conflicting recommendations at the same time as synergies are lost.

While a public debate on the appropriate mix of disclosure, separation and prudential supervision was possible, it was foreclosed by the global settlement reached on 20 December 2002 by the SEC, the New York Attorney General, NASD, NASAA, NYSE and state regulators with the ten largest investment banks.[18] The five key terms of the agreement were:

1. Firms are required to sever the links between research and investment banking, including analyst compensation for equity research and the practice of analysts accompanying investment banking personnel on road shows and pitches.
2. The practice of spinning is banned.
3. Each firm is required to make public its analyst recommendations,

including its ratings and price target forecasts.

4. For a five-year period, each of the brokerage firms will be required to contract with no less than three independent research firms to provide research to the brokerage firm's customers. An independent consultant 'monitor' for each firm will be chosen by regulators to procure independent research from independent providers to ensure that investors get objective investment advice.

5. Each firm in the settlement will pay a fine, which is partly retrospective relief, independent research and investor education. The total is more than $1.4 billion.

While it remains to be seen how the terms of this agreement are implemented, there are some good and some alarming features. Overall, it seems as though the Act aims at making analyst information a purely public good. By effectively socializing research, firms no longer compete for customers by the quality of their research if it is all made public. By taxing the firms to fund independent research, there will be an incentive to decrease their own internal analysis. What will be produced will probably be of lower quality. There is less incentive for quality information, as the banks do not control the information that they are being forced to acquire. Fortunately this is only for a five-year period, but it should not be renewed.

The stock market boom produced enormous opportunities for exploiting conflicts. Without a new spectacular rise in the market, there will be few incentives to favour issuing customers at the expense of investor clients. Banning spinning will, however, ensure that insiders do not take advantage of outsider investors. Although the executives did not always profit, they benefited by the underpricing of issues in the booming market. Banning spinning, which exploited the lack of information about how shares were distributed, will not affect the efficiency of the market.

Although it is appropriate for some separation between analysts and underwriters with firewalls, complete separation is mistaken. In light of the failed attempts to separate commercial and investment banking under the Glass-Steagall Act (described in Chapter 5), this remedy is extreme. Given that the market already discounted lead underwriter analysts' recommendations, firms were subject to some market discipline. Separation means that firms will have to have a separate staff for underwriting to perform the analysis, raising costs and thereby losing some economies of scope. Failing to let firms be disciplined by loss of reputation and litigation where conflicts were exploited by individual firms, may weaken the competitiveness of investment banks.

To overcome the information asymmetries, the New York Attorney-General-SEC's global settlement relies on separation and the socialization of research as remedies. The alternative approach would be to allow the market to discipline firms that have been required to provide increased disclosure to investors of the firm's underwriting relationships, complementing this with supervisory oversight where disclosure would result in the loss of proprietary information.

3 Accounting: Conflicts of Interest in Auditing and Consulting

3.1 Introduction

Information asymmetries between suppliers and users of capital create potential conflicts of interest that can limit the efficient allocation and use of capital. If shareholders, creditors and other stakeholders are confident that managers are maximizing shareholder value and meeting the firms' obligations, funding will be available. If, however, they suspect that managers are exploiting conflicts of interest, the flow of capital will dry up. One way in which managers have tried to reduce information asymmetries is to provide a set of 'accounts' that reflect how they have utilized the resources under their control.[19] The simple presentation of the information in a set of reports or accounts does not, however, eliminate the inherent agency problems. As a result there is a demand for an external monitor to opine on the reliability of the accounts. This role is most commonly taken by an auditor, or more recently an audit firm, that is independent of the managers preparing the accounts, to attest to the quality of information in the financial statements produced by the management.

This simple description leads to several important questions to be considered when examining the apparent audit failures that we have experienced recently. What is the nature of the opinion that is sought and delivered? What is the source of an auditor's comparative advantage that leads to value creation for suppliers of capital? What ensures that an auditor is unbiased and/or independent? This last question is particularly pertinent to issues surrounding the conflicts of interest that exist for auditors. Finally, what is the evidence on whether the market is able to discern differences in the quality and services delivered by auditors? To answer these questions, we provide some historical background to understand how existing institutions arose to meet the challenges faced by auditors and how the current crisis of confidence in auditing emerged.

3.2 The evolution of auditing, standards and regulation

From the earliest days of separation between managers of resources and their owners, there has been a role for an auditor to provide some credibility, certification or validation of the financial information being conveyed (O'Connor, 2002). Each nation can trace its auditing roots back to examples where managers were separated from and reporting back to the owners or creditors.

In the United Kingdom, the South Sea Bubble in 1720 highlighted a need for independent monitoring of claims made by promoters of share offerings in a public stock market. It was more than a century later, however, before the audit profession was created as a by-product of the industrial revolution, with the enactment of company legislation. The first professional organization of accountants was the Institute of Chartered Accountants of Scotland (ICAS), which received its Royal Charter in 1854, followed 26 years later by the combination of several local professional accounting societies in the Institute of Chartered Accountants of England and Wales (ICAEW). These professional accountants and auditors also played a significant role in the development of the accounting profession in the United States as they were sent there to 'protect' the capital provided by British investors to develop American railroads and industry in the late nineteenth century (Davidson and Anderson, 1987). Of the 'Big 6' global audit firms that operated in the 1990s, all but Arthur Andersen can trace its roots back to members of the English or Scottish Institutes. The professional society of accountants in the United States evolved from a small local organization founded in New York in 1887 to become the American Society of Certified Public Accountants in 1921 and finally the American Institute of Certified Public Accountants (AICPA) in 1957 (O'Connor, 2002). In many other countries either where the role of accounting reports was more closely matched with tax reports, or where governments played a larger role as suppliers of capital to industry, a 'statutory auditor' was appointed to report on compliance with laws rather than on economic activity.

History suggests that a private demand for audit services exists whenever managers are separate from the suppliers of capital. The services provided and the scope of the 'reports' that are made by auditors will vary with the nature of this demand. For example, in Germany the large universal banks 'owned' the audit firms to ensure independent validation of the accounts of companies to which they supplied capital.[20] When we consider that much of the early capital, especially in countries with universal banking systems, was provided by 'private placement' of debt rather than equity issues, it is likely that early voluntary audits provided sufficient information to support a 'credit rating'. Thus, the creation of a separate rating business, discussed in the next chapter, is not independent of the changing role of auditing over time. More generally, the auditor's role evolved from providing information to a select group of suppliers of capital to a broader set of users, with a transformation of the auditors' reports from a private to a public good.

While private demand for audits providing independent validation of accounts existed for centuries, the growth of public markets for equity was the primary catalyst for a shift of the audit report to a public good. The two largest equity markets at the beginning of the twentieth century were in the United Kingdom and the United States. The United Kingdom had already enacted its Companies Act that made audit opinions a statutory obligation. There was, however, no similar federal legislation in the United States until the stock market crash of 1929 convinced the public that auditors were not sufficiently independent of managers. The US regulatory response was the Securities Act of 1933, which led to the requirement that companies offering shares to the public must submit regular financial statements certified by an independent public or certified accountant. The Securities Exchange Act of 1934 created the Securities and Exchange Commission (SEC), which was given jurisdiction over the accounting profession and its rules.[21]

From the New Deal until the recent enactment of the Sarbanes-Oxley Act of 2002, the SEC delegated its accounting and auditing rule-making authority to private standard setting bodies with self-regulation and SEC oversight. In financial accounting, standard setting was initially delegated to AICPA committees; but perceived conflicts of interest led to a series of reforms that gradually evolved into an independent Financial Accounting Standards Board (FASB) in the early 1970s.[22] For auditing, in contrast, the AICPA retained its standard setting role with the Auditing Standards Board writing the principles and rules for independentauditors. Most of these rules pertained to the conduct of an audit and the nature of the reports the auditor provided, but there were also rules for oversight and self-regulation. Specifically, under the AICPA rules, auditors were required to have other audit firms perform peer reviews of their work; and there was a Public Oversight Board that provided an additional level of oversight on auditors and audit firms.

In response to the recent spate of business and audit failures the AICPA's self-regulatory efforts have been called into question. As a result, the Sarbanes-Oxley Act of 2002 established the Public Company Accounting Oversight Board (PCAOB). Under the SEC's oversight, the PCAOB will register public accounting firms, and establish rules for auditing, quality control, ethics, independence and other standards. In addition, it will conduct inspections of accounting firms and when needed carry out investigations and disciplinary proceedings and impose sanctions. The PCAOB has indicated its intention to take over the rule-making authority for auditing standards, while leaving accounting rules in the hands of the FASB, at least for now.

The evolution of accounting and auditing standards has followed a similar path in the United Kingdom, with the ICAEW having responsibility for standard setting in both areas until recently. An Accounting Standards Board (ASB) was created along the lines of the FASB in 1990. The United Kingdom's ASB is appointed by the Financial Reporting Council (FRC), a body that is supposed to be independent of the professional societies, being the 'guardian' of the 'Combined Code' of the Listing Rules and the accounting and auditing aspects of the Companies Act (ICAEW, 2003b).

Recently most European countries have sought to find a balance between their national standards, which evolved independently, and the regulations imposed by the European Commission on EU members. In 2002, the European Commission published a report, 'Statutory Auditors' Independence in the EU: A Set of Fundamental Principles', that the ICAEW (2003c) accepted as best practice in areas not already covered by existing guidelines, in advance of a comprehensive review. The European Commission has also mandated that by 2005 all European listed companies, with a few exceptions, should employ the International Accounting Standards.

3.3 The value of the audit opinion

It is probably not an exaggeration to state that audited financial statements are central to the efficiency of the capital market and that these statements are broadly relied upon as the key information source in assessing both past stewardship and expected future use of capital provided to firms.[23] The current audit opinion is expressed in a report attesting to whether the financial statements provide a 'fair presentation' or 'true and fair view' of the financial performance and financial position of the entity at a point in time or over a period of time. The form and content of the report, and thus the nature of the opinion, has evolved from detailed reviews and comments when audits were a result of private demand to the often 'boiler-plate' versions we see today.

By reducing the information asymmetry between management and investors, the certification provided by an audit should have a measurable value. Favourable opinions issued by audit firms with a strong reputation should be valued more than those issued by firms with weaker reputations. The available empirical evidence confirms that if the top firms have the strongest reputations, obtaining opinions from them lowers the required rate of return on issuing company bonds.[24]

The standard presumption is that a 'clean' or unqualified audit opinion represents a certification of quality and reliability of the information being reported. Studies suggest, however, that there is a large difference between the perception of what an audit opinion is intended to convey and what it actually does (McEnroe and Martens, 2001). Results of the Commission on Auditors' Responsibilities (1978) sponsored by the AICPA revealed that some users believe that an unqualified audit opinion indicates that the entity is financially sound. Users also expected auditors to have performed audit functions to penetrate into the company's operations and management and detect any illegal acts or fraud. (McEnroe and Martens 2001) These expectations are widely held in spite of the fact that in the United States the audit opinion only indicates that management's presentation of the financial information is a fair presentation of the financial position and performance of the company is in conformity with generally accepted accounting principles (GAAP). This difference in perception versus reality is known as the 'expectations gap'. An expectations gap exists in Europe also but may not be as great. In the United Kingdom and in many European countries since the 4th Directive of the European Commission, an auditor's opinion refers to whether the financial statements present a 'true and fair view' of the company's financial position and performance.[25] In these countries the audit process arguably has a focus more aligned with users' expectations than in the United States, although in many countries (like France) 'true and fair' has no simple translation and has made little impact on the nature of the opinion.

One possible cause of the expectations gap is from the difference between what auditors report to the company versus what they report to the public. As in earlier times when audits were driven by private demand, auditors still provide management (and audit committees where they exist) with a post-audit report that details a number of accounting, internal control and even business issues they discovered during their audit. Yet, these issues are inevitably 'resolved' to the point where the regular 'clean' opinion on the published financial statements can be made. Thus, market participants may presume that large-scale problems do not exist.

In the face of this large and perhaps growing expectations gap, it is important to emphasize that despite perceptions that accounting is a precise measurement system, there is no system of rules that can be written to eliminate the need for judgement in accounting decisions that are required for periodically reporting on a company's financial position and performance (Wallman, 1996). The external auditor's primary role is to provide an unbiased opinion on a company's financial information provided by management to the financial markets.

Given the complexity and subjectivity of many accounting decisions, it is necessary for an auditor to have both the professional expertise to evaluate management's judgements, and independence from management (Ryan *et al.*, 2001). Auditor independence is the key factor in ensuring there is no actual or perceived conflict of interest with the managers of the firms supplying the information (Wallman, 1996). If expertise and independence are the two primary attributes of a professional auditor, reputation is the primary asset of value to the auditor and especially the audit firm. Thus, we would expect all the auditor's actions to be guided by an overriding desire to avoid damage to this critical asset.

The current crisis of confidence in capital markets, arising from widespread massive business failures, is clearly exacerbated by the perceived failure of the auditors to enforce accurate reporting of companies' true performance and to identify fraudulent activities in several cases. Many of the companies that failed spectacularly had unqualified audit opinions prior to their demise. While audit failures are not a new occurrence, the growing list of assumed audit failures at large companies has damaged all auditors' reputations, and brought into question the auditor's primary role as an independent expert and monitor of financial statement information.

There are three interrelated potential explanations for the perceived audit failures:

1. The expectations gap of the auditor's role may have increased. The rise of class action lawsuits against audit firms on behalf of shareholders may reflect this rising expectations gap.
2. The bull market of the late 1990s, propelled perhaps by overly optimistic investor sentiment, may have increased the incentives for management to manage earnings, increasing the difficulty of audits. The post-bull market catharsis revealed the intense accounting management that attempted to meet earnings expectations to sustain high stock valuations.
3. There were systemic problems from the lack of auditor independence, creating conflicts of interest that were exploited.

All the explanations have some validity and interacted to create a crisis of confidence, tarnishing the reputations of the largest audit firms.

3.4 Conflicts of interest

In auditing, threats to truthful reporting arise from several potential conflicts of interest. The conflict most frequently discussed in the popular financial press arises from an auditor providing non-audit services, usually in areas of tax, accounting or management information systems and strategic advice, commonly referred to as management advisory services (MAS). In an early empirical study of the potential audit/MAS conflict, Simunic (1984) defined an auditor's conflict of interest as 'a setting where an auditor must evaluate (trade-off) the benefits and costs of truthful reporting', adding 'In general, any situation which increases the probability that an auditor will not truthfully report the results of his audit investigation can be viewed as a threat to independence'.[26]

Despite the potential cost from conflicts of interest in provision of joint services, there are also offsetting efficiency gains from economies of scope. For example, auditing firms are natural consultants to companies because they gather and assess a wide array of information leading to their attestation of financial performance reported in the financial statements.[27] Based on the historical evolution of auditing we described, it has long been common practice for auditors to supply management with an assessment of the company's systems and practices at the end of an audit. There are clear economic efficiencies in using the information already gathered to move to an advisory role in related areas.

As companies became more complex and as technology advanced, corporate accounting systems were increasingly computerized. It was a natural step for the advisory role of auditing firms to specialize in computerized management information systems. This practice developed rapidly, and from the early 1980s, the auditing firms emerged as major powerhouses of the consulting business. The largest auditing firms entered the ranks of the top ten of global consulting firms. At the head of this list was Andersen Consulting, which was almost solely a systems-oriented consulting firm.[28] All audit firms provided systems advice, although not to the same scale as Andersen Consulting.

To function efficiently in their primary audit attest function, audit firms need to invest in specialized industry knowledge that enables them to evaluate management accounting decisions. Such investment in industry expertise has natural information synergies with traditional strategic and structuring consulting services. Thus, all audit firms have industry specializations that served both audit and non-audit businesses. For example, Arthur Andersen had a long-standing expertise in oil and gas and related energy businesses, which made it an obvious choice for Enron, an energy firm with Headquarters in Houston, the hub of the US energy industry. One of the conflicts that arose within Arthur Andersen was the growth of the non-systems consulting business that Andersen Consulting partners viewed as a threat to their franchise.[29] Tax advice is another complementary service that audit firms have increasingly provided. Accounting and taxation have often been closely associated in many people's minds, especially in those countries, notably Germany and Japan, with a clear link between the financial reporting and tax reporting systems.

Some sense of the growth of these non-auditing/accounting services can be obtained from Figures 3.1 and 3.2, although they only cover a brief period. From 1994 to 1996, the auditing fee revenue for the Big 6 rose slightly in absolute dollar terms but dropped by more than 10% as a share of total revenue. Fees from tax advisory services were flat in percentage terms at about 20%, while the areas of gain were consulting and other MAS services. Following the dramatic revelations at Enron and other major corporations, there was a sharp increase in 2001 and 2002 in auditing and accounting fees both in absolute and percentage terms. The change in percentages was driven in part by the separation of the consulting businesses by the end of 2002 in all the companies except Deloitte Touche and Tomatsu.

These multiple services generate economies of scale and scope but create two potential sources of conflict of interest. The most commonly discussed conflict is the potential to pressure auditors to bias their judgements and opinions to limit any loss of fees in the 'other' services. The second more subtle conflict is that auditors often evaluate systems or structuring (tax and financial) advice that were put in place by their non-audit counterparts within the firm. With all the non-audit services, a potential boundary for the trade-off between economic efficiency and potential bias is between when the audit firm provides its expertise to solve issues raised by the client and when it 'sells' new ideas for structures, especially if these are at the edge of acceptable current practice. For example, one of the more publicized problems at Enron was its array of off-balance special purpose entities.[30] Arthur Andersen was discovered to be marketing some of these structures to Enron and other clients. Similarly in the tax area, two senior executives of Sprint PCS recently resigned after it was discovered they had employed certain 'aggressive' tax structures marketed by Ernst & Young.

Both conflicts lead to questions of independence and are assumed to reduce the likelihood of a negative audit outcome. These conflicts and debates about independence existed in the 1920s and became prominent again in the 1970s (Simunic, 1984). In 1976, the Metcalf Committee Staff Study argued that a conflict of interest exists when an audit firm supplies MAS and audit services, which it then has to audit for reliability and accuracy. The study claimed that any negative views on the systems arising from the audit could impose a cost on the

Figure 3.1 Percentage of fee revenues by business unit

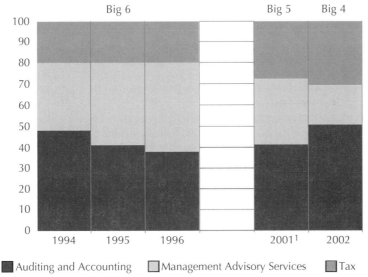

Notes: The years 1994-6 include revenue fee split percentages for the Big 6; 2000 and 2001 include revenue fee split percentages for the Big 5; 2002 does not include Arthur Andersen and therefore includes the revenue-fee split for the Big 4 only. Ernst & Young sold its consulting arm (MAS) prior to 2001. KPMG spun off its consulting business in 2001 and had no MAS revenues in that year. In 2001 Arthur Andersen's MAS revenues excluded the revenues of Andersen Consulting that was spun off in that year.
1   Arthur Andersen 2001 numbers are Bowman's estimates.
Source: 'The 2003 Top 100 Firms', *Accounting Today*, 17 March-6 April 2003, www.webcpa.com, pp 30-40.

Figure 3.2 Distribution of fee split revenues

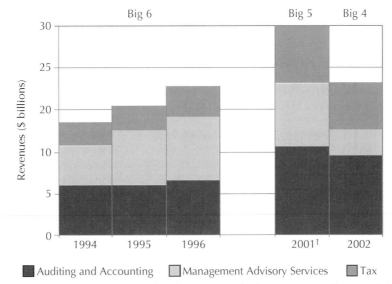

Notes: The years 1994-6 include revenue fee split percentages for the Big 6; 2000 and 2001 include revenue fee split percentages for the Big 5; 2002 does not include Arthur Andersen and therefore includes the revenue-fee split for the Big 4 only. Ernst & Young sold its consulting arm (MAS) prior to 2001. KPMG spun off its consulting business in 2001 and had no MAS revenues in that year. In 2001 Arthur Andersen's MAS revenues excluded the revenues of Andersen Consulting that was spun off in that year.
1   Arthur Andersen 2001 numbers are Bowman's estimates.
Source: 'The 2003 Top 100 Firms', *Accounting Today*, 17 March-6 April 2003, www.webcpa.com, pp 30-40.

whole audit firm as it would have a direct cost related to reimbursement for the poor non-audit service supplied and lead to a loss of reputation.

Several studies have tried to assess how the combination of audit and non-audit services affect efficiency and independence, providing some limited evidence on economies of scope. Using fee data collected from a sample of publicly held US companies, Simunic (1984) analysed a client's decision to purchase MAS and audit services when their production functions were interdependent. He tested for the existence and pricing effects of such knowledge externalities or spillovers and found significantly higher audit fees for clients who purchase MAS from their auditors relative to clients who do not. Simunic claimed that this result is consistent with the existence of efficiencies from joint production as the quality of audit services was improved. Extending Simunic's analysis, Palmrose (1986) uncovered similar effects when non-audit services were supplied by non-incumbent audit firms. Antle *et al.* (2002) produced results consistent with Simunic (1984) and Palmrose (1986) where higher audit fees led to higher non-audit fees and vice versa, consistent with economies of scope running in both directions.

Parkash and Venables (1993) examine differences in the frequency of purchase of recurring versus non-recurring MAS by audit clients. They suggest that audit clients have incentives to limit non-audit purchases from incumbent auditors. Their conjecture is that a perceived reduction in auditor independence reduces audit credibility incurring added agency costs for companies as the value of the auditors' monitoring role is reduced. Their empirical tests indicate that agency costs explained cross-sectional differences in the recurring purchase of non-audit services but the strongest factor was informational and cost efficiency arising from the industry specialization of the auditor. These results suggest that the economic efficiency can dominate agency costs.

More recently studies have examined whether auditors' fees for MAS are associated with abnormal accruals, used as a proxy for earnings management and hence biased reporting. Frankel *et al.* (2002) find results consistent with non-audit fees being positively associated with small earnings surprises and the magnitude of discretionary accruals. As Kinney and Libbey (2002) point out, however, the data and controls for omitted correlated variables makes the findings tenuous. Antle *et al.* (2002) used a UK data sample, where audit and non-audit fees have been disclosed for many years under the Companies Act, and an improved model specification to examine the issue. Their results were consistent with economies of scope when audit and non-audit services were combined. There was no significant effect of abnormal accruals on audit fees or non-audit fees, indicating that these fees were not used as inducements to obtain favourable treatment. They did find, however, that higher fees for non-audit services decreased abnormal accruals. They interpreted this finding as being consistent with a productive effect of non-audit services in lowering customers' receivables and inventories, for example. In addition, they provided evidence that audit fees had a positive effect on abnormal accruals, suggesting that the higher fees lead to more frequent acceptance of abnormal accruals.[31] DeFond *et al.* (2002) also find no evidence that non-audit service fees impair auditor independence and that auditors are more likely to issue going concern qualifications to clients that pay higher audit fees, consistent with a risk-based propensity to audit more. Using proprietary data from specific accounting firms, Bell *et al.* (2001) examined the relationship between audit fees and risk of the audit client and concluded that risky clients bear higher fees because of extra effort with more hours spent.[32]

Collectively these studies suggest auditors expend effort to address aggressive or risky accounting decisions made by clients, implying that the source of bias is in the accounting rather than in the audit effort. The conflicts of interest arising from auditors providing non-audit and audit services have been a concern for decades, yet the empirical evidence does not reveal a systematic pattern of these conflicts creating obvious biases. Nevertheless, regulators' concerns about compromises to auditors' independence grew dramatically in the late 1990s, in parallel with the dramatic growth in the share of the MAS practices relative to the audit firm's total revenue and profit.

3.5 Separation of auditing and related services

Concerns about the exploitation of conflicts of interest produced demands that auditing firms cease their non-auditing services. Yet, separation does not guarantee that problems will disappear, as former SEC Commissioner Wallman (1996) explained:

> 'the issue of independence and objectivity is not resolved by a separation of audit and non-audit work – in fact, continuing to focus on that issue misses the point about dependency. It is not a question of what service is performed, but a question of what dependency or conflict is created and how best to address it and ensure the reliability of the information presented to the public.'

While this nuanced approach has not been ignored, separation of services has become the popular remedy to the perceived failures of auditing.

Consulting services were popularly viewed as the key problem and new SEC rules forced changes in the non-audit services being offered (Securities and Exchange Commission, June 2000; Levitt, 2000), with several firms selling their consulting businesses. The major vehicle for separation as a remedy in the United States is the Public Company Accounting Reform and Investor Protection Act or Sarbanes-Oxley Act of 2002. Section 201 of this Act determines what services cannot be performed by auditors. The law holds that it is unlawful for a registered public accounting firm to provide any non-audit service to an issuer contemporaneously with the audit including: bookkeeping, financial information systems design, appraisals, actuarial services, internal audit outsourcing, management functions, broker, dealer, investment advisor, investment banker, legal services and any other service that the PCAOB determines are impermissible. The Board is empowered to allow for case by case exceptions, if services constitute less than 5% of the total amount of revenues paid to the auditor by a client.

Although at this time it is not clear how the law will be applied, it is certain to restrict the activities in which audit firms had previously engaged drastically. There are indications that the PCOAB will take a hard line. The SEC initially decided to allow audit firms to retain their tax services, but the PCOAB has indicated that this non-audit service may be eliminated.

3.6 The multi-product audit firm and auditor independence

While solutions for controlling audit independence are currently focused on restricting non-audit services, these remedies may be of limited help in our view because they are unlikely to solve the core problems of incentives and performance measurement in the audit process itself. In most countries auditing firms have been organized as partnerships with complex profit sharing rules and joint and several liability for losses. Until the early 1980s, the firms' managing partners, governance structure and profitability of the firms' divisions was clearly dominated by the audit side. Power within the firms began to change, however, as MAS activities and revenues grew dramatically with the growth in information technology. Not only did the consulting business see high revenue growth and high margins, but audit profits were under pressure at the same time. The profit pressure came from both the revenue and cost side. Audit services became increasingly competitive causing fee reductions, at the same time as costs ballooned, especially as auditors became subject to growing litigation risk (Palmrose, 1988 and 1991). Consulting partners began increasingly to question why they should 'share' their profit growth with their audit partners, as the partnership organizational structure meant that the non-audit partners also incurred a share in the audit risk with little ability to exert any control over it.

Nowhere was this conflict more extreme than at Arthur Andersen, where the audit and consulting partners fought publicly about power and profit sharing. It was clear from anecdotal evidence and press reports of infighting that a split was inevitable and that significant amounts of management effort were focused on trying to deal with the internal battles.[33] The internal conflicts moved to a difficult court battle leading to the final split of Arthur Andersen and Andersen Consulting in 2000. During this contentious period, Andersen's audit partners were pushed to focus on revenue generation and profitability as these were the focus of the 'battle'. Other firms had less contention between the audit and consulting services, with different routes taken to eliminate related conflicts of interest. KPMG spun off its consulting entity into a public company; PricewaterhouseCoopers and Ernst & Young sold their consulting businesses to other firms; while Deloitte and Touche recently decided to retain the consulting business.

There was, however, another very important dimension to the Andersen case. Many of the largest recent corporate failures that were Arthur Andersen clients – Enron, Worldcom, Qwest and Global Crossing – were also the largest companies in their local regions.[34] With an incentive structure that puts pressure on managers to deliver audit revenue and profit at every unit, the manager of a regional or city office would be wary of taking a negative stance on an audit that would risk the client selecting an alternative audit firm in that region. The loss of an Enron or Worldcom account would have been devastating to a local office and its partners, even if it was only a small part of firm-wide revenues and profits.[35] This pressure on any branch office would have been exacerbated by the competition withconsulting for power and profits within Arthur Andersen. Thus, the conflicts of interest may not necessarily have been linked to pressure to sell non-audit services to the audit client. The point is not to minimize the potential conflicts from the existence of non-audit services to a client but to emphasize that the elimination of conflict by separation of audit and non-audit services is unlikely to solve the problem if the incentive structures for the audit partners are focused on local short-term profitability, rather than sustainable quality that provides reputational value for the whole firm. From a strict economic perspective the firm-wide reputational cost of an audit failure has to outweigh any short-term benefits from avoiding a qualified audit. It is difficult, however, for local office performance measurement and incentive systems to capture such long-run costs.

In principle, in the United Kingdom, the United States and increasingly in other countries, firms have an audit committee of the Board of Directors that is supposed to monitor auditing to prevent any conflict of interest between the auditors and managers. Audit committees are, however, rarely in complete charge in practice, and it is the executive officers who are the primary decision-makers. If both the fees and the decision of which audit firm is engaged rests with the senior managers being audited, there is a conflict of interest that can only be remedied by a change in the governance structures. The dependence on local office auditors by managers probably became more acute over the last twenty years because of changes in the industry.

The role of the audit committees including board of directors and governance structures in the United States is under review as part of the Sarbanes-Oxley legislation. The United Kingdom has taken a slightly different approach. The Financial Reporting Council (FRC) appointed a committee chaired by Sir Robert Smith to prepare a report summarizing the guidance under existing codes and rules. The Smith Report entitled 'Audit Committees – Combined Code Guidance' includes specific guidance on reviewing auditor independence (ICAEW, 2003a). The approach recommended has three broad elements for the audit committee to consider:

1. fundamental principles to be followed by the auditor with objectivity being primary;
2. identification and consideration of threats to independence; and
3. consideration of safeguards.

The threats and safeguards are considered in some detail and as such a clear framework is set out for audit committees to evaluate and control auditor independence. The interesting point of the Smith Report is that it provides a framework for a governance-based supervisory process to control auditor conflicts of interest.

The 1980s and 1990s were a period of increased competition among audit firms and possibly excess capacity in the audit profession, especially as growth in corporate mergers and acquisitions reduced demand for audit services by reducing the number of firms. An audit firm became easily replaceable in the 1990s, as each firm was actively engaged in seeking out competitors' clients. This was a relatively new phenomenon beginning in the 1970s when the Federal Trade Commission, worried about an oligopoly of large audit firms, required the profession to change its standards and permit audit firms to advertise and compete for clients (Healy and Palepu, 2003). During this period of competition for audit clients, combined with pressures to compete with non-audit partners, the 'cost' of losing a client appeared to be steep. Contracting profit in audit activities contributed to the consolidation of the large accounting firms from the Big 8 to the Big 5 (and now the Big 4) as the firms sought to exploit scale economies. With competition for revenue intense, it was natural for audit firm partners to focus on who hires or fires them, as well as who negotiates the fee paid. In a highly competitive environment, local branches serving dominant firms, coupled with a lack of independence from management created the potential for lower quality audits.

3.7 Litigation risk and rules-based audits

While supplying non-audit services and fee pressure reduce the independence of auditors from managers, thus creating conflicts of interest, it is unlikely that these conflicts were exploited to an extent that can explain the recent, huge audit failures, as there is evidence that auditors understood that the audit firm's primary asset is its reputation. In fact, paradoxical as it may seem, it may have been audit firms' heightened concerns to protect their reputation and guard against litigation risks that were a driving factor in the audit failures. There was a sharp rise in litigation risk for US audit firms in the 1970s and 1980s in the United States, as class action lawsuits were filed on behalf of shareholders, claiming that declines in share prices were caused by faulty auditing (Palmrose, 1991). Litigation defeats provide both an immediate direct cost in the penalty and higher insurance costs, and an indirect cost in reputational loss that can cause firms to lose audit clients. For audit firms, the cost of defence in these lawsuits and the large settlements focused attention on reducing litigation risk. The national offices of audit firms began to perform risk assessments of clients and practices to manage these costs. Firms adjusted their activities to protect themselves from litigation.[36] The threat of such lawsuits against company managers increased the incentive for earnings management and, as auditors were often part of the litigation, there were large negative incentives to force companies to 'miss' earnings targets especially over 'judgement' calls.

One reaction to counter the growing legal threat to the auditing profession and the corporations themselves was to seek and rely on increased codification of auditing and accounting standards that facilitated a legal defence of compliance with rules (Dye, 1993). Since the creation of the Financial Accounting Standards Board in 1973, there has been a proliferation of codified accounting rules in the United States. These rules have allowed for a clear shift in auditors' focus from opining on whether financial statements fairly present the 'true' financial condition and performance of the company to a focus on compliance with the detailed 'Generally Accepted Accounting Principles' (GAAP) rules. This focus permitted managers to argue that audit opinions should concentrate on compliance with the rules, shifting attention from the 'true' condition and performance of the company. Managers and auditors could also use the rules to create structures that allowed them to obscure the true economic condition of companies by, for example, placing assets and obligations in unconsolidated entities.

The Enron debacle has all of the elements described above, including the focus on rules rather than the true condition of the firm. While it remains to be seen who bears legal responsibility for the failure of the firm, many of the conflicts discussed above existed at Enron. Several financial executives were ex-auditors from Andersen. Non-audit service fees were greater than the audit fees. Enron purportedly was the prize audit client of the Houston office and its growth appeared to be spectacular. In addition, it had complex structures that distorted the economic reality but were constructed, with the help of their auditors and legal advisers, to meet codified standards. Finally, Anderson was the only big firm to devolve decisions on some accounting principles to its local offices.

Two examples serve to illustrate how an audit and accounting system based on prescriptive GAAP rules aided in distorting the economic picture. Enron was listed in the top ten of the Fortune 500 companies based on its consolidated sales. The sales measure had no bearing on reality, however, as it reflected trading activity in energy contracts that were recorded on a gross rather than a net basis because of a GAAP rule EITF 98-10.[37] (This rule was recently rescinded.) Enron also created Special Purpose Entities (SPEs) that placed assets, associated liabilities and guarantees off the balance sheet. These SPEs were acceptable as long as there was a 'minimum' outside equity position based on interpretations of existing rules. When the chairman of Arthur Andersen testified before a congressional committee on Enron he commented that the problem was with the interpretation of the consolidation rules not that the structures had totally distorted the economic realities. This typifies the way in which many in the audit profession perceived their role, opining on compliance with arcane rules, irrespective of the economic substance.

The evolution of audit practice over the last 50 years has been rapid, especially in the United States. Increased competition for audit clients put pressure on audit revenue and pushed firms to cut costs to sustain profits. Simultaneously non-audit services, especially the installation of management information systems, grew dramatically leading to growing concern about auditors' independence. As the revenues from these non-audit services increased, profit-sharing structures that favoured audit partners created internal tensions that often led to audit partners and local offices being pushed to deliver audit revenues and profits. Furthermore, there was an increase in litigation against audit firms in the 1980s resulting in rising costs and damage to reputations. To defend themselves, audit firms sought to reduce litigation risk, most notably by demanding and obtaining legally defensible rules in regulatory accounting and audit principles, even if these practices limited the auditors' ability to provide relevant and reliable information about the financial performance and condition of firms. As competition for audits heated up and risks increased, the governance structure around hiring and audit-fee decisions shifted away from boards of directors to the senior executives of the companies being audited. Each of these factors contributed to the conflicts of interest in the audit system of the late 1990s that were part of the spectacular business failures.

3.8 Remedies

To address the problems of the audit industry and improve its ability to reduce the information asymmetries between investors and managers, a broad set of remedies are necessary. While the details of how the Sarbanes-Oxley Act will be implemented are in the process of being spelled out, the changes it promotes are not only insufficient but also in certain cases inappropriate.

The emphasis on isolating auditing from related financial industries does not solve the underlying problems. It will reduce the economies of scope that serve the interests of investors by broader monitoring of companies. Regulation of auditor independence that forces elimination of all non-audit work is flawed as it 'precludes activities that might benefit the public interest by limiting an auditor's learning about its clients' (Wallman, 1996). Regulation and supervision needs to focus attention on the individual, office or other units of the firm that make decisions with respect to a particular audit client (Wallman, 1996). Separation by activity has not proved to be an acceptable remedy in other parts of the financial industry. As will be seen in Chapter 5 on universal banking, the separation of commercial and investment banking and insurance was an unnecessary remedy for the problem of conflicts of interest. It is unlikely that the proscription of non-auditing services, as envisioned by Sarbanes-Oxley, would have prevented the recent audit failures. Greater transparency about the nature and role of non-audit services is valuable, however, to control the temptation to exploit conflicts of interest.

Leaving the problem of conflicts of interest to the market in auditing implies that audit firms' concern about the maintenance of their reputation is sufficient to limit the exploitation of conflicts of interest. For reputation to be an adequate instrument to ensure that auditors' opinions focus on the 'true' financial condition and performance of companies, however, several actions are needed. First, the corporate governance structure of companies needs to be altered so that auditors will report to, be hired by, and be compensated by an audit committee representing stakeholders other than management. Section 301 of the Sarbanes-

Oxley Act recognizes the importance of this arrangement, and the PCAOB will need to adopt regulations to ensure that it is properly implemented. The Smith Report in the United Kingdom also advocates this strong role for audit committees and provides useful guidance.

Second, there needs to be a fundamental shift away from detailed prescriptive accounting rules that will push companies and auditors' to be more transparent about their assumptions and choices made in measuring companies performance, thereby revealing more clearly any biases in the information. Continued focus on the codification of accounting and auditing standards, as appears to be implied in Sarbanes-Oxley, will not improve the quality of auditors' reports and may lead to more manipulative innovations to hide companies' true conditions. This issue will come to the fore when the SEC reports to Congress on whether accounting should be principles or rules-based. A specific remedy that has been debated periodically, but always rejected, is to replace the current published audit report with a more detailed report highlighting all the items addressed by the auditors with the audit committee. This remedy has its own implications, but seems like a path worth pursuing. As litigation risk has been a key element in driving auditors to focus on rules, firms will not be able to respond to changes in governance and incentives unless this risk is reduced.

The last major change that is required is for audit firms to adjust their internal governance and compensation structures to limit problems from large client dominance of local offices and from competition between audit and non-audit services. These changes are not ones that can easily be designed and may vary from firm to firm, depending on their configuration. The penalty for failing to make adequate changes has been brought home, however, by the stark reality of the collapse of the once proud firm of Arthur Andersen. While firms will need to devise their own structures, supervisory oversight from the PCAOB can help in this process. The PCAOB will need to monitor and encourage best-practice compensation and performance measurement structures inside accounting firms.

4 Rating Agencies: Conflicts of Interest in Credit Assessment and Consulting

4.1 Introduction

The significance of ratings in the financial system has expanded materially in recent years. Ratings are widely used by investors as a guide to the creditworthiness of the issuers of debt and in financial covenants. As such, they play a major role in the pricing of debt securities and whether particular securities are eligible to be held by particular types of investor. Changes in ratings have come to be used as 'triggers' in financial contracts, with downgrades requiring actions such as the posting of additional collateral, an adjustment in interest rates, or even the termination of the contract. Regulators, too, have placed additional weight on credit ratings for constraining the portfolio decisions of fiduciary intermediaries, assessing the risk level of their portfolios, and determining the size of the minimum capital cushion they are required to hold.

In addition, ratings have increasingly influenced the behaviour of borrowers and potential borrowers. Companies often structure their borrowing in order to achieve a desired rating. They have also established special-purpose entities with a view to receiving a higher rating for a portion of their obligations, thus reducing their borrowing costs.

As ratings have become more influential, the work of the rating agencies has come under closer scrutiny. Following the Asian financial crisis of 1997-8, the agencies were widely criticized for being too slow to recognize the deteriorating situation in Asian banking systems, and then for being too precipitate in downgrading the affected countries, thus compounding and spreading the original problem (Bank for International Settlements, 1999). Greater scrutiny by official bodies in industrial countries was triggered by the collapse of the Enron Corporation in December 2001, followed by a wave of corporate scandals. Enron enjoyed an investment grade rating until four days before its failure. Moreover, its business strategy and financial structure, especially the off-balance sheet special purpose entities, were strongly influenced by the objective of maintaining a high rating.

The US Congressional committee investigating the collapse of Enron found that the rating agencies had displayed 'a disappointing lack of diligence in their coverage and assessment of...' Enron (US Congress, 2002). As a result, the Sarbanes-Oxley Act mandated the SEC to prepare a report on 'The Role and Functioning of Credit Rating Agencies in the Operation of the Securities Markets'. This report has two parts. The first part (Securities and Exchange Commission, 2003a) is mainly descriptive, outlining some of the potential sources of concern about the agencies, reviewing earlier enquiries into their activities and discussing aspects of the functioning of the industry. The second part (Securities and

Exchange Commission, 2003b) is likely to suggest possible remedies. Other countries share many of the worries of the US authorities but have decided to await the outcome of the SEC investigation before reaching conclusions on what initiatives to take themselves (Financial Stability Forum, 2002).

The first part of the SEC's report raised the following important questions:

1. Should more information be released by rating agencies about their decisions, and should more information by issuers be disclosed?
2. Should improved procedures be introduced to avoid or manage potential conflicts of interest?
3. Is there any basis to allegations of anticompetitive behaviour in the industry, and if so, what should be done about it?
4. How, if at all, should rating agencies be recognized for regulatory purposes?
5. Should oversight of rating agencies be changed?

In this chapter, we address these basic questions and assess what remedies may be required to manage any existing or emerging conflicts of interest.

4.2 The role of rating agencies

Rating agencies play an important role in reducing information asymmetries in the market for traded debt securities, as well as in the assessment of non-traded debt. These asymmetries arise because potential purchasers of debt instruments lack the information or the capacity to assess accurately the creditworthiness of issuers. The issuers are aware of the true characteristics of the securities they issue, but are unwilling or unable to communicate this information credibly to potential lenders.

White (2001) notes that, if rating agencies do their job well, 'credit rating firms can help lenders pierce the fog of asymmetric information that clouds lending relationships.' In a speech in February 2003, the President of Moody's Investors Services (McDaniel, 2003) explained:

> '...the main and proper role of credit ratings is to enhance transparency and efficiency in debt markets by providing an independent opinion of relative credit risk, thus reducing the information asymmetry between borrowers and lenders. We believe this function to be beneficial to the market, as it enhances investor confidence and allows creditworthy borrowers broader marketability of their debt securities.'

Rating agencies thus act as 'delegated monitors' (Ramakrishnan and Thakor, 1984; Millon and Thakor, 1985) for holders and potential acquirers of debt. They have three potential advantages in performing this role:

1. they may be able to devote more resources and specialized expertise to credit analysis than individual investors;
2. they may be granted access to information not available to the generality of investors;
3. if they are believed to be independent, their credit assessments will have greater credibility.

If rating agencies are used by numerous investors, they can avoid duplication costs in the gathering and analysis of information. The assessment of creditworthiness has always been resource-intensive. It is arguably becoming more so as the complexity of companies' financial structures increases. Even if each individual creditor were capable of performing the required analysis, such an effort would be wasteful of resources from a social standpoint.

The fact that rating agencies are viewed as delegated monitors for debt-holders means that issuers may be more prepared to share confidential information with them than with any individual creditor. They are willing to do so because there is an economy of effort to convey information once rather than many times, and a firm may, for legal reasons, be more comfortable sharing sensitive information (such as longer-term earnings forecasts) with an entity that has no direct financial stake in the company but will use the information as input to a rating decision that is available to all market players at the same time.

The absence of a direct financial interest also increases a rating agency's credibility, and hence its effectiveness as a delegated monitor. Users of the rating agency's assessments assume that its interest is in preserving its reputation for high quality, unbiased judgement, and therefore its rating should reflect a genuine assessment of the creditworthiness of the company being rated.

4.3 Beneficiaries of an effective rating mechanism

Credit-rating agencies have always been viewed as an important instrument in the hands of investors to help guide their investment decisions. Ratings have also long been used as a means for wealth owners to constrain the actions of fiduciary agents (e.g., trustees). High quality borrowers are, however, also potential beneficiaries of a well-functioning credit-rating process. In the presence of asymmetric information, high quality borrowers will find it difficult to 'certify' the quality of their liabilities, and will thus have to pay a premium to lenders to compensate for their uncertainty about the quality of an issue. The existence of credible independent credit assessment permits the quality of an issue to be certified more easily than by any other means, securing access to funding on better terms than would be possible in the absence of credit-rating agencies.

It might seem that issuers of debt of below average quality would have less interest in ratings. Once the quality of above-average debt has been certified, however, investors will revise down their estimate of the average quality of non-certified debt.[38] Those issuers whose debt quality is above the average of this remaining debt would then have an interest in being rated. By this process, all except the lowest quality of debt issuers will have an interest in a credible certification mechanism.

More recently, regulators too have come to place increased reliance on credit ratings as part of their ongoing supervision of financial intermediaries. Regulators want to monitor risk-taking by financial intermediaries to ensure that risks are properly managed, disclosed and priced, as well as supported by sufficient capital to protect certain classes of claims holders, including depositors and policy-holders. Ratings have the advantage of being a readily available and independent source of assessment of credit risk. They thus avoid the substantial resource costs that would be involved in a regulatory agency undertaking its own credit assessment, to say nothing of the need regulators would then face to justify their judgements.

All of these potential benefits depend on ratings providing the financial market-place with information that is additional and credible. If rating agencies merely duplicated information that was available elsewhere; or if their assessments were biased; or if the reliance placed on such assessments were due mainly to a special status conferred by regulation, then their economic function would be open to question.

4.4 The evolution of the rating industry

The origins of the industry can be traced back to the mid-nineteenth century, when various firms began publishing analyses of the creditworthiness of commercial counterparties (Cantor and Packer, 1994). These reports responded to a need on the part of suppliers of goods to judge how much credit to extend to customers. The next step was to provide credit assessments of traded debt instruments. In 1890, Poor's Publishing Company (the predecessor of Standard and Poor's) began to publish Poor's Manual, which analysed various types of investment, including bonds. Moody's Manual of Industrial and Miscellaneous Securities followed in 1900 (Moody's, 2003).

With the growth in bond markets and the increasing number of investors, a demand arose to have a simple means of ranking the investment quality of public issues. By the early 1900s, securities assessment had already moved beyond analysis and had begun to classify bond issues into different quality groupings. The beginning of ratings as they are known today can be traced to John Moody, who in 1909 developed a methodology for translating various statistical measures of credit quality into a single rating symbol. Moody's Investors Services was incorporated in 1914, and was shortly followed by Poor's, the Standard Statistics Company, and Fitch Publishing Company (Cantor and Packer, 1994).

Initially, credit assessments were provided only to paying subscribers. After the establishment of the main rating agencies, these were generally institutional or large private investors. Even in the early days, however, ratings came to be relied on by users who were not subscribers. It became relatively common for private contracts to limit fiduciary agents' ability to invest in obligations below a certain credit quality, as reflected in their ratings grade. Regulatory oversight of financial institutions also took investment ratings into account. From at least 1930, bank regulators made a distinction between investment and non-investment grade securities in their assessment of banks' portfolios. The SEC, under its net capital rules for broker-dealers, required 'haircuts' from net worth to take account of the credit quality of securities held. In 1936, the comptroller of the Currency's Office prohibited federally chartered banks from holding non-investment grade bonds (Wakeman, 1984). At roughly the same time, US insurance supervisors also began to use ratings in their oversight of insurance underwriters (Partnoy, 1999).

Although ratings had thus grown in importance in the interwar years, their influence seems to have waned during the 1940s and 1950s. In a large part, this may have reflected the fact that bond prices were not volatile and defaults were few. This diminished both the demand for and the supply of relevant information. Partnoy (1999) characterizes this period as one of 'austerity and contraction' for rating agencies.

This situation began to change in the late 1960s and 1970s, when interest rates and credit spreads became more volatile again, and the number and size of debt issues began to increase. A defining event was the bankruptcy of the Penn Central Railroad in 1970. From that time onward the demand for informed credit analysis has grown continuously.

An important change in the structure of the ratings industry, with potentially significant implications for conflicts of interest, took place in the early 1970s.

Starting at this time, the major rating agencies began to charge issuers for ratings assessments. One reason was the diminishing viability of investor subscriptions as a source of financing ratings. Technological changes in the dissemination of information, including the spreading use of photocopying (White, 2001), had made it increasingly difficult to restrict the beneficial use of ratings assessments only to paying subscribers. Since ratings information quickly became available to most market participants, the free-rider problem intensified and the value of subscribing to a rating service was diminished.

It might seem that in such circumstances the effective demand for ratings would die away because they were becoming more of a 'public good'. That is, they are costly to provide, but once created they benefit everyone and not just those who have paid for their provision. Under such circumstances, it is well known that the product or service in question will be undersupplied unless some other financing mechanism can be developed.

In the case of credit assessment, however, asymmetric information means that issuers, as well as investors, have an interest in a credible certification mechanism for loan quality. As discussed earlier, the dynamics of the adverse selection mechanism mean that all debt issuers have a need to certify the quality of their debt. How much they are prepared to pay for a rating is an empirical matter, and depends on their assessment of how much a credible assessment will result in a reduction of their credit spread. In turn, this depends on the capacity of the rating agency to supply the market-place with credible additional information and analysis.

The fact that issuers are prepared to pay for ratings is consistent with all or one of three hypotheses. It could be that the rating assessment adds additional information or analysis that reduces information asymmetries. Investors are prepared to pay for this by accepting a lower yield on their investment, and borrowers can use part of the resultant interest saving to pay for the rating. It could also be that, because of custom or regulation, a rating is a necessary precondition for access to capital, regardless of its informational value. Or it could be that payment confers special benefits on the payer beyond simply the dissemination of credit information to the market.

While these explanations suggest how rating agencies were able to move to an issuer fee model as the scope for subscriber financing diminished, they do not adequately explain why the main agencies (Standard & Poors and Moody's) rate virtually all issues, regardless of whether the issuer pays. Nor does it explain why 98% of rated issuers nevertheless pay for their ratings (Partnoy, 1999).

One possible explanation is that rated companies are afraid that, in the absence of payment, the rating would be lower than justified by the underlying facts. The SEC reports allegations that rating agencies have used 'strong-arm' tactics to induce payment by issuers for unsolicited ratings (Securities and Exchange Commission, 2003a). The *Economist* (1996) has suggested that 'the suspicion exists that a borrower who asks and pays for a rating may receive more favorable treatment than one who merely attracts an agency's uninvited "hostile" attention'. The US Justice Department has investigated allegations on occasions in the past (*Economist*, 1996) but no prosecutions have resulted.

Even in the absence of abusive tactics by the agencies, there may still be reasons why issuers may choose to pay for ratings. For example, it may be that the issuer is in possession of favourable proprietary information on its prospects, which for various reasons it is unwilling or unable to communicate directly and credibly to the market. The 'screen' of an intermediary that has no direct financial interest could allow such background assessment to get into market perceptions and prices without revealing proprietary information, or exposing the issuer to legal risk. Companies that pay for ratings may have additional access to rating agency personnel to supply additional interpretation about their future prospects.

Another aspect of the evolution of the rating industry that deserves mention is the increased reliance of regulation on external ratings and the accompanying move to certify certain agencies as approved for such purposes. As already noted, external ratings had been used for supervisory purposes as early as the 1930s. Initially, there was no formal guidance about which ratings would be acceptable for these purposes. With the increasing use of ratings, however, and growing regulatory reliance, there was an obvious danger that ratings quality would vary across agencies, and the temptation to 'shop' for ratings would intensify. For this reason, the SEC introduced in 1975 the concept of the 'Nationally Recognized Statistical Rating Organization' (NRSRO). At the time, the SEC did not contemplate its designation being used by other regulators, as in fact turned out to be the case (Securities and Exchange Commission, 2003a).

The fact that some agencies are recognized, even though recognition is intended to reflect a market reality rather than convey approval, has influenced the competitive structure of the industry. It adds to the value of a rating from a recognized agency and further increases barriers to entry in the industry. The greater the range of regulatory purposes to which a rating is put, the greater the value of recognized status, and correspondingly, the harder it is to distinguish the intrinsic value of a rating from its regulatory value.

In fact, the range of regulatory uses to which ratings are put has tended to widen substantially in recent years. Various regulators in the United States have enshrined the SEC's NRSRO designation into their own procedures, and regulators in other countries have also developed practices for the regulatory recognition of ratings (Bank for International Settlements, 2000). A substantial further increase will take place when the new Basel Capital Accord comes into effect (Bank for International Settlements, 2001). The new Accord responds to criticism that the previous Accord (Bank for International Settlements, 1988) was insufficiently risk-sensitive, by classifying bank assets into a larger number of credit risk classes. For this purpose, banks following the so-called standardized approach to calculating risk weights will rely on external credit assessments, which will, in practice, mean ratings from approved agencies.

The regulatory use of ratings may have contributed to the striking degree of concentration in the rating industry. White (2001) notes that the number of rating agencies in the United States has always fluctuated between three and five, and that other countries have even fewer. Moreover, the incumbent agencies seem to have substantial staying power. There can be few, if any, industries in the United States where the three remaining recognized firms in 2003 were direct lineal descendants of the dominating firms of 80 years earlier.[39]

Concentration is partly a reflection of economies of scale and scope, and partly the result of barriers to entry. The cost of acquiring the necessary reputation to function as an effective rating agency is a natural barrier to new entrants, but its height may have been artificially increased by the procedures by which reputation is now officially recognized for regulatory purposes.

4.5 Do rating agencies add value?

The fact that ratings are widely used and that most issuers are prepared to pay to receive them cannot be regarded as conclusive evidence that agencies add value. The privileged position created by market practice and regulatory requirements could generate a demand for the services of rating agencies that is independent of the underlying value of their assessments (Partnoy, 1999; Wakeman, 1984; White, 2001). Analysis of the contribution of the agencies has therefore relied on other means of judging the quality and influence of their assessments.

One approach is to simply look at the accuracy of ratings. Since ratings are intended as a guide to the likelihood of the rated entity servicing its obligations on time and in full, correlations between ratings and subsequent default history provide an initial measure of their accuracy. Many studies have shown that, notwithstanding prominent counterexamples such as Enron, there is a reasonably close correlation between ratings and default probabilities (see studies reviewed in Bank for International Settlements, 2000). The agencies themselves also provide evidence of the relationship between their ratings and subsequent default history (Brand and Bahar, 1999; Keenan, 1999).

For several reasons, however, this cannot be regarded as demonstrating the value of the information supplied by rating agencies. In the first place, such correlations do not show how much rating agencies' judgements add to what can be gleaned from other indicators of credit quality, such as interest spreads, or other sources of credit analysis, including analysts' and auditors' reports. Partnoy (1999) surmises that the added value might be quite low, in view of the fact that the staff working in rating agencies are spread very thinly. For example, at Moody's an analyst rates an average of 35 issues.

Second, while credit agencies' assessments may reflect the relative risk at a point in time, the correspondence of ratings to default probabilities seems to be subject to substantial change over time (Cantor and Packer, 1994). If a given grade is supposed to measure probability of default, the correlation between rating grades and subsequent defaults should be more stable.

A more powerful test of the extent to which the market uses ratings is to look at how market prices respond to changes in ratings. If a rating provided information over and above that which was already reflected in market prices, it is to be expected that market prices would react in a systematic manner to changes in ratings. Most academic studies confirm this expectation, although the effects for downgrades are stronger than for upgrades.[40]

Even this cannot be regarded as conclusive. It is possible that observed relationships reflect an element of reverse causality. In other words, credit downgrades may not necessarily reflect an underlying weakening in credit quality; they may themselves be a determinant of credit quality via their influence on financing costs. This possibility appears to have become more realistic in recent years, as ratings have been increasingly used in bond covenants, and ratings downgrades are more often used as triggers for contract revisions. Such triggers seem to have played a significant role in the end-game of a number of recent corporate failures, such as Enron and Worldcom.

Another reason some observers have offered for questioning the finding that rating actions are associated with market reactions is that rating adjustments often come out contemporaneously with other news (Partnoy, 1999). In an effort to get around this problem, Kliger and Sarig (2000) analyse the rating refinement made by Moody's in 1982. At that time, Moody's effectively tripled the number of rating categories by adding a + or − suffix to existing ratings. Kliger and Sarig's contention is that the addition of a suffix provided previously unknown additional information about Moody's judgement, with no change in the situation of the entity being rated. If this information was regarded as having value, a systematic change in the relevant market prices for bonds should be observable. Their results show that there was a statistically significant effect, suggesting that the market values the judgements of rating agencies.[41]

Although there are few studies that attempt to determine whether rating agencies, analysts or other monitors contribute more information to the market, they do conclude that rating agencies independently provide additional information (Ederington and Goh, 1998). In any event, it is difficult to provide a conclusive assessment of the exact contribution of rating agencies because the picture is muddied by the regulatory situation. It is always possible for the agencies' critics to argue that the observed impact of rating agencies' judgements on the market is due to a reverse causation, in other words a downgrade leads to a weakening of a firm's prospects, rather than a weakening of prospects being identified by a rating agency and revealed to the market in a rating downgrade. The growing practice of tying interest rates on certain categories of debt to credit ratings is likely to amplify this effect.

One thing is hard to dispute, however. Agencies' ratings are a convenient shorthand for synthesizing information about credit quality (Wakeman, 1984; Bank for International Settlements, 2000). They are looked at by the market, and widely used in financial covenants. Borrowers expend considerable effort to secure a rating, so presumably they believe there are advantages in having a good one.

4.6 Vulnerability to conflicts of interest

How far does the structure of the rating industry, as it has now emerged, give rise to a conflict of interest? The potential for a conflict is clearly created by the fact that there are multiple users of ratings and, at least in the short term, their interests can diverge. The investor is interested in a well-researched, impartial assessment of credit quality; the issuer in a favourable rating. Regulators are interested in a stable relationship between ratings and default risk over time as well as the avoidance of moral hazard and the distortion of the competitive environment. The rating agencies themselves have their own interests as commercial enterprises. They are presumably seeking to maximize their revenues and market value. Moreover, if rating agencies are affiliated to other businesses (Standard & Poors is part of McGraw-Hill, for example), this can also create the potential for divergences of interest.

What specific conflicts could these divergent interests give rise to? An obvious risk is that the 'issuer fee' model could result in rating agencies implicitly or explicitly offering more favourable ratings in exchange for business. Since most bond issues are rated anyway, one could ask 'what exactly do issuers think they are paying for?' We referred earlier to the suspicion that could arise that payment for a rating led to more favourable treatment. As we will discuss later, any overt quid pro quo of this sort would tend to undermine an agency's reputation for impartial analysis, and thus the basis of its franchise. It seems unlikely, therefore, that it would arise in such a blatant way.

There are, however, two other mechanisms through which this type of conflict might come into play. One is if the compensation arrangements in a rating firm rewarded analysts for securing additional ratings business, an incentive for lenient treatment would be created.

The second is more conjectural. The behavioural finance literature has recently identified ways in which agent bias can arise, even when financial incentives have been removed, and agents believe themselves to be acting objectively. Moore *et al.* (2002), for example, undertake an experiment in which an agent who has been closely involved with one party to a transaction is subsequently placed in a position where they have no direct financial incentive, and is asked to act objectively. Placed in such a situation, agents nevertheless tended to adopt positions favouring the party with whom they had previously worked. Moore *et al.*'s test was in the context of auditing, but if valid, could also apply in the case of a rating agency analyst that had worked closely with a client firm.

A potential source of conflict could also arise in the ancillary businesses that rating agencies have recently begun to develop (Fitch, 2003). Rating agencies are increasingly offering advice on the structuring of debt issues, usually to help secure a favourable rating. Such consultancy business has aspects in common with the advisory business developed by accounting firms. Rating agencies have developed this business because clients often want to create financial structures that have a low probability of default and have this recognized by the market in favourable borrowing terms. To do so, they need the institutions that certify credit quality to give them a high rating. These institutions themselves are most familiar with their rating methodology. So they can charge for helping design a structure that will be accorded the desired credit rating. In this case, however, the credit-rating agency would be in the position of 'auditing its own work'.

Several observers have also noted that the increased use of ratings for regulatory purposes has implications for the extent and nature of vulnerability to conflicts of interest (White, 2001; Partnoy, 1999). For instance, it might increase the incentive to shop for the best rating, as the value of such a rating is increased when it results in a relaxation of regulatory constraints. For rating agencies, the acceptance of their rating for regulatory purposes greatly increases their franchise value.

Regulatory recognition also has the capacity to contribute to moral hazard. Market participants may misconstrue recognition as approval of the methodology used by rating agencies or of the ratings that result. They may therefore come to rely on rating assessment to a greater extent than would be justified by the additional information it contains. This in turn would complicate the task of judging the accuracy and effectiveness of rating. The observed influence of ratings' judgements on the market price of traded instruments could be the result of a false assumption that ratings convey more information than they in fact do (Partnoy, 1999).

Another potential source of vulnerability to conflict of interest could arise from concentration in the industry. The rating industry is dominated by a small number of players. In the United States, for example, there are currently only four NRSROs, and of these, two (Moody's and Standard & Poors) are much larger than their two competitors. Most other jurisdictions have even less competition (White, 2001; Bank for International Settlements, 2000). It is widely believed that the combination of economies of scale and regulatory privileges favouring incumbents constitute significant barriers to entry to the industry.

Lack of competition has offsetting implications for conflicts of interest. On the one hand, it could help reduce conflicts, since agencies will not be under short-term pressures to shade their judgements in order to win business. The business will come to them anyway, and they will be more conscious of their interest in maintaining reputation and discouraging the entry of competitors in the longer term. On the other hand, since the competitive position of the agencies is assured, they have less incentive to provide the best possible service. This could lead them to devote fewer resources (in quantity or quality) to the credit assessment process than would be justified by the fees received. They may also have added incentives to lobby to maintain their favoured status.

White (2001) documents that the profit margins of rating agencies are very high (up to 50% in the case of Moody's) so that there is some *prima facie* reason for believing that the services delivered do not match the fees paid. Oligopoly could lead to a conflict between a rating agency's private interest in maximizing its income and the economic function for which it has been given certain regulatory privileges, namely the provision of data and analysis that reduces information asymmetries.

4.7 Remedies to conflicts of interest

4.7.1 Market discipline

Rating agencies have usually contended that potential conflicts of interest are in practice limited by market forces and that attempts to impose regulatory remedies are neither necessary nor desirable (Fitch, 2003). It is certainly true that market forces are often capable of finding solutions to information asymmetries. Indeed, the history of the rating industry itself is that of market solutions to perceived conflicts of interest. The institutionalized separation of saving and investment in modern economies created a demand for information-generating intermediaries, including informational service firms such as rating agencies.

The market mechanism by which conflicts are controlled for rating agencies is that of 'reputational capital'. To the extent that if an intermediary is viewed as being conflicted, the demand for its services is likely to be curtailed. This creates an incentive for the intermediary to find ways of certifying its objectivity, in order to protect its reputational capital. If it is unsuccessful in doing so, then the market will seek out information-generating sources that are not conflicted.

The 'market solution' to the problem of potential conflicts of interest at rating agencies is to allow reputation to police any temptation on the part of the agencies to shade their judgement in order to favour debt issuers that pay for ratings. The argument is that a rating agency's franchise depends on its stock of reputational capital, and any compromise with objectivity would cost more in diminishing the stock of reputational capital than it would yield in additional fees. Eventually, failure to maintain high quality and objectivity in credit assessment would draw competitors into the industry.

While this argument is compelling in many markets, it may be limited for ratings agencies. First, the loss of reputational capital is likely to take place gradually. Biased judgements by rating agencies would probably not become visible until some time had passed, probably not until the down-phase of the cycle, when the externalities would be most damaging. The mechanism, therefore, while powerful, may not by itself be sufficiently timely to avoid substantial costs. Second, although a rating firm will have a strong interest in maintaining its reputational capital, this does not necessarily apply to individual agents within the firm. As was demonstrated in the case of auditors, an individual office or manager may have an interest in cultivating a particular client, even at the expense of the firm's long-run reputational capital. Establishing appropriate compensation arrangements within the industry is therefore important. By far the most important factor is, however, that the ratings industry is not a fully competitive market. There are a limited number of competitors, and significant barriers to entry. Regulatory privileges have distorted the incentives within the industry and altered the behaviour of its users.

These considerations tend to weaken the power of market discipline and suggest it may be necessary to contemplate ways in which this discipline might be reinforced or supplemented.

4.7.2 Reduce existing regulatory privileges

The reduction of existing recognitions by financial regulators would be a step in the direction of increasing the operation of market discipline on the industry. Critics of the industry have often argued that the demand for ratings arises mainly because of the regulatory use to which they are put, rather than to the additional information they convey (White, 2001; Partnoy, 1999). Regulatory privileges do not in themselves create a conflict of interest, but they may increase the incentive to exploit a latent conflict of interest, as well as raising the barriers to entry in the industry.

We see some justification, therefore, for reconsidering the uses to which ratings are put for regulatory purposes. Such uses have clearly expanded beyond what was intended when some rating agencies were granted recognized status as NRSROs (Securities and Exchange Commission, 2003a). It seems that those who have granted such recognitions also have reservations about the extent to which they have been used (Nazareth, 2003). The issue, however, is whether financial regulators have viable alternatives.

Regulators of financial institutions have been moving increasingly in the direction of 'risk-based supervision'. They have made financial institutions' risk management systems subject to supervisory review and have required minimum capital levels to be related to measured risk. To the extent that measuring risk involves an assessment of the asset portfolio of the supervised institution, some means of assigning credit risk weights to individual claims will be needed. Publicly available ratings provide a convenient way of doing this, without involving the regulator in detailed, resource-intensive and controversial judgements. It is probably unrealistic to expect supervisors to abandon this tool in the short term.

Still, we do not believe that this is the optimal solution for the long term. Supervised financial institutions should be encouraged to develop in-house credit assessment techniques (something that is already happening), which could then be reviewed on their own merits by the supervisor, rather than cross-checked for compatibility with published ratings. Where publicly traded securities are concerned, greater reliance on market judgements (as revealed in credit spreads, for example) could be used.

Our view, therefore, is that the increasing official reliance on private ratings is problematic and reducing it would be a reasonable objective of public policy. It would allow market disciplines over rating agencies to work much more effectively. In the interim, a less far-reaching move would be to ease the barriers that existing procedures present to the recognition of new agencies, while finding alternative techniques to guard against competitive laxity in the rating industry.

4.7.3 Provide for greater transparency

Transparency is also a tool of market discipline. In general, therefore, we favour the maximum degree of transparency, subject to one caveat. If an economic agent is required to be transparent about proprietary information, their incentive to generate such information may be reduced. Insofar as rating agencies produce information or analysis that could not profitably be produced if it was required to be made public, then we believe there is a case for protecting the confidentiality of that information.

Still, this leaves a wide range of information that we believe could usefully be disclosed, which would help users of ratings judge the potential for conflicts. This would include any relationships between the rating agency (or its employees) and the rated entity; the fees paid; whether a rating was solicited or unsolicited;

compensation structures within individual firms; and any adjustments to provisional ratings made after consultation with representatives of the rated entity.

A particularly important area, in our view, is that of the sale of advice. Where a rating agency provides advice on how to structure a financial contract in order to achieve a given rating, and then provides the relevant rating, the potential conflict risks become overwhelming. This does not necessarily presume any lack of diligence or goodwill on the part of the agency concerned: it may simply be that it believes, erroneously, that its credit assessment method is superior to others. We believe that all ratings of issues for which the rating agency has provided prior advice on financial structure should be clearly signalled.

4.7.4 Develop codes of conduct

As already noted, the credit-rating agencies are fully aware that doubts could emerge concerning the objectivity of their credit assessments, given the principal source of their revenues. To allay these concerns, all of them have instituted procedures designed to insulate credit analysis from undue pressures. To take Moody's as an example, these include: avoidance of commercial relations with any entity rated by the firm; the absence of forbearance out of concern for the consequences of publishing a rating; procedures to avoid conflicts of interest; the proper use of confidential information; and procedures to ensure that rating decisions reflect full and deliberate consideration (McDaniel, 2003). Is this sufficient?

In view of public concerns about potential conflicts of interest, we see advantages in taking this process further, and for the agencies to develop a comprehensive and uniform document codifying their practices. The agencies themselves seem to be willing to move in this direction: 'We are not opposed to a further consolidation of our policies and procedures into a single public document, such as a Code of Conduct. Nor are we opposed to oversight that can confirm that these policies are being followed' (McDaniel, 2003).

While we have some doubts about how far official oversight could appropriately go in providing continuous supervision of the industry, we think it could be helpful for the principal market regulator in each jurisdiction to give its opinion on the suitability of an industry-developed code of conduct and possibly help in its construction.

4.7.5 Prohibit activities creating conflicts

As we note in other connections (see Chapter 5 on universal banking), the prohibition of combinations of activities that create potential conflicts of interest risks may be too extreme a remedy, unless actual conflicts are severe. Such solutions can reduce the information available to markets, if synergies in information production and dissemination are forfeited. The question we will wish to ask concerning rating agencies, therefore, is what is the balance of advantages and disadvantages from prohibiting certain kinds of activity, or their financing in particular ways.

In the case of the rating agencies, the most visible potential conflict arises from the issuer fee model of financing the rating process. While we recognize this potential conflict, we do not regard the prohibition of this source of financing as a proportionate remedy. It would almost certainly lead to the severe contraction of the industry, and the loss of an important source of information and analysis. The conflicts to which the financing model gives rise can, we believe, be kept in check by market forces, especially if these are buttressed by the additional actions we have proposed.

A second source of conflict that may be set to grow in importance over time is the combination of advice and rating. We have suggested above that, at a minimum, rating agencies ought to reveal details of all cases where they are rating firms or issues where they have provided advice on financial structure. Should this be taken further, with separation being required between the activities of advice and rating? And if so, can this be achieved through firewalls within existing institutions, or would it require full legal separation?

We do not feel we have enough information to come to a definitive answer on these questions. Rating agencies have expertise in assessing the risk-sensitivity of different debt structures. They may be able to help firms structure their debt, particularly asset-backed securities, to reveal more information and so produce better credit ratings and a greater flow of credit. A unique advantage of the rating agencies, however, is that they have proprietary knowledge of their own assessment procedures, and therefore can supply clients with greater assurance that their advice will produce the desired result, that is, a lower rating. Moreover, given the regulatory advantages that will flow from a positive rating judgement, clients have an added incentive to use the rating agencies advisory services. This could be an artificial source of comparative advantage, rather than a genuine synergy. Thus, although we do not advocate prohibition of rating agencies involvement in these consulting activities, we do believe that supervisory oversight may be needed to make sure that conflicts of interest of interest do not damage the provision of information from rating agencies.

4.7.6 **Establish a regulatory regime**

The most far-reaching solution to the alleged problems in the rating industry would be to establish a formal system of oversight of the agencies, such as exists for banks, securities firms, and insurance companies.[42] The case for a regulatory regime is that, in the absence of such a regime, the market will produce distorted incentives with attendant negative externalities for the economy at large. The case against it is that official intervention will smother beneficial market incentives, encourage moral hazard, and permit the intrusion of extraneous objectives favoured by the political process.

In general, we are skeptical that a fully developed regulatory regime would produce the desired results. We do not see how it would promote genuine competition, generate improvements in the judgements made by rating agencies, or result in the provision of higher quality information to the market-place. It is more likely, in our judgement, to result in formalistic procedures and less effective competition.

Moreover, there is the question of how such a regulatory regime would be justified. Rating agencies have frequently stressed that what they provide are simply opinions and are thus protected by the First Amendment to the US Constitution, and similar free speech provisions under constitutional arrangements in other jurisdictions (Fitch, 2003). It seems unlikely that a direct attempt to regulate rating agencies would be successful, even if it were thought desirable.

Any supervisory approach would therefore have to work through limitations to existing regulatory recognitions. In other words, where ratings are currently allowed for certain regulatory purposes (such as assessing risk weights for capital adequacy purposes) they could be disallowed for agencies not following rules. This seems a disproportionate response to the problem at hand, and one that goes contrary to our preferred approach of reducing regulatory recognitions and relying increasingly on market disciplines.

4.8   Conclusion

Our overall conclusion is that conflicts of interest at rating agencies, while not to be dismissed, have so far been more latent than overt. Market discipline, working through the need for agencies to retain their reputational capital, has been instrumental in maintaining this situation. Nevertheless, there are troublesome aspects of the way in which the industry has developed, and the potential exists for conflicts to assume greater significance in the future. To guard against this, we believe it is important to ensure that market disciplines are provided with full scope to work in their intended way. This means an emphasis on transparency, and possibly supervisory oversight of new activities being developed by the agencies; a reduction in the scope of regulatory recognitions granted to approved ratings; and a diminution of barriers to entry of qualified new entrants to the industry.

5 Conflicts of Interest in Universal Banking

5.1 Introduction

Unlike the conflicts of interest in investment banking and accounting firms that played a central role in the recent financial scandals, the conflicts that arise from universal banking have had a long history in the United States.[43] Until a few years ago, these conflicts of interest seemed to have vanished, as the remedy of separation by creating distinct classes of financial institutions, each with its own niche of intermediation, seemed to eliminate them. As the barriers between commercial banking, investment banking and insurance have disappeared, however, concerns about conflicts may arise again. We focus on the United States because conflicts of interest have been discussed in greater depth in the context of US firms and have attracted greater public attention.

Although commercial banks, investment banks and insurance companies arose in nineteenth-century America as distinct intermediaries, by the turn of the twentieth century there were obvious economies of scope that could be attained by their combination. At a time when information costs were extremely high, commercial banks thrived because of their 'special' ability to collect information and monitor borrowers, overcoming adverse selection and moral hazard problems. In the absence of standardized accounting methods and rating agencies,[44] commercial banks had a decided advantage because their customer relationships provided detailed and specific information not available elsewhere. Commercial bank loans are still regarded as 'special' today, assisting borrowers who have poor or no credit reputations. Even for established firms, the market construes the announcement that they have been approved for new bank loans as a positive signal.[45] There are fixed costs of investigating a borrowing firm. If the firm turns out to be a good credit risk, it may be able to raise money from the securities market later. For a bank that has a lending relationship with a firm, it should be less expensive to perform due-diligence analysis for underwriting a new issue because of the reusability of information.

Economies of scope may also exist in building a reputation for financial institutions. If a universal bank can use the reputation acquired in one business to enter another, it will have an advantage over specialized banks.[46] There may also be economies of scope in serving the large customer bases that commercial banks, investment banks, brokerages and insurance companies create. The considerable overlap in the information they collect may reduce the cost of supplying these services jointly. Proprietary information obtained by information in securities issue and lending should improve the quality of their portfolios. Universal banking also increases the point of contact a bank has with a firm, expanding the number of services and improving its information acquisition and monitoring.

Universal banks thus offer many possible economies of scope that lower the cost of providing financial services. Yet, given that activities within a firm serve multiple departments, there are many potential conflicts of interest. If the potential revenues from one department surge, there will be an incentive for employees in that department to distort information to the advantage of their clients and the profit of their department. For example, issuers served by the underwriting department will benefit from aggressive sales to customers of the bank, while these customers are hoping to get unbiased investment advice. A bank manager may push the affiliate's products to the disadvantage of the customer, fail to offer dispassionate advice, and limit losses from a poor public offering by placing them in bank managed trust accounts. A bank with a loan to a firm whose credit or bankruptcy risk has increased has private knowledge that may encourage it to have the bank's underwriting department sell bonds to the unsuspecting public, paying off the loan and earning a fee. On the other hand, a bank may make below market loans to investors to finance the purchase of securities underwritten by an affiliate. A bank may also try to influence or coerce a borrowing or investing customer to buy insurance products (Saunders and Walter, 1994).

Given the multiple services provided by a universal bank, there are multiple opportunities for departments or individuals to benefit from the conflicts of interest. While other countries had long permitted some form of universal banking, the United States only recently re-opened the doors. Breaking down the barriers imposed by the Glass-Steagall Act, the Gramm-Leach-Bliley Financial Services Modernization Act of 1999 permits banks, securities firms, and insurance companies to affiliate within a new structure – the financial holding company (FHC).[47] Most of the research on conflicts of interest in universal banking has thus been focused on the pre-1933 era when commercial banking deeply penetrated the securities business.

5.2 American universal banking before Glass-Steagall

In the discussion of conflicts of interest in the financial industry, the debate over universal banking in the United States has been largely framed by the historical experience of the early twentieth century that was terminated by the Glass-Steagall Act in 1933. While the separation of commercial and investment banking by the Glass-Steagall Act is well known, it was a direct descendant of a much less familiar but important separation of insurance and investment banking engineered by state legislation a quarter century before. Both of these barriers were swept away by the Gramm-Leach-Bliley Act of 1999.

In both the 1890s and 1920s, rapid technological change in the economy produced a stock market boom where new firms and mergers flooded the markets with securities. Challenged to underwrite and distribute these securities, the financial industry reorganized itself to capture economies of scope and scale. When the stock market boom collapsed, the combination of insurance and investment banking and later commercial and investment banking were accused of exploiting conflicts of interest. While the remedy of complete separation was imposed in both episodes, there are striking differences in how the financial industry evolved to handle the conflicts of interest.

5.3 Investment banking and insurance

The formation of large vertically integrated manufacturing companies in the late 1890s created a new demand for capital. Huge new equity issues were floated for such industrial giants as US Steel. In addition, the reorganization of railroads brought about the issue of $1.2 billion of securities between 1900 and 1902 (Carosso, 1970). The size and risk of new industrial issues made underwriting by a single investment bank undesirable, leading one firm to take the role of manager, organizing syndicates of underwriting firms that could distribute the securities. Barred by law from holding equities, commercial banks could not be members of an equities syndicate.[48] In their place, insurance companies became major syndicate members.

The rapidly expanding insurance companies had large steady inflows of funds from their policy premiums, making them significant purchasers of securities. Coordination with investment banks was furthered as the insurance industry was highly concentrated with the Mutual, the Equitable and the New York Life Insurance companies garnering half of all policy sales.[49] New York Life was closely tied to JP Morgan. The Mutual was not tied to any specific bank but had important relationships with First National Bank and Speyer and Co., and the Equitable had an affiliation with the Harriman and the Kuhn Loeb investment banks. New York Life's portfolio was filled with Morgan railroads, US Steel and other Morgan issues, while Equitable's holdings reflected the railroad interests of Harriman and Kuhn Loeb (North, 1954). These insurance companies also gave investment banks loans and other assistance either directly or through their affiliated trust companies, in which they had large deposits (Carosso, 1970).[50] The primary device for coordinating these combinations of intermediaries were interlocking directorships, where insurance company officers were partners of investment banks and investment bankers served as directors or trustees of insurance companies.[51] Acutely worried by the potential conflicts of interest involved in these arrangements, progressives described this concentration of activity and power as the 'Money Trust'.

The boom and crash of the market are depicted in Figure 5.1. New industrial issues followed by a battle for control of the railroads drove the market to its peak in June 1901. Although there is no data for the number or value of new issues, the volume of trading on the New York Stock Exchange is available. Trading on the exchange peaked during the summer of 1901. The declining market hit a plateau until the summer of 1903 when in the 'rich man's panic' it tumbled again, apparently triggered by banks calling in loans to underwriting syndicates forcing them to unload securities. Contemporaries affixed the blame to the over-abundance of new, overpriced securities, and what a leading financial journalist called, 'revelations of fraud, chicanery, and excessive capitalization'.[52] Tumbling stock prices alarmed not only stockowners but also insurance policy holders (Mishkin and White, 2003).[53]

In the booming stock market, conflicts of interest received relatively little public attention. The public debate was joined when the stock market collapsed and a struggle over control of the Equitable broke out between its president and the majority shareholder James H Hyde. These events revealed institutional relationships and questionable management practices of which the public had been largely unaware. Disclosures in the press raised questions about whether investment banks had benefited at the expense of life insurance companies and whether insurance officials had personally benefited at the expense of policy owners and stockholders. In the case of the mutual insurance companies, it

Figure 5.1 Dow Jones, 1900-04

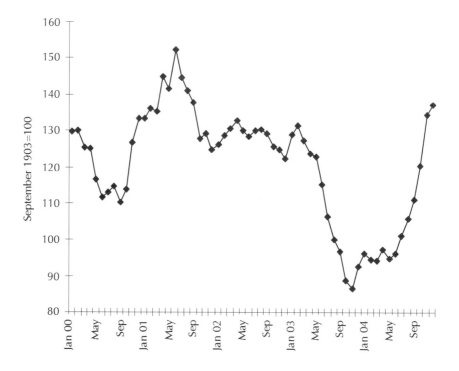

appeared that officers were in violation of their fiduciary responsibilities.

Insurance companies had sought syndicate participations to get large blocks of securities at reduced prices. They were not, however, treated equally with other syndicate members. Typically, insurance companies were not allowed to buy at the syndicate prices. Most of the securities they acquired for their portfolios were purchased at the public offering price, and they did not participate in the syndicate's profit. Yet, at the same time officers of the insurance companies, like Richard McCurdy, president of Mutual Life, participated as individuals or through private partnerships in the syndicate (Carosso, 1970). In the mutual insurance companies, the directors took considerable risks that they attempted to hide from state regulators. When a Morgan syndicate for the International Mercantile Marine was unable to sell the securities to the public, New York Life and other syndicate members were required to buy their allotments. To hide this transaction, New York Life sold the bonds to Morgan on 31 December 1903 only to repurchase them on 2 January 1904, providing window dressing for its annual report to the New York Superintendent of Insurance.

Some officers appear to have used the insurance companies to protect them from poor private investments. George W Perkins, a vice president of New York Life, belonged to a partnership investing in a syndicate for the Mexican Central Railroad. When the partnership was unable to take its allotment, Perkins arranged for New York Life to acquire the bonds. Similarly, James H Hyde of the Equitable formed a partnership that received the syndicate participations for the Equitable and divided them among the officers, the company and subsidiaries as he deemed appropriate (Carosso, 1970). Some bankers were concerned about the appearance of conflicts of interest implied by interlocking directorates. In 1901, when JP

Morgan invited Perkins to become a partner in his firm, he urged him to resign from the insurance company in order to avoid a possible conflict of interest as New York Life was a regular purchaser of Morgan sponsored securities. Perkins refused and Morgan reluctantly agreed to allow his new partner to continue at New York Life as chairman of the insurance company's Finance Committee (Carosso, 1970).

These revelations in the press led the New York State legislature to convene a special session that created the Armstrong Committee to investigate. Serving as chief counsel, Charles Evans Hughes questioned the bankers focusing on the role they played in determining the investment policies of the companies they were associated with, and demanded to know how they could serve the interests of both. Although the Armstrong Committee found it difficult to measure how investment banks or their managers had profited from their control of financial intermediaries through interlocking directorates, it registered its disapproval of the interlocking directorates and recommended that life insurance companies be prohibited from serving as underwriters (Carosso, 1970). In response, the New York State legislature passed a reform Bill in 1906 that was quickly copied by 19 other states, effectively making it the law of the land. These laws prohibited life insurance companies from underwriting securities, ordered them to break their interlocking relationships with investment banks, and compelled them to sell off their stocks.

While the pre-Armstrong combination of investment banks and insurance companies offered potential benefits to both, the use of interlocking directorates to manage the two firms seems, in retrospect, designed to offer the maximum opportunities to exploit conflicts of interest. Most companies were mutuals, and the few stock companies, like the Equitable, were dominated by one shareholder, diminishing the capacity of the policy owners and shareholders from monitoring the managers. The management structure and the transactions executed by managers on behalf of their companies were opaque to the public. While complete separation was an extreme solution, some reform was necessary. Afterwards when commercial and investment banks began to combine, this poor financial architecture was not repeated. Institutional innovation offered new and improved solutions to the problem of conflicts of interest.

5.4 Commercial and investment banking

The buoyant securities market of the 1890s was eclipsed by the post-World War I boom. Beginning in 1922, Americans gradually became convinced that the economy had entered a 'new era' of permanent prosperity. Inflation was near zero, unemployment was low and the economy was rapidly growing. As the stock market flourished, new issues flooded the market, concentrated in the 'high tech' industries (White, 1990). Educated by the government's wartime bond drives, more Americans invested in stocks and bonds directly or through investment trusts.

Figure 5.2 shows the well-known stock market boom of the late 1920s that peaked in September 1929 and crashed the following month. Although it briefly recovered, the market continued to decline, mirroring the long economic slump. The surge in trading that boosted prices is seen in Figure 5.3, as measured by volume on the New York Stock Exchange. Underwriting boomed with an explosion of new issues, concentrated in equities, as shown in Figure 5.4. At the same time, profits of the commercial banks were stalled. Drawn by this extraordinary opportunity, more and more commercial banks entered the securities business.

Figure 5.2 Dow Jones, 1926-32

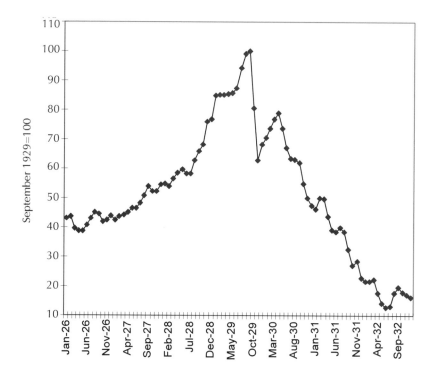

Figure 5.3 Monthly NYSE stock sales, 1920-30

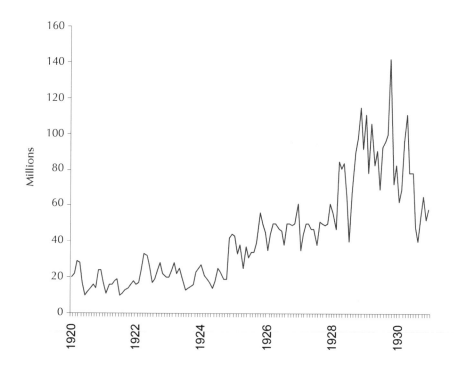

Figure 5.4 New stock issues, 1919-41

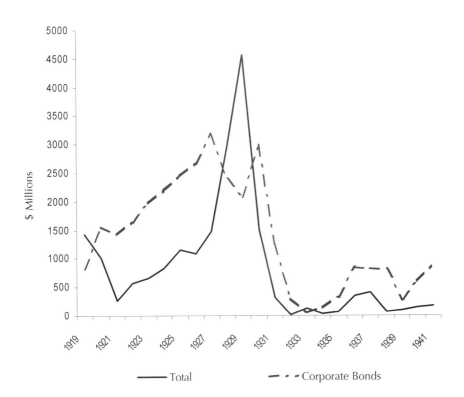

Unlike the case of combining investment banking and insurance at the beginning of the century, there was considerable experimentation in how to structure intermediaries that combined commercial and investment banking. Initially, most investment banking activities carried out by commercial banks were in internal bond departments.[54] The National Banking Act of 1864 only permitted banks to own or handle 'evidences of debt', thus excluding common stock. Furthermore, when commercial bank customers who were dissatisfied with investment advice or the bonds sold to them by a bond department sued national banks, the courts found that the plaintiffs could not recover damages because the banks were conducting a business that was *ultra vires* or beyond their corporate powers (Peach, 1941). Thus, although many banks operated bond departments, there was some doubt as to their legal status until the McFadden Act in 1927 explicitly permitted national banks to underwrite and deal in bonds.

While the McFadden Act clarified national banks' powers, it did not result in more bond departments, as securities affiliates became the preferred vehicle for a securities business. Incorporated under the general states' laws of incorporation and separately capitalized, affiliates had few restrictions on their non-bank activities.[55] Typically an affiliate had a name very similar to that of the parent bank; and its offices were in the same building. These affiliates were linked to their parent banks by one of four devices:

1. each shareholder of the bank became a pro rata shareholder of the affiliate;
2. the stock of the affiliate was held by a holding company that also owned the stock of the commercial bank;

3. the bank appointed a panel of trustees who held the shares of the affiliate in trust for the bank, appointed the same board of directors as the bank and delivered the dividends to be distributed to the shareholders of the bank;
4. the bank owned the stock of the affiliate as an investment.

The affiliates nominally had separate boards of directors, but they often shared some of the directors and upper management with the bank (Peach, 1941).

The number of banks operating a securities business in an internal bank department grew from 62 to 123 between 1922 and 1931. Even more rapid was the development of separate securities affiliates, which rose from 10 in 1922 to 114 in 1931. Among these were the industry leaders – the Chase Securities Corporation and the National City Corporation affiliated with the Chase National Bank (now part of JP Morgan Chase) and the National City Bank (the precursor of Citibank) respectively. Affiliates and the bond departments of commercial banks quickly penetrated underwriting. While the share of all bond originations for independent investment banks fell from 78 to 55% between 1927 and 1929, commercial banks' share climbed from 22 to 45% of the market from 1927 to 1929. Affiliates dominated this expansion, accounting for 41%, while internal bond departments attained only 4% (Peach, 1941).[56]

A commercial bank with an investment banking business could take advantage of an affiliates' larger and more specialized research staff to analyse securities for its purchases or use as collateral. Unlike investment bankers, which had had a small clientele of the well-to-do, commercial banks had large numbers of potential customers who could purchase some securities and place them in the banks' safe deposit boxes. The banks acted as the contemporary equivalents of 'discount brokers' charging a quarter of the fee of New York brokerages. This new clientele helped to broaden the market for securities. Thus, commercial banks found that underwriting, distributing and dealing in securities complemented their existing services (White, 1986). While drawn to the highly profitable securities business, commercial bankers were aware that the accompanying conflicts of interest would be damaging and many were very careful to maintain their reputations.[57]

Although the economy was already showing some signs of weakness in the summer of 1929, the stock market crash in October stunned the public. In two days, 28-29 October, the Dow Jones index fell 24%. In November it fell another 22%. Although the market enjoyed a brief recovery in early 1930, it continued to drop downwards during the next two years; and the public questioned why they had been induced to buy so much equity.

In response to public outcry and pressure from the White House, the Senate Banking and Currency Committee began an investigation that became known as the Pecora hearings. Among the various 'abuses' discovered by the Congressional hearings, several appeared to be conflicts of interest between commercial and investment banking.[58] First, bankers were blamed for selling new issues of 'unsound and speculative securities' generated by their affiliates to their customers. Second, commercial banks were accused of converting bad loans into security issues that were sold to an unsuspecting public or to affiliates and investment trusts managed by the bank. Finally, security affiliates conducted pool operations, often in the stock of parent banks, with officers as private participants, adding an element of personal conflict of interest.

The first charge arose in the depressed markets of the early 1930s. The public saw that the prices of their stocks that had plunged would not soon recover, and many bonds were in default. Securities firms were blamed for selling low quality bonds and stocks to uninformed or misinformed investors. It should be noted that examples provided in Congressional hearings and subsequently cited in the academic literature (see Carosso, 1970) are biased in their selection. Three issues underwritten by the National City Bank were investigated by the Senate Committee on Banking and Currency in 1933-34, but they were the only issues that were in default at that time (Benston, 1990). One of the supposedly infamous examples cited in Congressional hearings were the bond issues floated by National City Company for the Republic of Peru that went into default in 1931. Evidence was uncovered that representatives of the National City Company had written unfavourable reports about the condition of Peru in 1921, 1923, 1925 and 1927. They pointed out that Peru had a bad debt record, was an adverse moral risk, and the international situation was bad. Prospectuses distributed with the bond issues made no mention of this information, suggesting that the bank had concealed information from investing customers to the benefit of its underwriting business. Yet, the bank was not alone in its initial favourable assessment. These bonds were graded A by Moody's in 1927, and though they were downgraded to BAA in 1928, their market price exceeded the issue price until May 1930 (Benston, 1990). Many of the facts were publicly known and the default was primarily the result of the unanticipated worldwide depression. National City Company did not specialize in low quality issues, and Huertas and Silverman (1986) report that 85% of National City Company's underwritings were initially investment grade or better. Even if the bonds had been wholly purchased by the customers of National City Bank, which they were not, there does not appear to have been an effort to exploit a conflict of interest.

The second allegation of the Pecora hearings was the conversion of bad commercial loans into securities. One often cited example is the case of General Theaters and Equipment (GTE). Chase National Bank financed GTE's acquisition of the failing Fox Motion Picture Company in 1929 with a $15 million loan. This loan was repaid out of part of the proceeds from a $53 million issue of common stock and debentures underwritten by Chase's securities affiliate, Chase Securities Company. When GTE ran into trouble in 1930, Chase Securities underwrote another $30 in debentures; GTE went bankrupt two years later. The Congressional investigation concluded that a conflict of interest led Chase to underwrite 'poor securities to pay off its own loans', concealing or misrepresenting information (Wigmore, 1985). The conflict of interest may not have been the key factor, however, as the economy was in the middle of the Great Depression and Chase held most of the securities, taking a loss of $70 million, having been unable to sell them to the public (Benston, 1990; Kroszner and Rajan, 1994).

In a similar case, National City Bank loaned $30 million to Cuban sugar producers. When the price of sugar collapsed after World War I, the bank held these loans as 'slow and doubtful'. On 15 February 1927, the capital stock of the bank and its affiliate were each increased by $25 million. The next day, National City Company acquired the General Sugar Corporation (into which the producers had been amalgamated) at a price of $25 million, permitting the sugar company to pay the loans held by the bank. Peach (1941) commented that while this might appear to be a contribution of the shareholders to a write-off that would otherwise have reduced the bank's capital, the shareholders were not informed of the purpose of increasing the stock. Likewise, shareholders did not appear to have been informed when Chase National Bank converted credits for public works in Cuba into bonds with the intention of selling them to the public. When the bond prices sagged, the bank purchased the issue. Peach (1941) concludes that the Chase National Bank took $10 million into its portfolio in order to assist its affiliate.

The third charge of conflict of interest in the Pecora hearings was that managers had used their position and knowledge to privately benefit at the expense of the bank and its shareholders. The most common avenues for this activity were pool operations to support stock prices. During the boom period, it was common for security affiliates to conduct pool operations in the stock of parent banks. National City Company maintained an active trading position in the stock of National City Bank, as did many other affiliates for their parent banks.[59] The head of Chase, Albert H Wiggin formed six corporations for his family and other officers and directors of Chase National Bank and Chase Securities Corporation. They also used these corporations to allow them to participate in issues handled by the bank and its affiliates.[60] Perhaps the most shocking example occurred during October-November 1929. Wiggin sold Chase's stock short at the time Chase was a member of a banking group trying to support and stabilize the market (Carosso, 1970).

Congressional investigators were equally critical of Charles E Mitchell, the president of National City Bank and its affiliate, singling him out for failing to safeguard the interest of shareholders and investors while giving management bonuses and special investment opportunities. They objected to the management fund set-up using the annual earnings of the bank and its affiliates. The management fund guaranteed owners and managers a minimum return in the form of 8% dividends and fixed salaries. The remaining profits were distributed to owners and executives in a four to one ratio, ensuring executives received compensation as if they had been important shareholders.[61] While this appeared dubious to contemporaries, it looked much more like an appropriate attempt to align incentives properly so that top management would not attempt to favour one part of the bank in favour of the other, rewarding them for its overall performance (See Benston, 1990).

For these alleged problems, contemporary experts, like Peach (1941), offered narrowly targeted remedies. Peach believed that the Securities Act of 1933 and the Securities and Exchange Act of 1934 provided ample protections to investors by ensuring adequate divulgence of information for new issues. To block private profiting from pool operations, he recommended that it be made illegal for officers to participate individually in any business conducted by affiliates. Although somewhat critical of management funds, he felt that they should be better publicized. For the shifts of funding from loans to securities, he eschewed separation and promoted what would be considered today as prudential supervision. He felt that compulsory periodic examinations of security affiliates by federal authorities in conjunction with the parent banks would prevent the shifting of undesirable assets, pointing out that while one could not easily prevent banks from making bad loans, one could prevent them from being hidden by shifting them around.

The securities affiliates of commercial banks would have survived the New Deal's legislation in some regulated form, if the chairman of the Senate Committee on Banking and Currency, the influential Senator Carter Glass, had not insisted on a complete divorce of commercial and investment banking. Based on his firm belief in the fallacious real bills doctrine, Glass refused to permit banking reform to proceed, even though he was the only important advocate of this remedy.[62] Although Glass focused on the threat securities affiliates posed for the safety and soundness of their parent banks, White (1986) showed that securities affiliates did not weaken their parent banks. In fact, the presence of a securities affiliate reduced the probability of a bank's failure and had no deleterious effects on solvency or liquidity.[63] Nevertheless, in the depths of the depression, the Congressional hearings cast a pall over the affiliates, generating a myth that they destabilized banks. Ironically, although Senator Glass's concern centred on the effect of banks' soundness, belief in the importance of the 1920s conflicts of interest grew over time.

The remedy Congress chose, complete separation, was seen as eliminating both conflicts of interest and threats to safety and soundness. The Banking Act of 1933 revoked the securities powers of all Federal Reserve member banks. Sections 16, 20, 21 and 32 of the Banking Act became known as the Glass-Steagall Act. Section 16 limited national banks' powers to the purchase of securities on their own account and restricted them to dealing in some government securities. Section 20 ordered that after 16 June 1934 no member bank could be affiliated with any corporation, association or business trust engaged principally in the issue, floatation, underwriting, public sale, or distribution at wholesale or retail through syndicate participation of stocks, bonds, debentures, notes or other securities.[64] Section 21 made it illegal for investment banks to accept deposits, and Section 32 stipulated that no bank officer or director could be associated with any business engaged in these activities.[65]

The effect of the Glass-Steagall Act was to force commercial banks to eliminate their securities affiliates and shrink their bond departments. National City Bank liquidated its affiliate. First Boston Corporation was formed out of the security affiliates of Chase and First National Bank of Boston. Morgan decided to pursue deposit banking, while some of Morgan's partners left and created Morgan Stanley & Co. (White, 2000). For the next several decades, there was no challenge to the separation of commercial and investment banking and insurance.

5.5 Testing the myths

So firm was the acceptance of the legal separation engineered first by the post-Armstrong state legislation and the Glass-Steagall Act that there were very few studies of the actual behaviour of universal banks prior to the 1990s. No significant work has been carried out on the combination of insurance and investment banking prior to 1906. Of the three conflicts identified in the Pecora hearings, only the conflict between commercial bank lending and underwriting has received significant attention.

The central question addressed in the literature on conflicts of interest from combining commercial and investment banking is whether the benefits from the added 'certification' from a universal bank outweigh the costs from the exploitation of 'conflicts of interest'. In making and monitoring loans, commercial banks gain information about firms that is not usually known to outside investors. Investment banks also collect similar information; but by forming long-term lending relationships and providing transaction services, commercial banks may acquire complementary information. By combining commercial and investment banking, a universal bank will benefit in the reduction of costs from the economies of scope in information collection. Universal banks may thus be better informed than independent investment banks, and the issues they underwrite may be perceived as having better 'certification'. Similarly, universal banks may be considered to be better advisers for mergers and acquisitions. Given this synergy, the market should be willing to pay a higher price (or accept a lower yield) on securities that are underwritten by universal banks compared to independent investment banks.

The value of this superior certification by universal banks will be offset by any perceived conflicts of interest. Conflicts of interest between lending and underwriting may arise in several contexts. A firm that has obtained a loan from the bank may suffer an adverse shock that the bank, which is monitoring it closely, is aware of but which is unknown to the investing public. The bank may exploit its information advantage by issuing securities to repay the loan, selling them to the public. A bank could also exploit its superior knowledge of its clients by 'cherry picking', retaining the best clients to fund by bank loans and underwriting securities for the weaker customers. If the public fears that a bank will exploit conflicts of interest to its disadvantage and the advantage of the bank's shareholders, a conflict of interest effect will lead the market to demand a discount on the price (a premium on the yield) of securities issued by universal banks.

Whether the 'certification effect' or the 'conflict of interest effect' is stronger will depend on the bank's ability to persuade the market that there is no conflict of interest. The organizational structure of a universal bank may help to reduce the potential and the perception for conflicts of interest by creating appropriate incentives for managers and increasing the distance within the overall organization between lending and underwriting. If both lending and underwriting are conducted in departments within a bank, the public may not be able to discern if the two units are cooperating closely to exploit a conflict of interest. The creation of a separate affiliate or subsidiary for underwriting could provide a clearer picture of its activities within a bank. If, however, separation in a subsidiary is effective in containing conflicts of interest, it may also lead to a reduction in the information economies of scope. Thus, there is a trade-off in the closer integration of activities between economies of scope and potential conflicts of interest.

While contemporary critics of universal banking in the 1920s were thought to have made a persuasive case that conflicts of interest were pervasive, recent research has overturned this conventional wisdom. Not only was there a strong certification effect, but also universal banks learned how to improve their organization to convince the market that they were not taking advantage of conflicts of interest.

Examining all securities issued from January 1927 to the end of the third quarter of 1929, Puri (1996) found that industrial bonds and preferred stock underwritten by bank securities affiliates had lower yields than similar issues underwritten by independent investment banks. In a related study, Ang and Richardson (1994) estimated that bank affiliate issues had lower *ex-ante* and *ex-post* yields. This certification effect was stronger for more junior securities and less seasoned issues.[66]

There also appears to be no support for the view that universal banks inflicted low quality securities on the public. Kroszner and Rajan (1994) collected a sample of industrial bonds underwritten by the securities affiliates of commercial banks and by independent investment banks for 1921-29. Measured by Moody's Manuals and Poor's Manuals ratings, the quality of bonds fell over time for both classes of underwriters as the stock market boom proceeded, although the affiliates originated higher quality bonds. In tests of matched industrial bonds and logit regressions, Kroszner and Rajan found that there were fewer defaults among the affiliate-originated issues, measured in number and dollar value. Furthermore, the losses for defaulted bonds originated by universal banks were no different than the losses sustained by defaulted bonds issued by independent investment banks.[67] Examining the cumulative default rates of universal bank and investment bank underwritten securities issued between 1927 and 1929 with a probit model, Puri (1994) found that issues underwritten by universal banks issues defaulted less frequently. Ang and Richardson (1994) similarly found that bonds underwritten by bank affiliates had lower default rates. Thus, the public's faith and the rating agencies' judgements were upheld by experience.

Security affiliates and investment banks did not underwrite the same mix of securities, however. It appears that affiliates shied away from underwriting smaller, more junior securities and concentrated on underwriting larger older firms with an emphasis on senior securities. Kroszner and Rajan (1994) argued that investors were aware of the potential conflicts of interest but could not easily see behind the scenes to judge whether the banks were exploiting them. While investors did not have the information that would have allowed them to discriminate between issues that were tainted and untainted by conflicts of interest, they responded by applying a 'lemons-market' discount to these bonds. Evidence for this problem is suggested by the fact that ratings were good predictors of default for investment bank underwritten issues but poor predictors for affiliate underwritten issues. Universal banks compensated by underwriting higher quality securities, which were less information sensitive but for which they still enjoyed advantages in information collection.

What is even more striking is that the commercial banks engaged in investment banking recognized that they could reassure the public of the value of their certification by using a securities affiliate. Initially most banks in the United States in the 1920s underwrote bonds through a securities department inside the bank, like a German universal bank. In addition to allowing them to issue equities, however, banks soon appear to have found that they could mitigate conflicts by moving underwriting to an affiliate, thus distancing this activity from lending and gaining credibility for their certification. By creating a securities affiliate, the managerial hierarchies could be separated and questions of information and coordination would be handled by top management instead of at the department level. The incentives and compensation of the managers of the affiliate could be quite distinct from those of the loan officers. The balance sheets, income statements and accounting information for the parent banks and their separate affiliates provided greater transparency.

Kroszner and Rajan (1997) found strong evidence for the ability of commercial banks to signal their control of conflicts through their organizational structure. Drawing on all new public securities issued for the period 1925-29, they examined 906 securities underwritten by 43 internal bond departments and 32 securities affiliates. Adjusting for characteristics of the bonds and the banks, the difference in the yield to maturity at the offering date for the bonds was 14 to 23 basis points lower. The market seemed alert to even more subtle indications of separation. Affiliates whose board of directors exactly matched the parent bank's board of directors had the issues that they underwrote discounted by approximately the same degree as those of internal bond departments. Furthermore, securities departments and affiliates underwrote different mixes of securities. Compared to internal departments, affiliates tended to underwrite more junior securities and issues for smaller, younger and more indebted firms. These attributes suggest that affiliates had more credibility to certify these more information intensive securities.

Contrary to the impression in the Congressional hearings, the potential for conflicts of interest was not something discovered the day after the 1929 crash of the stock market. Some bankers were well aware of the problem even in the middle of the decade, before the market heated up. The Farmers' Loan and Trust Company of New York told the *Commercial and Financial Chronicle* in 1925 that:

> 'Due to our policy and firm conviction that, as a trustee, we should never place ourselves in the position of a buyer and seller of securities at the same time, we have never had a bond department. Our whole security department is organized for the impartial study of securities for the benefit of our customers and not for the sale of bonds to the public' (quoted in Kroszner and Rajan, 1997).

Over time, managers became aware that the prices of issues underwritten by internal departments could be increased by switching to the more credible form of a securities affiliate. Not only did new entrants choose the affiliate form to enter the securities business, but many bond departments were also converted to affiliates. While the two organizational types divided the number of new issues almost exactly in half in 1925, separate affiliates garnered 82% of all issues by 1929 (Kroszner and Rajan, 1997).[68] Thus, recent scholarship has almost completely overturned this conventional wisdom about universal banking in the critical era of the 1920s.

5.6 Contemporary universal banking in the United States

While we now see that most allegations made during the Congressional hearings cannot be supported by accumulated evidence, the myths propounded in the hearings ensured that the New Deal legislation imposed a long halt on the movement towards universal banking in the United States. Constrained by the Glass-Steagall Act and vigilant regulators, commercial banks largely ignored the securities business.[69]

Only in the 1960s did commercial and investment banks again attempt to enter each other's turf and pressure regulators to change some regulations. Commercial banks sought to persuade the Federal Reserve to expand the permissible activities for bank holding company subsidiaries. This opening remained tightly controlled, however, with revenue generated from formerly 'ineligible' activities initially limited to 5% of a subsidiary's revenue and with firewalls imposed between the subsidiary and the bank. On this limited basis, member banks moved into underwriting commercial paper, municipal revenue bonds and mortgage and consumer receivables backed securities.[70]

In 1987, the Federal Reserve enabled commercial banks to re-enter investment banking by permitting them to set-up bank holding company subsidiaries under Section 20 of the Glass-Steagall Act in order to underwrite corporate securities. By limiting their gross revenue from underwriting to 10%, the Federal Reserve considered these subsidiaries not to be in violation of the Act that prohibited affiliation with any firm that was 'principally engaged' in investment banking. These new entities could underwrite commercial paper and were allowed to underwrite corporate debt in 1989 and equities in 1990. Section 20 subsidiaries were established subject to the erection of firewalls to limit information, resource flows, and financial linkages with the affiliated commercial banks. The revenue limit was later raised to 25% in 1996, and some of the more restrictive firewalls were removed.

The re-emergence of universal banks has not resulted in any perceived exploitation of conflicts of interest; in fact, the market appears to believe that commercial banks' subsidiaries provide valuable information. Gande *et al.* (1997) examined the characteristics and pricing of securities underwritten by the top 20 underwriters (four Section 20 subsidiaries and 16 investment banks) for 1993-95. Like their pre-Glass-Steagall predecessors, they found that bank subsidiaries underwrite relatively smaller issues compared to independent investment banks.[71] Over time, as banks gained experience, the average issue size has declined even further. This fact points to the special role of commercial banks in the financial system and their ability to assist the firms facing the greatest asymmetric information hurdles, increasing small firms' access to the market.

Since the repeal of Glass-Steagall, one new concern has arisen with the reappearance of universal banking in the United States. Newly organized universal banks have been increasing their share of the investment banking market, often by giving clients credit facilities, which investment banks traditionally did not provide, on favourable terms (Cairns *et al.* 2002). This development may reflect economies realized from the combination of commercial and investment banking or a conflict of interest that favours investment banking units at the expense of the commercial banking units in universal banks. The policy issue is that large cheap credits may increase the risk to commercial banks, and potentially the safety net.[72]

Although there may be concerns for the safety net, recent experience suggests that issuing firms have gained from the entry of commercial banks. The investment banking subsidiaries of commercial banks have provided strong certification for investors. Gande *et al.* (1997) found that when the commercial bank has a significant lending stake in the issuing firm, the yield was 27 basis points lower for lower-rated issues compared to investment banks. If the issue is used to refinance part of the commercial bank debt and the parent bank still holds a stake, the yield was 42 basis points lower. In the case where the loans are completely refinanced, the market does not penalize the subsidiary underwriter and there is no significant difference in yield between debt issued by subsidiaries or independent investment banks. They concluded that the firewalls are not so high as to prevent banks with subsidiaries from more effectively certifying securities. For the economy, Gande *et al.* (1999) believe that there are significant benefits from commercial bank entry into corporate debt underwriting. Focusing on the period 1985-96, they determined that underwriter spreads, *ex-ante* yields, and market concentration has declined. Increased competition was most apparent among the lower-rated smaller debt issues. While underwriting spreads for corporate bonds have declined, there is no trend for equities, where commercial banks do not yet have a significant presence.

The presence of substantial firewalls may limit conflicts of interest that might emerge if regulations were not drawn so tightly. Gompers and Lerner (1999) investigated whether conflicts of interest were exploited when underwriting investment banks hold stakes in the issuing firms through venture capital subsidiaries. Their sample covered venture-backed IPOs from 1972 to 1992, a period over which this type of IPO increased substantially. In this analogous, but unregulated case, there is no evidence to support the limitations imposed on combining commercial and investment banking. The market appears to be concerned with potential conflicts of interest and offers a lower price for the securities, even though IPOs underwritten by investment banks with stake-holding subsidiaries had the same or higher five-year excess returns and fewer failed compared to IPOs of unaffiliated investment banks. Like the universal banks of the 1920s, the response of the investment banks with equity stakes is to underwrite less information sensitive issues, and investor discounting is mitigated by the reputation of the bank.[73]

5.7 Universal banking and conflicts of interest outside the United States

The literature on conflicts of interest may leave the impression that it is only a US problem. The US banking system's characteristic of arms' length transactions instead of relationship banking certainly heightens the awareness of conflicts of interest. While the potential problem may not be as visible, however, the issues remain.

Although the Canadian banking system has some important structural differences with the US system, the Anglo-Scottish tradition of arms' length transactions allows the examination of potential conflicts of interest. Until the Bank Act of 1987, Canadian chartered banks were prohibited from underwriting corporate securities and offering investment advice. This legislation permitted Canadian banks to enter investment banking by organizing a direct subsidiary of the bank. Hebb and Fraser (2002) compared the yields on all Canadian corporate bonds underwritten by commercial bank affiliates and independent investment banks between 1987 and 1997. Controlling for other factors, regression results show that the former have yields that are 19 basis points lower. Even the presence of a commercial banking relationship does not alter this difference, suggesting that any conflict of interest effect is dominated by the certification effect.[74] This result was stable over time, which may be noteworthy since Canadian banks quickly dominated investment banking, achieving a high level of concentration.

While the Canadian case provides similar evidence of general absence of exploitation of potential conflicts of interest, one study of the Israeli system suggests the opposite. Examining Israeli IPOs in the 1990s, Ber *et al.* (2000) found that issuing firms whose equity was underwritten by an affiliate of a bank that had provided credit to the firm had significantly lower than average stock performance but better accounting profitability. If an investment fund managed by the bank bought into the new IPO, the stock performance was even lower. They tentatively concluded that bank affiliates provide more certification, but that there is some exploitation of the conflict of interest between banks and their investment funds.

The most widely admired system of universal banking appeared in nineteenth-century Germany, where there were no legal constraints on universal banking. First private banks then joint-stock banks combined commercial and investment banking. Providing both loans and investment banking services and taking lead roles in founding and managing industrial companies, they have been viewed as essential to the rapid industrialization of the then backward German economy (Fohlin, 1999; Guinnane, 2002). The banks' size and prominence relative to markets was reinforced by German law. A transactions tax encouraged banks to settle securities trades internally, and the requirement that any issue must be fully subscribed before a company could begin operation gave advantage to large banks, which could carry the issue. These universal banks' information advantage has been seen as arising not only from the provision of commercial and investment banking services, but also from their ability to place representatives on firms' supervisory boards. In accordance with the pecking order theory of corporate finance, the ability of universal banks to service firms better has been viewed as a consequence of their ability to adjust financing as companies matured, making use of their accumulated information (Calomiris, 1995).

This German relationship banking may have allowed banks to manage and distribute risk better than banks that had more arms' length transactions, but it also produced a highly concentrated industry. By 1913, the three largest firms in Germany were banks, and they comprised 17 of the largest 25 German firms. They were able to exercise considerable power to promote the business of clients and cartels. Case histories of the banks (Guinnane, 2002) indicate, however, that they protected clients' national and international projects, but also decided which of their own clients to favour. In a vast literature on the subject, there is almost no discussion of conflicts of interest, although there was clearly potential. In one exception, Fohlin (1999) suggests that internalization of securities trading within universal banks may not have provided investors with the best execution of their trades. The literature does consider the ability of the concentrated and sometimes collusive banking industry to extract rents from industry, which suggests some exploitation of asymmetric information by less than transparent banks.

Unfortunately, just as there are no historical studies of conflicts of interest in European banking to compare to those examining the United States, there is an absence of research on conflicts of interest in contemporary European banking, in spite of the fact that the diversity of regulation provides a natural laboratory. Surveying European countries, Santos (1998) found that, as of 1997, all Western European countries permitted securities activities both within the bank and through a bank subsidiary. Although regulations varied considerably, banks in Austria, Finland, Germany, Italy, Luxembourg, the Netherlands, Sweden and Switzerland conducted their securities operations directly. Greece and Ireland preferred to use a subsidiary; and there was no dominant type in Portugal, Spain and the United Kingdom. While there are no empirical studies, there are perceptions of conflicts of interest. In Germany there are concerns about conflicts of interest where banks serve clients in more than one capacity. Potential conflicts are seen in the fiduciary responsibilities of a bank and its role as investment banker, assisting mergers and acquisitions, and the stuffing and churning of portfolios (Saunders and Walter, 1994).

5.8 Remedies for conflicts of interest

While there is currently debate over increasing the regulation of investment banks to reduce the internal analyst-underwriter conflicts of interest, the debate over universal banking is focused more on reducing regulation to gain from economies of scope without inducing the exploitation of conflicts of interest. Universal banking focuses on deregulation because until recently US public policy was guided by the Glass-Steagall Act that has inclined towards the most extreme remedy of separation.

5.8.1 Separation

Separation of the activities of a financial intermediary is a matter of degree not kind. There are basically three degrees of separation:

1. separate in-house departments;
2. separately capitalized subsidiaries of a bank or bank holding company;
3. a prohibition on a combination of activities by any organizational form.[75]

The gains in economies of scope and the potential costs from conflicts of interest will depend on the degree of integration and the organizational structure. Presumably, there is a trade-off – the greater the degree of separation, the smaller the economies of scope and the lower the potential conflicts of interest.

At one extreme, prohibiting any form of universal banking eliminates the conflicts of interest but deprives banks of any benefits from economies of scope. The US Glass-Steagall Act of 1933, copied by the Japanese, exemplified the complete separation. Although it is difficult to disentangle the costs of this regulation, it may have contributed to the relative decline in the domestic and international competitiveness of US commercial banks (Saunders and Walter, 1994). Competitive pressures on the banks, coupled with the new evidence discussed above, convinced Congress to allow firms to combine commercial and investment banking through separately capitalized affiliates of bank holding companies, each with its own management and accounting records. Flows of information, personnel and other inputs are controlled. Limited liability is aimed at protecting each unit's shareholders and depositors from losses if another unit fails. Separation also permits different compensation for each unit's management that can reduce incentives to exploit conflicts.

Essentially, this is the new banking regime in the United States under the Gramm-Leach-Bliley Financial Services Modernization Act of 1999 that allows banks, securities firms and insurance companies to affiliate within a financial holding company. Evidence from the early, more limited, expansion of commercial banks into investment banks strongly suggests that firewalls were not so high as to prevent gaining some economies of scope. According to Saunders and Walter (1994), the firewalls were found by a 1990 General Accounting Office study to be sufficiently stringent that no conflicts of interest were found between Section 20 subsidiaries and their affiliated banks. While it is too early for any judgement about the effects of the 1999 Act, banks have moved to take advantage of the law presumably to gain potential complementarities.

Although keeping investment banking in a subsidiary may not allow it full exploitation of the economies of scope, it may be appropriate if a closer affiliation would expand the safety net in banking. If the safety net were not a concern, a bank could select the most efficient organizational form, providing some investment banking services in-house and others through subsidiaries. In the presence of distortions created by deposit insurance and the doctrine of too-big-to-fail, segregating investment banking activities in a subsidiary may be an inferior choice of corporate form from a pure efficiency point of view, but it may limit the potential liabilities of deposit insurance. At the same time, it will prevent universal banks from benefiting from the safety net in competition with independent investment banks, keeping the playing field level.

While substantial firewalls are thought to play a key role in the emerging system of American universal banking, it is generally believed that legally and operationally separate units are not truly independent. There are strong incentives to manage them as an integrated entity to gain economies of scope rather than as a portfolio of independent companies. Studies of US banking holding companies indicate that policies are usually centralized at the holding company level. Furthermore, universal banks have incentives to protect their units from bankruptcy because they are fearful of reputational effects; and the courts may hold the parent companies legally liable. Thus, the holding company does not necessarily restrict connections, and banks can provide capital infusions, offer credit, exchange information or purchase assets and services from their subsidiaries (Santos, 1998). These considerations may help to explain why the Congress and the Federal Reserve have allowed the weakening of some firewalls beginning in the 1980s. The Gramm-Leach-Bliley Act is certainly not the final word on financial architecture, as further deregulation will, no doubt, await the evaluation of the performance banking under this new regime.

5.8.2 The problem of compensation and incentives

Central to the decision of the degree of corporate separation is the problem of setting the incentives and compensation for managers. The pre-1933 experience in the United States of universal banking shows, in extreme form, the dangers when incentives are not adequately aligned for managers. The ability of officers and directors to benefit from establishing their own partnerships that participated in syndicates with their insurance companies and securities affiliates created unusual opportunities for exploiting conflicts of interest. The partnerships established by officers of Enron are the contemporary equivalents. The conflicts are blatant as they provide compensation to officers that directly diminish the revenues of their companies. These problems may be eliminated either by regulation or ensuring that relationships are sufficiently transparent to the shareholders.

Within a bank, incentives also need to be properly aligned. If there is a booming stock market, with soaring revenues from IPOs, any misalignment of compensation of executives within a firm may induce an exploitation of conflicts of interest. As seen in Chapter 2, underwriters may pressure analysts and commercial bankers to assist them. How to design a management compensation scheme that maximizes shareholder value is the central problem. While there is no simple guidebook, the example of the National City Bank's management fund is an insightful approach. By pooling the revenues from commercial and investment banking and allotting them to the shareholders and managers in a fixed ratio, managers were treated as large shareholders. There was no incentive for them to favour one unit of the bank over the other unless it maximized shareholder wealth.

One danger that arises from even the best-designed management compensation system is if the time horizon of managers differs from shareholders. Managers might be willing to favour underwriting customers over depositors, brokerage clients or insurance policy holders if the profits from underwriting are high in the short-run and they have a short-run horizon. In this case, they will not be concerned about the long-term reputational effects of this favouritism on commercial banking, brokerage or insurance. Whether shareholders can effectively monitor managers to ensure that their behaviour is aligned with maintaining the reputation and value of the firm depends on the bank's transparency and disclosure.

5.8.3 Reputation, transparency and prudential supervision

Except for the problem posed by the subsidization of intermediaries by the US government's too-big-to-fail doctrine, some economists are convinced that the market offers sufficient monitoring discipline to ensure that conflicts of interest are minor problems at worst. Rajan (1995) argues that the belief in the 'naïve investor' who is prey to conflicts of interest is a 'patent fallacy'. Empirical studies of universal banking in the United States before 1933 and in the 1990s find that the market offered the correct incentives. Universal banks appear to have been rewarded for their greater ability to certify new issues with higher initial prices, and the investors were rewarded by their superior performance. The market *also* displayed a preference for the securities issued by affiliates over internal bond departments where conflicts of interest may have been greater. Affiliates thus became the pre-eminent form of corporate structure. In both periods, given that they could signal a reduced likelihood of conflict of interest, subsidiaries were able to underwrite more junior, more information-intensive securities, thereby improving the efficiency of the financial system.

For the German banking system, where market discipline rather than regulation is allowed to discipline conflicts of interest, the Monopolies Commission Report (1976) and the Gessler Commission Report (1979) found no evidence of exploitation of conflicts by universal banks. There are, however, few studies of the German system, and as Saunders and Walter (1994) point out, the official studies have been treated with some skepticism.

Looking at the UK financial system, Benston (1998) makes a similar case for the sufficiency of market discipline through reputation. Disparaging government regulation of financial products and contracts and mandatory disclosure, he concludes that:

> 'most financial institutions have considerable investments in their charters and in customer goodwill. Hence, they have strong incentives to treat customers fairly. In the event that they do not, either because of corporate policy or inability to control salespersons' mis-statements, they can be sued and be subject to judgments, which reinforces their incentives to avoid engaging in fraud and misrepresentation. Probably of greater importance, however is that at low cost consumers can shift their businesses from suppliers with doubtful reputations to their competitors, because similar financial products are delivered by many firms. Thus, financial product institutions have strong incentives to maintain reputations for honesty and fairness.'
> (Benson, 1998, pp. 55-6)

The ability of the market to adequately monitor and discipline financial intermediaries depends, however, on the disclosure of information to the market. Apart from the costs of disclosure, firms may not be willing to provide all the needed information if some of it is proprietary and its disclosure would reduce the gains from information collection. Banks should disclose their commercial banking terests in a firm to their investment bank/brokerage clients and vice versa. Mandatory disclosure of these relationships will ensure that information asymmetries are reduced, limiting the ability to exploit them. Nevertheless, there are some cases, such as mergers and acquisitions, where banks may not be able to divulge information of a relationship without giving an advantage to their competitors. Supervisory oversight is then necessary if disclosure is limited to protect propriety information.

Banking supervisors already have powers to supervise universal banks and to monitor universal banks' internal control procedures to make sure that they do not take on excessive risk. Bank supervision has been expanded in recent years to focus on so-called operational risk, and conflicts of interest can easily be viewed as a particular form of operational failure. Thus, having bank supervisors focus on universal banks' internal controls and compensation mechanisms with regard to conflicts of interest is a natural direction to follow. Controlling conflicts of interest in universal banks also has a growing importance for preserving the safety and soundness of banks (and so is important from a prudential perspective) because banks now may have strong incentives to make loans on overly favourable terms in order to obtain fees from activities like underwriting securities. Just as bank supervision has become more oriented to focus on risk management in recent years, it needs to increase its focus on control of conflicts of interest.

The general acceptance that the market, combined with appropriate disclosure and prudential supervision, should be the primary remedy to restrain the exploitation of conflicts of interest between commercial and investment banking represents a remarkable change in the United States. The stock market collapse of the 1930s induced the acceptance of the most extreme remedy – complete separation. A key lesson of this episode is that the panic to find a remedy resulted in the adoption of a very costly solution when more modest remedies would have sufficed. The potential problems from deposit insurance dictate that investment banking should be separated from commercial banking in a separately capitalized intermediary. This degree of separation may, however, be close to a market solution for some firms, as indicated by the evidence from the 1920s. While the market can discourage the exploitation of conflicts of interest and set appropriate incentives for managers and banks, mandatory disclosure of multiple banking relationships will help to ensure that information asymmetries are reduced. Coupled with regulatory and supervisory oversight, conflicts of interest in universal banking can thus be limited.

6 Overview and Conclusions

In the previous chapters, we examined conflicts of interest in four basic areas of the financial system: investment banking, auditing, rating agencies and universal banks. We examined the theory and empirical evidence to assess how serious particular conflicts of interest are and what remedies might correct them. In this chapter, we step back from the details and identify the basic themes that arise in our analysis of the different types of conflicts of interest.

6.1 When are conflicts of interest a serious problem?

Our analysis of conflicts of interest starts with the observation that conflicts of interest present their main problem for the financial system when they lead to a decrease in information flows that make it harder for the financial system to solve adverse selection and moral hazard problems that reduce the flow of funds to productive investments. Even though a conflict of interest exists, it does not necessarily reduce the flow of information because the incentives to exploit the conflict of interest may not be very high. Exploitation of a conflict of interest that is visible to the market will typically result in a decrease in the reputation of the financial firm where it takes place. Given the importance of maintaining and enhancing reputation, exploiting the conflict of interest would then decrease the future profitability of the firm because it will have greater difficulty selling its services in the future, thus creating incentives for the firm to prevent exploitation of the conflict of interest. Our reading of the evidence indicates that these incentives do work to constrain conflicts of interest in the long run, but the extent to which they are effective in the short run depends on factors such as transparency and incentive structures within firms.

One example occurs in credit-rating agencies. At first glance, the fact that rating agencies are paid by the firms issuing securities to produce ratings for these securities looks like a serious conflict of interest. Rating agencies would seem to have incentives to gain business by providing firms issuing securities with higher credit ratings than they deserve, making it easier for them to sell these securities at higher prices. If, however, rating agencies were to attempt to exploit this conflict of interest, by giving higher credit ratings to firms that paid for ratings, this would result in decreased credibility of the ratings, thus making them less valuable to the market. The market is eventually able to assess the quality of biased ratings down the road because it can observe poorer performance by individual securities. The resulting loss of trust in the information provided by the rating agency when this conflict is exploited would lead to a costly decline in its reputation.

Similarly, the apparent conflicts of interest when commercial banks underwrote securities before the Glass-Steagall Act do not appear to have been generally exploited. When a commercial bank underwrites securities, it may have an incentive to market the securities of financially troubled firms to the public because the firms will then be able to pay back the loans they owe to the bank, while the bank earns fees from the underwriting services. The evidence for the 1920s suggests that the presence of this conflict of interest caused markets to find securities underwritten by bond departments within a commercial bank to be less attractive than securities underwritten in separate affiliates where the conflict of interest were better contained. In order to maintain their reputation, commercial banks shifted their underwriting to separate affiliates over time, with the result that securities underwritten by banks were valued as highly as those underwritten by independent investment banks. When affiliates were unable to certify the absence of conflicts, they focused on more senior securities where there was less of an information asymmetry and conflicts were less severe. Again, we see that the market provided incentives to control potential conflicts of interest. It is important to note, however, that the market solution was not immediate and took some time to develop.

The responsiveness of the market can also be seen in the apparent conflict of interest for investment banks when underwriters who have incentives to favour issuers over investors puts pressure on research analysts to provide more favourable assessments of issuers' securities. It has been observed that lead underwriters make more buy recommendations for their IPOs than do other firms' analysts for the same securities, yet the stock prices of firms recommended by lead underwriters declined during the SEC's 25-day quiet period while other banks' picks rose. Hence, the market appears to recognize the difference in the quality of information when there is a potential conflict of interest. There are fewer empirical studies in auditing, but even this limited evidence suggests that the market perceives and adjusts for potential conflicts of interest. There is evidence that clients who are concerned about conflicts of interest from the joint provision of auditing and management advisory services will reduce the value they attach to audit opinions and limit non-audit purchases from incumbent auditors. These examples do not indicate that the market can always contain the incentives to exploit conflicts of interest. Sometimes, information needed to contain conflicts of interest would reveal proprietary information that would help a financial firm's competitors, thus reducing the incentives to reveal this information.

As brought out in the recent scandals, what are particularly worrisome are conflicts of interest whose exploitation leads to large gains for some members of the financial firm even if it reduces the value of the whole firm. Compensation mechanisms inside a firm, if inappropriately designed, may lead to conflicts of interest that not only reduce information flows to credit markets but end up destroying the firm. Indeed, the story of the demise of Arthur Andersen illustrates how the compensation arrangements even for one line of business, like auditing, can create severe conflicts of interest where partners in regional offices had incentives to please their largest clients even if this was detrimental to the overall firm. The conflict of interest problem can become even more severe when several lines of business are combined and the returns from some activity – underwriting, consulting – are very high and expected to be brief, so that a compensation scheme that worked reasonably well at one time may become very badly aligned.

The extraordinary surge in the stock market created huge temporary rewards, permitting well-positioned analysts, underwriters or audit firm partners to exploit the conflicts before incentives could be realigned. In the most severe cases, opportunistic individuals were able to capture the firm's reputational rents. The exploitation of these conflicts of interest clearly damaged the reputation of such investment banks as Merrill Lynch, Salomon Smith Barney of Citigroup, and Credit Suisse First Boston, and perhaps the credibility of analysts in general. Audit firms have lost much of their non-audit business, while Arthur Andersen was destroyed.

6.2 Evaluating remedies

In designing appropriate remedies, we believe that it is important to remember that conflicts of interest did not create the boom or bubble in the stock market. Rather, the conflicts were opportunities to exploit the very rapid rise of stock prices in certain sectors. Conflicts may be largely eliminated by a complete separation or segregation of each specific type of financial activity, but clearly that would impose a huge cost on financial intermediation by drastically reducing the economies of scope. Stock market booms are clearly infrequent events. The only cases that parallel the events of the late 1990s are the late 1920s and possibly 1986-87. To impose segregation remedies on the financial industry to prevent the exploitation of conflicts in the rare spectacular bull markets will result in excessively high costs. The imposition of the Glass-Steagall Act's separation of commercial and investment banking after the boom of the 1920s is a clear example of an excessive response that imposed large and unnecessary long-term costs on financial intermediation. Exploitation of conflicts of interest that we have examined was never uniform across each industry. Litigation may be the appropriate response to discipline specific firms and individuals as part of an overall market solution. Legal liabilities and penalties need to be carefully designed, however, as witnessed by the behaviour of audit firms seeking to avoid the extremely high litigation risk from class action lawsuits.

In evaluating specific conflicts of interest, it is important to ask the two questions posed at the beginning of this book:

1. Do markets have the information and incentives to control conflicts of interest?
2. Even if the incentives to exploit a conflict of interest are strong, would a policy that eliminates the conflict of interest destroy economies of scope, thereby reducing information flows?

If the answer is 'yes' to either question, then the case for a policy to remedy a particular conflict of interest is substantially weakened. Putting the remedy into practice would be likely to reduce the overall information in the market place, thus doing more harm than good.

This perspective provides a framework with which to examine the five generic approaches to remedying conflicts of interest:

1. market discipline;
2. mandatory disclosure for increased transparency;
3. supervisory oversight;
4. separation by function;
5. socialization of information.

The first approach, market discipline, is the least intrusive, avoids overreaction and can hit where it hurts most through pecuniary penalties. Also market forces can promote new institutional means to contain conflicts of interest, for example, by generating organizational structures to reduce conflicts of interest. We observed this development when security affiliates took pre-eminence over in-house bond departments in universal banks in the United States in the 1920s. Market-based solutions may not always work, however, if the market is not able to obtain sufficient information to punish firms that are exploiting conflicts of interest. Thus, to make the market work in constraining conflicts of interest, the second approach to induce increased transparency may be needed. Mandatory disclosure of information that reveals whether a conflict of interest exists may help the market to discipline financial firms that exploit conflicts of interest or enable investors to judge how much weight to place on the information the firm supplies. Although regulating for transparency may be intrusive, it should be seen as a complement to market solutions because it can help the market control conflicts of interest.

Mandatory disclosure is not without its problems, both because financial firms may hide relevant information and because disclosure may reveal so much proprietary information that a financial institution's incentives to generate valuable information would be compromised. The problems of mandatory disclosure suggest that the third, somewhat more intrusive approach, supervisory oversight, may be needed to constrain conflicts of interest. Supervisors can observe proprietary information about conflicts of interest without revealing it to a financial firm's competitors and can take actions to prevent financial firms from exploiting conflicts of interest.

Where the market cannot get sufficient information to constrain conflicts of interest because there is no satisfactory way of inducing information disclosure by market discipline or supervisory oversight, the incentives to exploit conflicts of interest may be reduced or eliminated by an even more intrusive approach: regulations enforcing separation of functions. Separation by function has the goal of ensuring that 'agents' are not placed in the position of responding to multiple 'principals' so that conflicts of interest are reduced. Moving from less stringent separation of functions (different in-house departments with firewalls between them) to more stringent separation (different activities in separately capitalized affiliates or prohibition of the combination of activities in any organizational form), reduces conflicts of interest. More stringent separation of functions reduces synergies of information collection, however, thereby preventing financial firms from taking advantage of economies of scope in information production.

The most radical response to conflicts of information generated by asymmetric information is to socialize the provision or the funding source of the relevant information. The argument for this approach is that information is a public good and so it might need to be publicly supplied. Of course, the problem with this approach is that a government agency or publicly funded entity may not have the same strong incentives as private financial institutions to produce high quality information, thus reducing the flow of information to financial markets. Furthermore, there is a compensation problem in government agencies because, as a practical matter, they may not be able to pay market wages to attract the best analysts.

In evaluating remedies it is also important to remember that there are many types of agents in the financial system who provide information to the market, ranging from those with the least access to proprietary information to those with the most. Analysts have the least access, and rating agencies have more. Auditors probably have the most privileged access along with government regulators charged with supervisory oversight. This gradient of access to proprietor informa-tion should reflect the ability of agents to discover the true financial condition and performance of the firms that they observe. Agents' ability to discover this information will also be determined by their compensation and the other incentives provided to them. Although these agents provide some overlapping information, one is not a substitute for another. This lack of substitution is not solely because they provide different types of information or signals to the public. These agents are all subject to various pressures and conflicts of interest that may diminish their ability to perform their task of discovery. Analysts may be well compensated and have substantial research resources at their disposal, but they may be too favourable to the firms for which their bank is lead underwriter and they have the least access to proprietary information. Rating agencies are more insulated from conflicts of interest and have better access to proprietary information; but enjoying an oligopoly, their research effort may be reduced. Auditors enjoy superior access to proprietary information and operate in a competitive industry, but the value of their opinions may be reduced by conflicts between audit and non-audit activities, pressure from management, and a litigation-risk induced focus on rules rather than principles. Finally, regulators/supervisors may have the best access to proprietary information, yet their capacity to monitor is limited by the resources they have been allocated and political pressures for forbearance.

To ensure that the capital markets are adequately served, it is necessary to have multiple agents who work to reduce the information asymmetries. One may become less useful at one point in time, but maintaining the quality of information delivered by these different agents engaged in overlapping work is more likely to provide sufficient monitoring of companies. The remedies we find appropriate are intended to increase the effectiveness of all four types of agents.

Our review of the evidence on conflicts of interest suggests that the market is often able to constrain conflicts of interest to a considerable degree, even though at first glance they seem to be severe. Furthermore, we think that it is dangerous to prevent exploitation of synergies in information production because this could substantially reduce the amount of information available in financial markets, thereby reducing the efficiency of these markets in chanelling funds to those with productive investment opportunities. We may be showing our biases as economists, but we believe that, when it can be made to work, the market is the most effective and desirable way of disciplining conflicts. So the first focus of solutions to remedy conflicts of interest should be on strengthening market discipline. Only when we are convinced that market discipline cannot constrain serious conflicts of interest that reduce information flows, do we recommend non-market solutions. We also should note that market solutions work in the long run; non-market solutions work in the short run, but they can hinder or prevent the emergence of more efficient market solutions in the long run.

6.3 Recommendations

Using the information-oriented framework we have developed in this study leads us to recommend the following remedies for controlling conflicts of interest in the financial services industry.

1. Increase disclosure for investment analysts, credit-rating analysts and auditors to reveal any interests they have in the firms they analyse. Disclosure plays an important role, enabling markets to acquire information that can be used to punish financial firms that exploit conflicts of interest.

Provision of this information makes it more likely that financial services firms will develop internal rules to ensure that conflicts of interest are minimized so that their reputation remains high, thus enabling them to continue to profitably engage in the information-production activities. Recent efforts by the SEC and other government agencies to increase disclosure of conflicts of interest are moves in the right direction.

2. Improve corporate governance to control conflicts of interest. Remedies for controlling conflicts of interest cannot be effective in a vacuum. Without good corporate governance, markets are unlikely to work well and so the remedies discussed here would be unlikely to solve conflict of interest problems. Improving corporate governance is a huge topic that is well beyond the scope of our study, and thus we have not addressed the broad topic here. There is one area of corporate governance that we think is critical to the quality of information in the financial system. Auditors need to be hired by, compensated by, and report to audit committees whose responsibility is to represent stakeholders other than management, as provided for in the Sarbanes-Oxley Act. Proper implementation of this reform is an important job for the PCAOB.

3. Establish codes of conduct to control conflicts of interest, developed by industry participants in cooperation with supervisors. Given their experience, financial service providers in the private sector are capable of designing effective internal controls and codes of conduct. Government supervisors can help, however, because they can monitor internal controls at many firms and observe what is best practice. It is important that these codes be dynamic. The market-place in financial services is continually in a state of flux and best practice to control conflicts of interest will of necessity change over time.

4. Increase supervisory oversight over conflicts of interest. Mandatory disclosure may not always be sufficient to enable the market to constrain conflicts of interest, especially as it may be necessary to limit disclosure of proprietary information. We thus see a strong role for supervisory oversight. Supervisory oversight has an important role in containing conflicts of interest because many of the most damaging conflicts of interest arise from agency problems within firms, the result of poorly designed, internal compensation mechanisms that are difficult for markets to observe.

   Banking supervisors already have powers to supervise universal banks and to monitor universal banks' internal control procedures to make sure that they do not take on excessive risk. Bank supervision has been expanded in recent years to focus on operational risk and conflicts of interest can easily be viewed as a particular form of operational failure. Thus, bank supervisors' focus on universal banks' internal controls and compensation mechanisms with regard to conflicts of interest is a natural development. Controlling conflicts of interest in universal banks also has a growing importance for preserving the safety and soundness of banks (and so is important from a prudential perspective) because banks may lend on favourable terms in order to obtain fees from other activities, like underwriting securities. Just as bank supervision has become more oriented to focus on risk management in recent years, it needs to increase its focus on control of conflicts of interest.

   The SEC and its equivalents in other countries have a clear interest in the activities of investment analysts to monitor whether they are exploiting conflicts of interest that undermine market integrity. In the past, however, they have often focused their attention on other issues such as insider trading. Clearly, the recent corporate scandals and legal actions against financial service providers indicate that a greater focus on conflicts of interest is needed in agencies that supervise securities markets.

The newly created PCAOB has the authority to monitor internal controls at accounting firms and the creation of this oversight board by Sarbanes-Oxley is one of the most desirable features of this legislation. An important task of the PCAOB will be to ensure that auditors are independent of management and report to audit committees. Also, the PCAOB will need to monitor and encourage best-practice compensation mechanisms inside accounting firms that continue to conduct auditing and management advisory services under the same roof.

5. Provide adequate resources to supervisors to monitor conflicts of interest. Supervisors must have sufficient resources to monitor conflicts of interest. Supervision has failed when supervisors were starved for resources. In the 1980s, limited resources weakened supervisors during the US banking crises.[76] Only after the recent emergence of serious conflicts of interest that shook the financial system, did the SEC have its funding raised substantially. Starving supervisors of resources is often the result of strong lobbying efforts by the supervised industry. In the financial service industry this problem may become worse during good times when financial service providers are making huge profits. Although resources for supervisory oversight of the financial service industry has risen recently, it is important that the lessons of the 1990s are not forgotten and that supervisors continue to be given adequate resources and their employees compensated to ensure high quality talent is available.

6. Enhance competitiveness in the rating agency industry. While analysts, auditors and most financial institutions operate in highly competitive markets, rating agencies are protected from competition by high entry costs and the official sanction of their ratings by regulators. The barriers to competition for rating agencies need to be reduced to enhance the discipline of the market and ensure that adequate resources are invested in their activities.

7. Prevent the co-option of information-producing agents by regulators and supervisors. Currently a severe problem arises from the increasing standardization of ratings and their designation for regulatory purposes. This practice should be limited as it encourages firms to package their financing to meet certain targets. Excessive dependence of supervisors on rating agencies limits their effectiveness as monitors and thus their potential contribution to information.

In a similar vein, overly standardized, detailed prescriptive accounting rules have the unintended consequence of decreasing the amount of information in auditors' reports. Instead, the focus should be on a 'true and fair view' of the financial performance and financial position of the audited firm.

8. Avoid forced separation of financial service activities except in unusual circumstances. We are generally skeptical of forced separation of financial service functions to solve conflict of interest problems. In many cases, the market leads financial service firms to separate activities, either with firewalls or by setting up separately capitalized affiliates, in order for the firms to attest to the quality of the information they provide and thus sell

their services profitably. This is exactly what happened in the banking industry before the advent of the Glass-Steagall Act. In hindsight, we know that this Act created a costly and rigid separation of commercial and investment banking that reduced the efficiency of the financial system and prevented the development of market mechanisms to contain conflicts.

Both the segregation of the audit business envisioned in the Sarbanes-Oxley Act and radical changes for analysts imposed by the global settlement by the New York Attorney General, the SEC and other regulators appear to us to be misdirected and excessive responses to the collapse of the bull market. Because they segregate the activities of auditors and analysts, altering the compensation and forcing a sharing of information by the latter, economies of scope will be reduced and the quantity and quality of information may well decline. Complete segregation is an extreme and, we believe, inappropriate remedy. Litigation, industry standards and supervisory oversight should be sufficient to erect the limited firewalls needed in most cases, while the market disciplines firms that are perceived to exploit conflicts of interest.

We do see some role for regulations enforcing limited separation under unusual circumstances. For example, forcing banks to have separately capitalized affiliates to conduct investment banking, insurance and other non-banking activities makes good sense in order to limit extending the safety net beyond banking activities. A government safety net for banks has the rationale that it is needed to prevent bank panics. A government safety net, however, creates moral hazard incentives for risk-taking that requires more extensive regulation and supervision to ensure the safety and soundness of the banking industry. This problem is even more severe because the government cannot credibly commit to avoid a too-big-to-fail doctrine. Extending the safety net to other financial service activities has a much weaker rationale and would create further incentives for risk-taking that could be highly damaging to the soundness of the financial system.

9. Do not socialize information for the financial service industry. Socialization of information carries many hidden dangers for the quality of the information generated, and is generally unwarranted. Socialization could potentially take a variety of forms, including official provision of certain services (for example, research, auditing), and the financing of independent private sector services by taxation or a levy. We are, however, most skeptical of any remedy that mandates the socialization of information production in financial markets. In its extreme form, this approach negates the benefits of multiple, competing agents. Even where service providers themselves remain in the private sector, there are threats to the quality of information provided. For example, if rating agencies are protected from competition and their ratings are standardized and mandated for risk assessment, they have little incentive to devote effort to thorough analysis or to improve their assessment techniques. If auditors are induced to produce opinions that are exclusively rules-based rather than principles-based and the rules are tightly defined by the regulators, then they too become part of the regulatory system and do not contribute any independent judgement. A form of socialization has been incorporated in the global settlement reached with the largest investment banks, where firms are required to purchase outside research and share their own research. Although socialization of information production would reduce incentives to exploit conflicts of interest, it is likely to reduce the quality of information in the market-

place, and therefore make the financial system less efficient, rather than more efficient.

Overall, these nine recommendations rely on the combination of market discipline, supplemented by mandatory disclosure of conflicts, and supervisory oversight to keep conflicts of interest from damaging information production in the financial system. In other words, policies should almost always be based on our first three approaches to remedying conflicts of interest. We see these three approaches as being complementary and ones that are oriented to helping make markets work better. Market discipline, supplemented by mandatory disclosure and supervisory oversight is usually sufficient to control conflicts of interest. It is important to recognize that markets do not immediately create optimal structures to solve conflict of interest problems. As the history of universal banking suggests, financial markets move to manage conflicts effectively over time.

We think that radical solutions to conflict of interest problems, which involve socialization of information production or very stringent separation of financial service activities, are likely to do far more harm than good. We believe that with increased disclosure of information and supervisory oversight plus additional reforms of rules governing audit opinions and official use and sanction of ratings, the problems created by conflicts of interest can be minimized. More radical approaches have the potential to reduce, rather than increase, the quality of information in financial markets, with the result that chanelling funds to those with productive investment opportunities, which are so crucial to strong economic growth, could be severely compromised.

Our study has for the most part focused on conflicts of interest in the US context. This is not accidental. The problems of conflict of interest have been much more dramatic in the United States than in Europe and other countries; moreover, the generally greater transparency in the United States has revealed governance shortcomings in that country that may have remained hidden elsewhere. In addition, the greater importance of securities markets in the United States and the extremely competitive environment in the United States makes it more vulnerable to temptations to exploit conflicts. Nevertheless the lessons we have drawn from this study are important ones for Europe as well. With the advent of the European Monetary Union and the growing integration of financial markets in Europe, the financial system there may well become more like that in the United States. The importance of securities markets is growing in Europe and the financial environment is becoming more competitive. Conflicts of interest of the type we have described here are thus likely to become more important in Europe in the future. We hope that the framework we have developed here to understand conflicts of interest and what should be done about them will be just as useful in the European context as it is in the United States.

Discussion and Roundtables

Session 1: Analysts and underwriters

Hans-Jörg Rudloff
Barclays Capital
Hans-Jörg Rudloff opened the session by observing that thinking about conflicts of interest as an issue regarding 'analysts and underwriting' is a narrow approach. The extent of conflict during the last few years remains exceptional both in magnitude and frequency, it is much larger and more complex than specific conflicts of interest. The role of analysts has been minor relative to that of syndicate managers, traders and to outright market manipulation. In a big bear market there is usually a hunt for culprits and finger-pointing becomes the rule. Since the handling of the problem in the press has been rather primitive, Rudloff expressed the hope that the forthcoming discussions would allow us to advance further into the understanding of the fundamental causes of conflicts of interest.

John Lipsky
JP Morgan Chase
John Lipsky congratulated the authors for their work on a widely debated topic. He noted, however, that substantial changes in the role of analysts, the outcome of regulatory and legal decisions, are not fully discussed in the Report and yet have had an important impact on the profession. More generally, he argued that conflicts of interest must be seen in the broad context that have resulted from the securitization of markets and the changing role of intermediaries. These factors will continue to have a substantial structural impact on the role of research in financial markets. He outlined six main points:

1. There is a potential and inherent conflict of interest between the primary and secondary sides of the market. It is, however, in the interest of the securities' firms to control this type of conflict because reputation is critical. Difficulties arise when there is a perception of a failure there, and the recent past has provided some severe lessons.

2. The Glass-Steagall Act followed the burst of a bubble that led to the Great Depression. The current situation is different. The end of a so-called 'new era' and the burst of a bubble have not resulted in a serious decline in economic activity. In fact, it may well be the case that productivity has permanently increased, at least in the United States. Investors are not convinced that the new economy was just an illusion. Misvaluation was mostly concentrated in the Nasdaq market, it has primarily affected a

limited number of entrepreneurs, the 'Nasdaq billionaires', who owned the bulk of the stocks of their own companies.

3. In practice, most of those guilty of conflicts of interest are less than evil; mostly they did not really know what they were talking about. The serious and most visible exceptions concern analysts who failed to disclose personal interests in the firms they were reporting on. Such interests should be disclosed and firms should control potential conflicts within their own staff and, in fact, most firms require their employees to do so.

4. In the old days, equity analysts were particularly powerful. They were implicit purveyors of what otherwise might be called insider information. They enjoyed privileged access to corporate management, which would provide them with hints and specific information that were not available to others. Recent press commentaries still emphasize the role of the analyst as an industry visionary, but this view does not survive even the most casual examination. To a certain degree, analysts are being held up in public commentaries to a standard to which no institutional investor would ever have subscribed. The Spitzer criteria for judging industry analysts is unconvincing. Do we really believe that the value of the analysts lies in the accuracy of their buy and sell recommendations? Analysts cannot judge according to the accuracy of their forecasts which depend on assumptions about the broader economic situation. They are usually not directly responsible for such assumptions. Any investigation of the analysts' performance must be more subtle than is currently the case.

5. Most discussions in the Report focus on equity, but many underwriting firms have both corporate credit analysts – fixed-income research groups dealing with the credit quality of companies – and equity analysts. Both an equity analyst and a fixed-income analyst may be assessing the same firm and there is no obligation for their judgements to be identical.

6. Finally, the Report does not discuss the FD ('Fair Distribution') regulation in the United States. This regulation prevents corporate management from providing differential access to information. If, by law or regulation, management must provide the same information to everybody, the ability for research to differentiate itself in a way that was traditionally considered to be the heart of the business disappears. The Spitzer solution will have dramatic effects for the differential value of independent research on specific firms. There is already a substantial disinvestment in company research. Equity and company analysts are becoming providers of basic research. Moreover, the securitization process has already changed the nature of research as intermediaries become investors and have no more responsibility for providing credit analysis than do 'end investors'. The responsibility for research is switching to 'end investors'. Index funds have no interest in research. Hedge funds and private equity funds are only interested in proprietary research. To do better than the market, institutional investors need differentiated information. In a nutshell, the Spitzer solution already belongs to the past. It treats a problem that is not well defined and complicates an existing tendency of disinvestment on the part of underwriting houses to provide differentiated research. By legally separating research and investment banking, the Spitzer solution further accelerates the chances that there will be a substantial decline in the commitment of underwriters to provide independent research.

Benoît Coeuré
Agence France Trésor, French Ministry of Finance
Benoît Coeuré noted that the Report deals mainly with the stock market and not so much with other assets such as government bonds. Since information is the essence of financial markets, conflicts of interest are unavoidable. The important issue is not whether such conflicts exist, but the amount of price distortion that is generated and whether investors are equipped to cope with such distortions. He thought that the Report is very helpful in sorting out several sources of price distortions, and mentioned some additional ones such as market fragmentation, badly functioning derivative markets and insufficient liquidity. Whether the distortions created by conflicts of interest are of first order of magnitude depends on the kind of security under consideration and may even differ across countries. The Report focuses on the United States, emphasizing conflicts of interest and financial analysis whereas in Europe what matters most is market fragmentation and insufficient integration.

A useful criterion to investigate the differences across markets is the type of information that is embedded in the securities. In some markets information can be very idiosyncratic while in others – such as in the foreign exchange, money and to some extent government bond markets – aggregate information may matter much more. For instance, it is very difficult for an analyst to gain access to private information on government bonds. On the other hand, where information is largely private, conflicts of interest may develop and the quality of the analyst is crucial. This is an important issue *per se*. The market must be able to discriminate among analysts, which underscores their compensation structure and calls for learning about their qualities. This has really nothing to do with conflicts of interest. The time horizon of financial markets must be long enough for this process to take place.

Coeuré next focused on important differences across segments of a particular market. For corporate bonds, the elasticity of the price with respect to recommendations is very high, the credit spread can move by large amounts in reaction to an upgrading or a downgrading and, therefore, analysis remains very important. For government bonds the situation is quite opposite and the key issue is rather why the market reacts with such a low elasticity to information. At any rate, the role of analysts remains very limited.

Things change over time. The Report focuses on a period characterized by a bubble and changing productivity trends, when information is aggregate in nature. What happened in the late 1990s was the result of both a collective mistake and disproportionate attention on sectors with a very high content of private information such as the IT sector or Internet companies. In the face of such abnormal events, it is not clear that changes in the structure of the market will make it more robust to sharp market reversals.

Hans-Jörg Rudloff
Barclays Capital
As it takes its role very seriously, namely channelling savings into their most productive uses, the underwriting industry dogmatically believes that the market is the best allocator of scarce resources. Many commentators would argue, however, that the latest period was characterized by a massive misallocation of capital. Visibly, the industry and the intermediaries have failed. Rudloff pointed out that no more than 20 firms in the world carry out the underwriting business. These firms are organized in such a way that there is always a sponsorship and credit committee, which decide whether to underwrite and

sponsor a public offering. Management is part of this committee and the analysts do not represent a problem for new issuances. In fact, new issuances require the publication of a prospectus that contains all the necessary information. Moreover, breaching legal obligations and responsibilities can be highly costly. In the end, it is the management who decides and takes the responsibility for the accuracy of the information provided to the investors and the markets. Then, intermediaries deal with the selling. It is difficult to see the impact of analysts on this situation and to point out conflicts of interest. The situation is quite different in the United States where investment banks sell directly to their customers.

Although reputation is key in financial markets, that period of euphoria over the last three years was characterized by corruption and market manipulation. We are now back to normal times and it has become much harder to raise money. There must be sanctions and these must be hard. The focus should really be on the management, not on the analysts. If the former is not able to control the latter, the managers should be sanctioned. Indeed, analysts' compensation is really in the hands of managers. The basics are good management and control, which enhance reputation. There is too much focus on players who are only instruments in a firm.

General discussion

David Lipton thought that the Report should adopt a more sophisticated analysis of the economics of information. It asserts with justification that the gathering of information is central for economies of scope, but it does not assess where information is gathered within businesses, what its costs are and what its value is. We must distinguish between the economics of information gathering and the economics of what information is gathered and distributed by analysts. Are analysts a valuable form of information gathering within financial institutions?

Avinash Persaud, who thought that the discussion was too soft on investment banks, made three comments. First, we need to distinguish between retail and institutional investors. It is possible that the latter ignore the buy and sell recommendations but still read the contents of the prospectus. This content is not disconnected from the recommendations. If the industry is only getting one side, it is difficult for investors to make an unbiased conclusion. In the end, the retail investors were fooled, especially in the last three months of the bubble when they were the main buyers. Second, will the quality of research decline as a consequence of lower compensation? If the market as a whole reduces analysts' compensation, it should not affect the quality of research. There will, however, probably be less research provided by investment banks, mostly because of unbundling. Finally, Persaud argued in favour of more separation. As an example, independent analysts often self-censor themselves because the cost of being wrong is massive.

Hans-Jörg Rudloff agreed that anyone who believes that research in an investment bank would have the opportunity to write negative reports about that bank's customers is not living in the real world. The Glass-Steagall Act may not have been so detrimental as we thought until recently.

Charles Freedman commented on the trade-off between economies of scope and conflicts of interest. The Report provides little justification for economies of scope and the economic literature leaves their importance as an open question. The Report should pay more attention to economies of scope on which its conclusions crucially depend.

Eugene White agreed that it remains difficult to identify economies of scope, as well as economies of scale. A key part of the problem lies in the lack of economic data. Yet, practitioners and, perhaps more convincingly, investors think that there are sizeable benefits to be reaped from economies of scope. Moreover, retail investors weighted disproportionately on the policy response.

Session 2: Auditors and rating agencies

Edward J. Kane
Boston College
According to Ed Kane the key word in this debate is 'disinformation'. The issue is to get disinformation out of what is called the information flow. Disinformation is not just misinformation but information that has been cleverly designed to persuade people that adverse developments will not occur. The issue is then how hard the watchdogs dig to find the disinformation and to what extent they are willing to keep things to themselves. In truth, incentives for revealing disinformation are weak. The premise of the Report is that corporate managers, accountants and credit rating agencies are responsible to all stakeholders, but feel no compunction to treat all interests equally, especially in the short run.

The first line of defence has to be the personal ethics of the watchdogs and the people being watched. A common belief is that the trade-off between feeling good about the cleverness of exploiting others and the sense of shame for doing it has worsened over time. The second line of defence is the watchdogs, who must be known for both barking and biting. The concern is that the bark of the watchdogs is much greater than their bite. The importance of auditors has already been stressed; that of rating agencies is to provide an outside check on the reliability and economic meaning of the information that rating agencies produce. Auditors and rating agencies are subject to bias and coercion, euphemistically called conflicts of interest in the Report. Formal standards of accountability for estimates produced by both types of firms are incomplete and statistically shallow.

The next question, therefore, is to ask what the internal and external watchdogs really do. Internally, a firm's board of directors and auditing team have a duty to impose sound reporting safeguards and to detect deviations from these standards. This duty is not adequately performed in many cases and this is why external watchdogs are needed. External watchdogs include outside auditors, stock analysts, credit-rating agencies, standard-setting professional organizations, regulators, government examiners, law-enforcement personnel and information media (the 'press'). The first session emphasized the force of reputational penalties for watchdog dishonesty. These penalties can be overcome if insiders can temporarily deflect market prices from their full-information or 'inside' value through deceptive accounting reporting. Counterincentives can be created against disinformation activity through compensation that lets insiders and formally 'independent' external watchdogs profit extravagantly from temporarily boosting a firm's accounting condition or performance.

In principle, watchdog institutions that have no kinship ties to, or important commercial dealings with, insiders help outside investors to identify and ignore disinformation. In practice, however, managers can and do increase their firm's perceived profitability by concealing unfavourable information, and watchdogs are often fooled or persuaded to cooperate in the concealment. Accountants are also persuaded to participate by earning substantial profits from certifying loophole-ridden measurements that temporarily conceal adverse developments from outside stakeholders. Similarly credit-rating agencies can earn handsome fees for not challenging accounting information reported by contractual clients as conscientiously as figures reported by other firms. The ethics of watchdog professions limit their accountability for producing 'unsafe' informational products. The major weakness in the information production system lies in the link between the internal corporate governance of firms and the ethics of the watchdogs. The profession needs new codes to take away some of the protection that they have in courts to lessen the temptation of selling and cooperating in disinformation.

The major problem is the narrow defence that is provided by the so-called 'safe-harbours loophole'. The Sarbanes-Oxley Act of 2002 continues to assume that the formal independence of watchdogs is key to reliable authentication. The Act ignores the dangers of leaving US accounting rules riddled with safe-harbour loopholes. The Act asymmetrically imposes stronger disclosure obligations on CEOs, CFOs, attorneys and investment analysts but not on accountants. Auditors only need to confirm that specified procedures were followed without having to express an opinion about the accuracy of the information being transmitted. Standard-setting agents know very well that such safe-harbour loopholes limit accountants' professional obligations, and their exposure to both reputational damage and civil and criminal penalties. Corporate fraud, bribery and illegal-gratuity statutes limit this exposure even further by setting hard-to-prove standards for punishing deceitful reporting. Persuading accountants to certify misleading reports proved to be easy in scandalous cases such as Enron.

The greater scandal is the survival of safe-harbour loopholes and the difficulty of assembling evidence that can prove auditor or rating-agency malfeasance. These phenomena testify to the effectiveness of these professions' lobbies and to the strength of the incentive conflicts these lobbies transmit to government officials. Sooner or later, the practical ethics of the accounting and credit-rating professions must make their members more energetically embrace their twin common-law duties of rejecting corrupting forms of compensation and assuring the economic meaningfulness of the income and net-worth figures their clients publish.

Avinash Persaud
State Street Bank and Trust Company
Avinash Persaud agreed with most of the Report and focused his comments on the areas with which he was in slight disagreement. When discussing regulation, it is always wise to determine what the market failure that we are trying to address is, since there is often a large gap between the market failure and the regulatory solution. Indeed, there are two key market failures with auditing companies and rating agencies.

The first market failure is the principal-agent problem of shareholder capitalism. In many places, although not all, the board is neither independent from the managers, nor acting in the sole interest of their shareholders, nor appointing auditors who will dig deep to find if there is any disinformation. Often the management is key to the appointment and reappointment of the board, to determining whether they are on the sub-committees of their choice, knowing that the sub-committees may give remuneration. Persaud's favourite solution to this problem is directors' liabilities. In almost every occasion the company pays for the insurance liability of the directors removing the cost that they face of being sued for their liabilities if the company fails. Persaud said that this is the wrong approach. The correct way to deal with corporate governance issues and the correct appointment of auditors who dig deep is to ban companies from paying the insurance liabilities of their directors. The director should pay and the company should pay a good enough, non-exact remuneration that would meet the average director's liabilities. This is a very good way of enabling the market to function, since directors with a bad insurance rating will be priced out of the market.

Even when independence is achieved, another issue to bear in mind is the interest of future shareholders. Even if there is an independent board concerned with existing shareholders, it might not be good enough to ensure that there is correct auditing. Who then can make sure that the interests of both current and future potential shareholders are best served? In trying to break the link between management and auditing, other people than the board could appoint these auditors. There are two possibilities to do so. One is related to the listing agencies; when a public company is listed there are various commitments to comply with and one of these could be that the listing agent will appoint an auditor. There are many issues and problems with this approach and a danger of added bureaucracy, added costs of listings when listing should to be made easy to encourage companies to come to the market.

Persaud was biased to a second solution, which is the rotation of auditors, despite being aware that it also raises some concerns. The rotation should be of a long enough period, maybe three to four years, so that the auditors will be concerned about an explosion happening on their watch. A counter argument is that with rotation the auditors do not have enough time to understand the company. Persaud dismissed this argument since good management is transparent and clear and thus making it is easy for someone coming from outside to take over and understand what is going on.

The second market failure is the reputation capital, which is the last refuge of the anti-regulators. It is true that it is a powerful tool, but less so in an environment of uncertainty and oligopoly, as is the case for rating agencies. Persaud was very concerned, however, with rating agencies advising on the creation of a debt structure, which is then sold with their rating on it. Persaud acknowledged some sympathy with rating agencies and said that one should be careful in the finger-wagging exercise. There will always be problems uncovered at the end of booms, but rating agencies have not been any better or any worse than other market participants. The reputation capital should have made sure that they had behaved better than other market participants, but the problem is that reputation capital is not plentiful in a duopoly. In an uncertain environment two rating agencies basically move their ratings in line with each other. Where can the reputation loss come from? When one agency gets it wrong, so does the other. The reputation capital is very slim in such an environment and indeed it is slimmer than the reputation required for the industry as a whole. Thus, more competition is needed in the ratings industry. There is a danger that the regulation is reinforcing the existing establishment, creating higher barriers to entry. There are often requirements (from the investors' side, rather than the regulators' side), saying that a particular instrument has to be rated by more than one agent. This has created a market where there are two to three players. What would happen if the requirement said that you had to be rated by more than three? Regulation should be used to encourage competition in that industry.

To conclude, there is a risk of creating more regulatory approvals for auditing companies and rating agencies, reinforcing their oligopoly status and raising the barriers to entry. Regulation should be used to support competition, to create reputation capital and break the link between the management and the auditors.

Ernst-Ludwig von Thadden
University of Lausanne

Ernst-Ludwig von Thadden, praising the Report for an impressive blend of practitioner and academic insights, focused his discussion on the audit side which is mostly concerned with the problem of accounting, and less on the rating side. As an example of what accounting is about, he quoted from Enron's *Risk Management Manual*: 'Reported earnings follow the rules and principles of accounting. The results do not always create measures consistent with underlying economics. However, corporate management's performance is generally measured by accounting income, not underlying economics. Risk management strategies are therefore directed at accounting rather than economic performance'. What are, then, the incentives of accounting?

According to the Report, the recent accounting scandals have brought to the fore three aspects. First comes the distinction between rules-based and principles-based accounting. The former allows the auditor to hide behind formalities. In a society that puts a strong emphasis on litigation, rules-based accounting may be the best response of the profession. Second, the internal organization of audit firms matters. The argument, not often made in this context, is that decentralization forces local offices to accommodate local monopolists. This is highly similar to what in banking is called concentration risk. The last component of scandals is the governance of the firm-auditor relationship. Auditors who are hired and remunerated by management instead of the board have the wrong loyalties.

Von Thadden said that these points are well-taken but more interesting is that the Report exonerates two of the most publicly accused culprits. The first is the decay of ethical standards, and the second is the provision of non-audit consulting services by audit firms. He fully agreed with the report on the first point, arguing that ethical decay is typically too easily invoked and too little quantified. He pointed out, however, that the second issue might deserve more attention. The authors exonerate service bundling because of the opportunity cost of separating audit and non-audit services. Yet the authors are silent about the potential costs arising from the bundling of these two services. In fact, the 'dependency or conflict' may depend precisely on the 'question of what service is performed'. So the two activities cannot be as easily separated as suggested by the Report.

Von Thadden proposed to make his point with a little thought experiment of what the auditing industry might be about. Consider a firm that may be either well managed (IBM) or mismanaged (Enron). Call this state, $x \in \{0,1\}$ with $proba(x=1)=q$. An auditor exerts effort $e \in [1/2, 1]$ to find out about x. Given their effort, they learn about x through a signal $s \in \{0,1\}$ which is such that

$$proba(s = 1 | x = 1) = proba(s = 0 | x = 0) = e$$

Once the auditor has observed s, they announce their audit that is either bad or good, $a \in \{b, g\}$. In the long run, the state of the firm, x, is revealed publicly. The auditor's objective is $p(x,a)$, reflecting the potential trade-off between having a good reputation and being on good terms with management. In particular, we have $p(1,b) \ll p(1,g)$ with $p(0,g)$ and $p(0,b)$ in between. $p(1,b)$ is what you get if the firm is good and you state that it is bad. This is the worst thing that can happen to an auditor. He is getting on bad terms with the management and he is losing his reputation for being a good forecaster. On the other hand, $p(1,g)$ is the best that can happen to an auditor because he is having the right forecast and being on good terms with the management.

$p(0,g)$ and $p(0,b)$ are in between. If the firm is bad and the auditor is making a good forecast, that is *p(0, g)*, the auditor is on good terms with management but since the forecast is wrong, that may be bad for his reputation. *p(0,b)* is the other way around; the auditor makes the right forecast but the management does not like it. How to solve this?

The auditor has two possible strategies for her reporting: (strategy H being the honest strategy):

Strategy H: a(0) = b, a(1) = g
Strategy A: a(0) = a(1) = g

A simple comparison shows that strategy H yields more than strategy A if and only if:

(1-q)ep(0,b) + q(1-e)p(1,b) > (1-q)ep(0,g) + q(1-e)p(1,g)

This is likely to be the case if:
- *p(0,g)* and *p(1,g)* are small: gains from the firm-auditor relationship are not too large.
- *e* is large: auditors monitor carefully.
- *p(0,b)* is large: high professional standards in auditing.

If these conditions do not hold, the auditor is likely to fall into the 'Andersen trap', namely, provide favourable audit opinions when it is not justified by the data.

Of course, this is just a very simple example; but it is not grossly implausible and describes a situation in which the 'dependency or conflict' depends precisely on the 'question of what service is performed'. Von Thadden's overall conclusion was that although there are reasons to believe that the Sarbanes-Oxley Act is a case of premature and half-baked legislation, the argument against it in the present report needs to be strengthened.

General discussion

Richard Portes argued that the picture was even worse than that described by the Report. Recent work in game theory overturns the conventional views about the value of reputation. It says that developing reputation can be a bad strategy that could lead to minimum rather than maximum profits in the long run, therefore suggesting more arguments for regulation. He also commented on the idea of directors paying for their liability insurance. There is an example of such a solution in the United Kingdom with charities that cannot buy the liability insurance of their trustees. Implementing this more broadly does not seem implausible. Finally, he discussed the value of rating agencies. In the sovereign debt market, the market processes risk reasonably well. Historically, after market crashes, the data on sovereign bonds suggests that during the lending in the 1920s; the bank lending of the 1970s; and the sovereign bonds issued in the 1990s the real rate of return *ex-post*, taking into account the defaults, is almost the same, about 2%. In fact, the market is pricing the risks of default without any particular help from the rating agencies. These make things worse *ex-post*, after issuance, because they contribute to the self-fulfilling nature of financial crises. Therefore, we ought to question the value added of rating agencies, at least in that market.

Charles Freedman commented on the role of litigation risk in explaining developments and behaviour. The high risk of litigation may be one of the reasons why the United States has adopted a rules-based approach to accounting standards, while Europe, with less litigation risk, has tended to use a principles-based approach. It has also been argued that an enhancement of the ability to sue accounting firms may give them greater incentives to function better.

Trevor Harris answered that from an economic efficiency perspective, internal controls could be more efficient. Performance measurement and the way incentives are provided actually create the split, however. From a more macroeconomic point of view, the split will globally raise the costs because it will take away the efficiency that exists. Harris argued that it is true on the analysts' side as well.

Avinash Persaud elaborated on the idea that rating agencies encourage selling when they are downgrading. The problem is that there are covenants in the private sector by which private companies are forced to sell bonds with low ratings. This can trigger a vicious circle since when the bond price falls, and the rating agency downgrades it, private companies are in turn forced to sell. Persaud admitted not knowing how to eliminate these covenants in the private sector, however.

Session 3: Universal banking

Gertrude Tumpel-Gugerell
Vice Governor, Economics and Financial Markets Department, Oesterreichische Nationalbank, Vienna
Gertrude Tumpel-Gugerell opened the third session by observing that various conflicts of interest can arise in a universal bank, notably between investment and loan businesses. While universal banks are less dependent on the revenues from individual business lines, the incentive structure is usually defined on a business line level. An additional conflict of interest is whether universal banks should expand loan business or develop the capital market. Turning to the issue of bank failures, she identified three main weaknesses:

1. a low level of checks and balances, so that a certain group of players has too much power relative to others;
2. weak risk control systems, including imperfect separation of functions; and
3. weak auditors.

The excessive exploitation of conflicts of interest is also a bank failure, yet one that does not lead to insolvency, at least in the short run. Remedies must be designed on a systemic basis.

Antonio Borges
Goldman Sachs International
Antonio Borges adopted a more general definition of conflicts of interest. The current environment features very large losses and the focus is now on finding scapegoats, magnifying the issue and neglecting or overlooking the empirical evidence. In this sense, the Report provides an interesting contrast with the current situation.

Clearly, the stock market boom must remain central to the analysis. Without a bubble, most of the issues of conflicts of interest would have been of little concern. Indeed, banks can be blamed, as well as other players such as rating agencies, auditors, opinion leaders, business leaders and academics. Everybody followed in the great wave of euphoria leading to important distorted behaviour. Herding behaviour should also be debated; the excesses stem more from this than from the flaws of the financial system.

The historical focus of the Report is appreciated. It is amazing to see the similarities between the crises of the early 1990s and those of the 1920s. The statements and the way in which people describe the current situation are a carbon copy of what happened in those times: similar problem, similar behaviour, similar explanations and similar excessive remedies. We have not learned from history, in particular about the role of monetary policy in preventing the emergence of bubbles.

Governance is also an important issue. Financial markets have a key role in allocating capital efficiently. Yet the information that they provide has a value in itself beyond the efficiency argument. Notably, the lack of such information would make it virtually impossible to exercise scrutiny over management. An independent evaluation of management requires significant information, most of which comes from financial markets. Therefore, when this information is not sufficient, the problem is far more severe than just an inefficient allocation of capital. The most positive outcome of the recent crises is the emphasis on disclosure, transparency and more rigorous financial information.

It is very myopic to argue that whenever conflicts of interest exist, they will always be exploited. Reputational capital is crucial. In the particular case of universal banks, having the opportunity to exploit a conflict of interest rarely leads to taking advantage of it. There are, however, some cases where reputational capital is not sufficient. To start with, a collective failure does not allow for distinction between players, and poor performance becomes the norm. Reputation by itself is not a sufficient check on behaviour. This issue has been very important in recent years. In addition, in desperate situations long-term concerns are downplayed and the short run takes a disproportionate importance. Powerful players can take advantage of conflicts of interest to obtain the short-run relief necessary to survive.

Borges also argued that there must be some truth behind the argument of economies of scope in universal banking, despite the lack of strong empirical evidence. There is a continuum of institutions from very specialized entities to full-blown universal banks. Increasingly complex structures bring about additional costs which do not exist in smaller firms. Therefore, there must be significant additional benefits which justify the very existence of universal banks.

The most difficult issue in universal banking is the combination of investment banking and credit granting. Is universal banking a superior model? Does it raise special concerns? The evidence is that conflicts of interest remain rather limited, and whenever they exist, they are rarely exploited. Borges thought that the most serious conflict between investment banking and loan granting has a different dimension than that expressed in the Report. Investment banking features high barriers to entry and large resources are required to establish a sufficient market presence. New entrants use credit granting to enter the market, thereby subsidizing their investment banking through underpricing of loans. As a consequence, there is significant mispricing of credit and excess demand for it. This does not seem to be of any concern to regulators, although the consequences for regulation are serious. On the loan granting side, entering institutions benefit from a regime that does not apply to specialized investment banks.

Borges concluded that in terms of remedies, disclosure and transparency are very important. The market participants should make their own judgements, provided that they have all the relevant information.

Hans Genberg
Graduate Institute of International Studies

Hans Genberg emphasized two elements: the importance of reputation and the role of market discipline. The Report focuses essentially on conflicts of interest in the US banking industry before the Glass-Steagall Act of 1933 in order to look at the source of the Act, at the facts, and to determine whether it was justifiable. The legislation was the result of the perceived faulty behaviour of a relatively small number of actors, and not of a careful analysis of the importance of conflicts of interest for the market as a whole. Furthermore, the legislation came in the aftermath of large stock market declines, suggesting that it was at least in part the result of popular pressures on the legislators. The same process might be at work nowadays. Proposed solutions to the excesses of the recent period are driven in part by the losses of small retail investors and not by careful economic analysis. Discussing what is optimal should take into account what is feasible in terms of political economy analysis.

Genberg returned to the separation of commercial and investment banks in the Glass-Steagall Act. The evidence shows that it cannot be justified empirically. To a significant extent this evidence is based on findings that bonds and stocks underwritten by affiliates of universal banks had lower yields, hence higher prices, than corresponding liabilities underwritten by independent investment banks. The idea is that the certification value offered by universal banks lowers the cost of capital to the borrowing firms. Considerations of conflicts of interest were not important in the market. To explain the empirical findings, the authors of the Report state that investment banks had learned to improve their organisational structure so as to 'convince the market that they were not taking advantage of conflicts of interest'. Genberg asked how this statement should be interpreted. Does it mean that there were no conflicts of interest, or rather that the banks had convinced the market that there were none? It remains unclear whether comparing prices of liabilities underwritten by different institutions shows the importance of conflicts of interest.

Genberg wondered whether in a market equilibrium model, universal banks can benefit from exploiting conflicts of interest. On the one hand, this would lead to added costs for borrowers. On the other hand, the certification benefits lead to benefits for the borrowers. In equilibrium these effects should offset each other as banks optimize at the margin. Thus, there should not be any difference in the prices or yields of the underlying assets depending on which institution has underwritten them. From this perspective, investors should be neither penalized nor favoured by the legal structure of the underwriting.

Finally, Genberg commented on the Gramm-Leach-Bliley Financial Services Modernization Act of 1999. In particular, two issues in this context are relevant for the discussion contained in the Report. First, the limitation of merchant banking embodied in the Act may not be reasonable. Second, the supervisory challenges inherent in universal banking appear to be particularly important in the context of the United States. There are separate regulators for separate activities and it would be appropriate to discuss this issue in the Report.

Tommaso Padoa-Schioppa
European Central Bank

Tommaso Padoa-Schioppa touched upon four points. First, the notion of conflict of interest is useful to catch many of the pathologies that have emerged from the Enron case. It can be misleading, however, if it is used to transmit implicit normative statements, such as the removal of all conflicts of interest whenever they exist; or the fact that every person or institution should serve only one interest. Similarly, it would be misleading if remedies were drawn too hastily.

Padoa-Schioppa expressed a more problematic view of conflicts of interest since they, as well as other concepts like moral hazard or systemic risk, can be managed, reduced, but cannot, and probably should not, be suppressed. Moreover, conflicts of interest are not easily distinguished from conflicts of objectives, or trade-offs. In a world of contractual relations, fraudulent behaviour must be separated from shrewd business behaviour. Whereas the former is sanctioned by criminal law, the latter should be controlled by *caveat-emptor* type of defences. The problem, however, is that it remains very difficult to draw the line between these two types of behaviour; and the delimitation may shift over time along the cycle. Furthermore, it depends on the profile of the two contracting parties. Overall, when we must think about conflicts of interest, we must bear in mind that these cannot be suppressed and must be managed at all levels from the individual agent to the whole economy. Finally, there is an ethical dimension in this issue that ultimately remains part of the world of ethics and not that of legislation.

Second, Padoa-Schioppa recalled that the chapter of the Report on universal banking deals almost exclusively with the historical experience of the United States. As such, it is implicitly a chapter on the differences between Europe and the United States. The response to the crisis of the 1930s was a sharp separation of activities in the United States whereas no European country enacted any legislation like the Glass-Steagall Act. The problems of conflicts of interest have not been fundamentally eradicated by this Act, however. More generally, there are other differences between the two continents, which may give better explanations of why some of the problems do not seem to be as acute in Europe. The European context is typically characterized by widespread public ownership of banks and corporations; less competition in the banking industry; the existence of very pervasive public pension systems with little space left for private schemes; a smaller equity-based nature of the economy; and principles-based rather than rules-based accounting standards. Moreover, the European continental system has a very strict approach that requires a licence for banking business. Such an approach is weaker in the United States and to some extent in the United Kingdom. The granting of a licence allows for more activities than under a system where licensing is softer but the regulation of activities harder. More generally, there are also broader differences such as a lower degree of social mobility, a different measure of success, and some of these factors may explain how players react in financial markets.

Third, investors are very diverse. Some are very sophisticated, others less so. In finance, there are different risk-return combinations that are available. Normally, higher return portfolios should in the long run receive a higher return, and some face losses. Over the long run investments in equity yield higher returns than those in risk-free assets. Now the question is: 'Should access to the more sophisticated types of finance be barred to relatively unsophisticated investors?' There is a problem of somehow discriminating between types of investors, maybe through a market mechanism, which must be addressed. Clearly, the type of defence differs across categories of investors.

Finally, Padoa-Schioppa raised the public side of the issue of conflicts of interest. It is important to be aware that there are notable conflicts also in the public and regulatory sides. The public servant must serve the public interest. In continental Europe some problems arise from the life-time duration of public employment. Moreover, price and financial stability must be ensured, even if difficult trade-offs are involved. There is a trade-off between opacity and transparency. Although central banks were very opaque in the past, transparency has taken increasing importance. In general, there should be two agencies that preside over two objectives.

Angel Ubide
Tudor Investment Corporation

Angel Ubide recalled the definition of a conflict of interest as a decline in available information that lowers the efficiency of financial markets. There is thus a trade-off between the benefits of certification (economies of scope in information collection) and the (perceived) cost of conflicts of interest. The Report assesses whether underwriting activity is affected by such conflicts. The yield is typically lower when a commercial bank has a lending stake in the issuing firm. Moreover, universal banks are biased towards smaller firms, thus increasing the access to market for these firms.

With a worldwide trend toward universal banking, interest-rate margins are compressed to very low levels. The main strategy in banking currently seems to be to focus on fee-based activities and to use lending as a strategy to secure new business. Lending has become a crucial activity: customers demand credit in return for mergers and acquisitions and underwriting business, and banks are offering credit below current market rates as a sweetener to win investment banking contracts. As a result, this practice artificially improves the balance-sheet of corporations while increasing the risks on the balance-sheet. Is this really a conflict of interest as defined in the Report? Or is it a supervisory concern? Or both?

The increase in the use of derivatives has been dramatic. A first result is that the activity is highly concentrated in a few banks: the top three derivatives dealers hold 88% of total US bank derivatives notionals; 89% of contracts which are not related to interest rates; 88% of apparently unmatched positions; and about 75% of credit exposure. Furthermore, although some activity is directed at hedging, there are large unmatched market values inside the banks. Are universal banks playing with the safety net? Moreover, there has been a large expansion in credit default swaps. A conflict of interest might arise if the credit default swap department of the bank is pricing an issue, which involves the use of bond and loan information from the commercial banking part of the conglomerate.

In certain countries, banks can hold equity stakes in non-financial firms. In many cases bank managers sit on the board of the firms to which they lend. Even in the United States, a third of large corporations have bank directors on their board. It remains unclear whether such a situation is good or bad from the point of view of conflicts of interest. Long-term equity stakes increase the incentive to cooperate with the borrower in case of financial distress. Studies of *Keiretsu* show how banks went out of their way to help distressed borrowers. On the other side, the arrangement allows for an improvement in the monitoring of credit risks, which is beneficial. Another issue is that the interest rate charged is based on a long-term assessment of the firm rather than on the intrinsic risk of particular projects. Having a stake in a company reduces the conflict of interest between shareholders and the lender by aligning incentives. In the end, there is better monitoring but a less transparent pricing of risks. Does this increase or reduce the information that is available for the market?

Are there lessons to draw from the European experience with universal banking over 50 years? European banking is based on reputation to ensure a steady flow of future business, while the Anglo-Saxon arm's length banking relies more on courts to enforce explicit contracts. Relationship banking is largely self-governing, whereas arm's length banking is heavily regulated. The legal and cultural superstructure is key: governmental influence, notably through national champion strategies, accounting based on principles rather than rules, more concentration in the banking sector, and a regulatory framework tilted towards larger banks. Can universal banking avoid the exploitation of conflicts of interest without changing this superstructure towards relationship banking?

Finally, conflicts of interest must be related to Basel II. There will be greater discretion to determine capital needs and as a consequence, the scope for conflicts of interest may widen. It should, however, put a higher value on enhanced monitoring and relationship banking, thereby bringing about a higher level of information. The supervisory review process should enhance the control of incentives, although it is not clear that supervisors will deal with conflicts of interest. Finally, market disclosure will bring additional information. In the end, will Basel II increase or decrease the potential for conflicts of interest in universal banking?

General discussion

Edward Kane noted the absence in the Report of any reference to event studies showing that decisions relaxing the restrictions on banking activity generally helps large US banks and is detrimental to US securities firms. Even more disturbing evidence, though, is that the Gramm-Leach-Bliley Act of 1999 hurt non-financial corporations, especially corporate customers of large banks that are active in the securities business. As taxpayers, corporations may be contributing to the extension of the safety net. Furthermore, lesser safety-net subsidies for securities firms would reduce the number of such firms, thereby relaxing the disciplinary effect of potential market entry.

Neal Soss pointed to an identification problem. Lending, securities activity and ratings are observed simultaneously. How much is really observed that is due to the market power of customers of the banks?

Eugene White emphasized that in the period prior to the Glass-Steagall Act, the different organizational structures setting up securities subsidiaries attempted to mitigate the problems of conflict of interest by providing more transparency. In general, exploitation of conflicts of interest by financial conglomerates was controlled. Although there is less work on whether the holding of direct equity stakes by banks creates exploitable conflicts of interest, the small literature indicates that this has not been a serious problem.

Antonio Borges came back to the risks associated with credit granting. Investment banking generates very high returns. Since this is a permanent feature, there must be some barriers. to entry in this market. Given the change in regulation in the United States, large universal banks could use their size and financial strength to make their way into the investment banking market through subsidizing credit. The central issue is mispricing of credit and this generates an excess demand for credit.

Gertrude Tumpel-Gugerell concluded the session by saying that conflicts of interest are always a complex problem. The views about more regulation are split, although there is a broad agreement that more transparency and disclosure is beneficial. Moreover, behavioural aspects such as the loss of business ethics must be taken in consideration.

Session 4: Remedies

Karen Johnson
Federal Reserve Board

Karen Johnson was very much in agreement with the basic approach and conclusions of the Report, despite the fact that she differed in some instances with particular points or recommendations. She agreed with the fundamental point that a market solution to the conflict of interest problem should be preferred. Examining a variety of experiences, both failed and successful ones, would seem to be a fruitful approach to assessing the relative merits of the alternative remedies. Such a comparative review is not developed in the Report. In order to come to conclusions with respect to remedies, it is necessary first to judge the relative seriousness of the different elements of the problems caused by a potential conflict of interest. The cure should not turn out to be worse than the disease. In that context it is necessary to step back from the problems of the financial sector and take a broader perspective.

Clearly the Report cannot address all aspects of conflicts of interest. Still, it is worthwhile remembering that conflicts of interest and principal-agent problems exist throughout the corporate world – both financial and non-financial. It cannot be expected that solutions to conflicts of interest will provide general solutions to corporate governance. This is especially true with respect to the issue of audit firms. Johnson thought that it would be a mistake to approach reform of the incentives facing audit firms as if they were to be the policemen bringing malfeasance in corporate management under control. The Sarbanes-Oxley approach is correct in addressing the behaviour of both financial and non-financial corporations and putting responsibility for truthful reporting squarely at the highest level of management. The Sarbanes-Oxley Act should be judged from the broad corporate governance perspective. Success within the financial sector may depend on resolving problems in the non-financial sector.

The Report very correctly emphasizes the importance of transparency and thus the potential benefit of regulation that promotes transparency. Transparency by itself, however, will not achieve very much. Indeed 'leave it to the market' and 'regulate for transparency' should be combined into one strategy. Public policy to promote transparency is not needed for the really big players to make good decisions. The Report provides several examples of markets achieving the right balance, such as underwriting in the United States before the Great Depression where the large firms saw their own interests clearly. At least in the United States, most regulation with respect to transparency is for consumer protection. This is why regulations must forcefully meet the needs of smaller, individual investors. Open publication of the record of analysts' recommendations judged against outcomes might be one way to alert them to possible biases by particular analysts and firms.

Johnson differed from the Report on the question of rating agencies, particularly with respect to structured finance. It is a complicated, changing area of financial innovation and practice. Involving the raters in the structuring of a particular issue *ex ante* rather than *ex post* does not amount to rating their own ratings. It is rather a question of at what point in the process is it most efficient for the special expertise of the rating agencies to be relevant. The Report's conclusions with respect to separation of ancillary services by the rating agencies go a step too far. Problems arising within firms – for example in what department is the earning power of the firm greater and whether a short-run or long-run perspective is taken – should not be labelled 'conflicts of interest' in the usual sense since they are by their nature internal to the firm. Market-based solutions to conflict problems are precisely designed to internalize the negative consequences of certain behaviour. These are management problems of a more straightforward variety, which still are serious, warrant attention and need a remedy.

As a conclusion Johnson reiterated her view that market discipline combined with transparency was the primary course of action to be taken. Turning first to a market solution is desirable because market forces are better able to respond and adapt to change, and prompt and flexible remedy is essential. There are instances where regulatory oversight and/or separation are needed, but these should be kept to a minimum. Socialization of information is the right answer only in very special cases – such as weather forecasting.

James Sassoon
HM Treasury
James Sassoon welcomed an important contribution to an on-going debate and talked about the UK Government approach of working with market practitioners to help frame policy responses to the problems outlined by the Report. The starting point for the analysis is the hypothesis that conflicts of interest in financial services can pose a real problem to prosperity and growth by undermining investors' confidence in financial markets. It is important that the conflicts be identified and addressed, but it is also crucial that the policy response does not stifle risk-taking. Regulation should not kill off animal spirits. Three points should be kept in mind. First, the policy response must be proper and proportionate and deal broadly with the corporate world and not narrowly focused on one element or sector. Second, the solution should be developed in association with market participants and not be left to lawyers. Finally, the new regime should be based on principles rather than rules.

The UK approach, very much in line with the recommendations of the Report, provides a good example of how to apply these general principles, and shows some differences to the approach of the United States.

One of the foundations of the UK approach has been to increase the involvement of investors and shareholders. The Paul Myners review of institutional investment highlighted the importance of getting the incentives right for the management of transaction costs, soft commissions, the bundling of services and the arrangements between investment banks and fund managers. It deserves more attention than it is currently getting in the United States.

Investors also need to have confidence in the quality of financial information that companies produce. The UK Government's coordinating group on audit and accounting issues made several important recommendations to strengthen the regulation and oversight of auditing and accounting including recommendations on the rotation of audit partners and key audit staff. The approach is, however, cautious on banning non-audit services especially regarding tax advisory services. A preferred solution is greater disclosure in corporate annual reports, revealing to shareholders exactly what fees were paid to audit firms and for what services, and although this is going to be statutorily underpinned, companies may well begin to introduce it voluntarily. In a second stage, new audit oversight bodies will have a closer look at non-audit services.

Among other developments in the United Kingdom, audit firms have voluntarily committed to publish a full annual report about their activities, management structures, a breakdown of their fees and their approach to remuneration. This is a progressive approach, using a light regulatory touch, which has not been introduced in the United States.

Another important factor in strengthening the position of shareholders is the role played by independent, non-executive directors. The Higgs review of the role and responsibilities of non-executive directors recommended that independent non-executive directors should play a stronger role on company boards; that more attention should be paid to their suitability, skills and training; and that the definition of independence should be drawn more tightly. One or two of the recommendations – relating to the role of the company chairman – have generated some lively discussion. But most recommendations have been almost universally accepted.

More broadly, the UK Government is actively encouraging constructive shareholder activism: one topical strand is the so-called 'rewards for failure', i.e. managers who are able to walk away from corporations with large pay-offs. Transparency is at the core of the UK system where the concept of 'comply or explain' underpins the corporate governance regime. As the EU now focuses on corporate governance action plans, Sassoon hoped that 'comply or explain' will be adopted as a basic approach by the Commission. Under this approach, agreed principles and guidelines for corporate governance are set down (for example that audit committees should comprise only non-executive directors). The 'comply or explain' principle requires that companies either comply with this guideline, or otherwise explain why they have chosen not to. This has the dual advantage over more rigid, rules-based systems insofar as it still permits companies to adopt structures and procedures that they feel best suit their needs, while providing the necessary transparency to keep shareholders and potential investors fully informed. As a result the market will decide if they think companies' strategies are justified.

Although several key measures can be brought in voluntarily, there are some areas where new legislation or regulation has been necessary. Among these is the regulation of the audit profession through a new professional oversight board and enhanced financial reporting council that, among other things, examines the corporate annual reports. A Financial Services Authority (the UK financial regulator) consultation document on equity analysts is currently under discussion, again seeking to give investors greater confidence in market information. It does not go as far as the SEC but identifies many of the same problems. It is more principles-based and slightly less rule driven and allows global firms to operate under a somewhat more permissive regime.

To conclude, Sassoon stressed the UK view that the market has a primary role to play in dealing with conflicts of interest to ensure that they do not create severe distortions. In the long run the market will penalize those that try to exploit conflicts of interest, but careful regulation and oversight can and should minimize these opportunities without restricting the flow of high quality information that the market needs.

Lars Nyberg
Sveriges Riksbank
Lars Nyberg was concerned that overreaction may create a bigger problem than those posed by conflicts of interest. The market is currently adapting to now apparent misconduct and it is important to let that process take place. The European process, however, particularly worried Nyberg because directives tend to be written with the largest rather than the smallest common denominator. The trouble is that public confidence has to be restored quickly, even the market will eventually sort out its problems. Markets tend to forget, however, which is a point that the Report should stress. The better are market conditions, the quicker they

forget. The question is how to make sure that best practice is adopted and does not slowly deteriorate over time. What has really to be put into regulation and what can be solved in other ways? Conflicts of interest are very old, they have been neglected for a very long time, and in fact they were out of fashion as recently as three years ago.

One remedy, outlined by the Report, might be to strengthen internal rules and procedures in financial institutions. This approach is inline with the market orientation. Supervision, as argued by the Report, may come afterwards to ensure that these rules are not forgotten. Indeed, quite a lot can be achieved through appropriate codes of conduct or ethical standards.

Nyberg then turned to investment banking. The Report states that separation is desirable. For a central banker, this is an extraordinarily good idea because the central bank would not like to pay out more than is really necessary if something happened in the banking system. Why should risks from underwriting and investment banking be included? On the other hand, this is hardly an issue in most European countries, especially in Scandinavia where the investment banking part of the big local banks is relatively small and has not really generated conflicts of interest. Incentives to exploit the conflicts of interest may simply be very low.

Finally, Nyberg talked about the mutual life insurance sector, not dealt with in the Report but where the same type of principal-agent problem arises. In this sector, the customers are really the owners of the company, without necessarily being aware of it. If it is already difficult for a specialist to understand the balance sheet of these institutions, it is impossible for an ordinary customer. In addition the commitments are so far away that it remains impossible to know what will happen in the long run. This is the reason for regulating this sector, but the industry itself already solves a lot of the principal-agent problems that have been uncovered in many European countries.

General discussion

Jean-Pierre Landau said that, before thinking of remedies, one must first ask why conflicts of interest arise in the first place. The Report takes the view that they develop because some firms undertake multiple functions. So, when looking at the remedies, there is a trade-off to be considered between the economies of scope generated by such a bundling of activities and the risk of conflicts of interest. Another explanation would see conflicts of interest as a by-product of the difficulty – or impossibility – of charging a proper price for services such as ratings, analysts or audit. In an efficient market one should not have to pay for information since it is already in the price. It is costly, however, to collect and process information, so the question arises as to how it gets into the price in the first place. This is a well-known paradox about market efficiency. So we could ask whether conflicts of interest result from attempts to circumvent this paradox, by getting investors to pay indirectly for information. This can be done in many ways. The first one is cross-subsidizing activities so that information can be produced, although people will not buy it for its real price. Analysts cannot recover their costs, and that is why they have been used for other purposes. This cross-subsidization is at the source of conflicts of interest. The second way is to exploit the rents created or consolidated by regulatory privileges. This is obviously the case for rating agencies. At issue here is not so much a conflict of interest but the quality of the information produced in an environment of very low competition.

Information is a public good and attempts to treat it as a private good are bound to create distortions, some of them in the form of conflicts of interest. Would it not be more appropriate to recognize from the start that we are faced with a public good problem? The goal, then, is to find the least distortive way of financing these public goods. Would partial 'socialization' be a solution in some cases? It might not be necessary for audit services. A mix of good governance and supervision might work. The question of paying for information does not arise in this case, because companies are legally required to have their accounts audited and pay for it. As far as rating agencies are concerned there must be a way to finance them, while at the same time taking the rents out of them. This calls for encouraging entry in that market and by helping the creation of new agencies, possibly through subsidization. In the case of analysts, a degree of public intervention is provided in the 'New York' settlement, by the obligation to buy research from independent firms. So the obligation to pay for information is made transparent and explicit. Landau identified this as a progressive move, since it will create and stimulate the independent research industry. He admitted that he could not see the drawbacks and questioned whether there is any empirical basis to the argument that it will lower the quality of information. After all, top qualified people – including the present Chairman of the Fed – have made a career in independent research companies.

Frederic Mishkin agreed with the first part of Landau's argument, that the impossibility of charging people for the information which may be used for multiple uses is a source of conflicts of interest. This does not mean, however, that the firm as a whole cannot charge for information. Mishkin disagreed with the second part of the comment dealing with socialization. Bundling is a way to charge for information. This is not only true for the financial services industry but also for many other industries where synergies exist between different activities or components. For example, cars come with radios and, yet, we think that the market works well.

Mishkin also agreed with the view that solving the conflict of interest problem in the financial services will not solve the key corporate governance problem. He also agreed strongly with the need for market participants to be involved in the design of policy. This is exactly the way good supervisory oversight operates: public authorities should gather the view of the market participants and synthesize them in the policy framework.

Alexander Swoboda said that many recent problems that have received so much attention in the popular press are not real issues of conflicts of interest; rather they reflect basis misconduct and outright crime and should be reported as such. Transparency is necessary, but not sufficient to generate adequate information. As shown by the bubble or the international financial crises, there are periods when the incentives to use the information are downplayed for psychological or other reasons. This is where it would be most important to have good rules in place because the costs of conflicts of interest are hidden during the upward part and only get revealed after the crash. It remains important to have codes of conduct and best practices, as they provide the regulator with a benchmark on which to judge whether the compensation scheme is adequate. It is difficult, however, to devise the scheme and also to ensure that it does not become a hard regulation that is stifling to the development of innovation.

Antonio Borges commented on corporate governance, and pointed out that there can be a conflict of interest among shareholders. One of the key differences between the United States and Europe is the way in which companies are controlled. Companies within the United States are widely held by numerous shareholders and the principal-agent problem is acute. Managers sometimes act against the interests of shareholders, and get away with it. In continental Europe the vast majority of corporations are controlled by so-called reference shareholders, players with very large blocks of shares, often majorities, who have complete control over management, and who replace the agent at the slightest hint of a principal-agent problem. That is why many of the problems analysed here do not occur in Europe. The real problem in Europe is that management and majority shareholders collude against the minority shareholders. This is a real conflict of interests. Recent reports have emphasized the role of auditors, of powerful independent directors, of a strict regulation to require disclosure of transactions between corporations and officers and between corporations and significant shareholders, and the fact that there would be much less opportunity for taking advantage of minority shareholders if all of that were publicly known. Unfortunately this is not happening in continental Europe.

Endnotes

1 Full disclosure includes revealing the identity and relationships of highly compensated employees, shareholder rights beyond those of ordinary stockholders, insider loans, fairness of contracts between the company and insiders, stock options, pensions, stock purchase plans, up to five years of audited earnings, and 'comfort letters' from accountants attesting to the dependability and accuracy of the financial information (Bloch, 1986).

2 For one theoretical treatment of how synergies arise between brokerage and underwriting, see Stefanadis (2003).

3 Customers may also reward a firm with overall trading business rather than trading in a specific stock. Also large traders may place orders with multiple broker-dealers to avoid fully revealing their intentions.

4 There are also European, Latin American, Japanese and other Asian polls.

5 The rankings are posted on the Institutional Investor's website, www.institutionalinvestor.com.

6 For example, AT&T chose the lead underwriter for Lucent Technologies IPO on the basis of investment bank analysts reports on AT&T (*Wall Street Journal*, 13 July 1995).

7 One CFO of a company making a new IPO remarked: 'Since nobody knows you, and all of your numbers are pro forma, the analyst must paint the picture for prospective investors' (Galant, 1992).

8 For IPOs, technology firms are defined to include companies in the internet, computer software and hardware, communications, medical and electronic equipment, but not biotechnology, see Ritter and Welch (2002).

9 See Loughran and Ritter (2002) for a survey of the literature.

10 D'Avolio *et al.* (2001) argue that the growing number of newer, younger investors reduced the market's sophistication. Likewise the quality of analysts declined as they grew in number.

11 One Wall Street observer, James Grant acidly commented: 'Honesty was never a profit center on Wall Street, but the brokers used to keep up appearances. Now they have stopped pretending. More than ever, securities research, as it is called, is a branch of sales' (quoted in Shiller, 2000).

12 In 2001, the US House of Representatives Financial Services Committee's Subcommittee on Capital Markets, Insurance and Government-Sponsored Enterprises held hearings on analysts and their conflicts of interest. The chairman, Richard H Baker, opened the meetings stating: 'As a free-market conservative, I am the last person interested in government putting the market on trial.... However, the foundation of the free-market system is the free flow of straight-forward, unbiased information. And I must say I am deeply troubled by evidence of Wall Street's erosion of the bedrock of ethical conduct' (quoted in Boni and Womack, 2002, p. 96). Surveying the practice of spinning, Rep. John LaFalce (D NY) ranking member of the House Financial Services Committee commented: 'The fact that investment banks can hand out IPO shares to individual clients who generate more underwriting business for the banks creates potential conflicts of interest across the

entire investment banking industry that we cannot simply ignore' (*Wall Street Journal*, 3 September 2002, p. C1).

13   If firms find that their reputations have been impaired, meaning that their ability to compete for investment banking business is weakened, they may restructure the firm to signal to the market that they are controlling conflicts.

14   In a simple exercise to attempt to distinguish between conflict of interest and selection (and implicitly cognitive) bias, Michaely and Womack (1999) conducted a survey of MBAs in investment management and investment banking, asking them to interpret their empirical results as the result of one effect or the other. Although the sample was small, all 13 investment managers and 10 out of 13 investment bankers believed that the differences in their study were attributable to conflicts of interest.

15   If investors were caught up in a bubble mentality, they may not have paid attention to fundamentals even if the correct information was readily available.

16   In the commercial banking industry, prudential supervision is already in place to assess risk management. The movement towards a reorganization of the US financial industry as a universal banking system implies some complementary expansion of prudential supervision.

17   Boni and Womack (2002) report that most institutional investors do not believe that firewalls exist currently or that they could be credibly enforced.

18   The firms are Bear Stearns, Credit Suisse First Boston, Deutsche Bank, Goldman Sachs, JP Morgan, Lehman Brothers, Merrill Lynch, Morgan Stanley, Salomon Smith Barney, UBS Warburg.

19   The most rudimentary form of accounts are known to have existed since ancient times (O'Connor, 2002).

20   The largest audit firm in Germany was Deutsche Treuhand Gesellschaft, managed by Deutsche Bank before regulation forced it to become 'independent'. This firm eventually merged with KPMG Peat Marwick.

21   Sutton (1997) notes that in 1933 the US Congress was contemplating the establishment of a corps of government auditors; but Congress was persuaded by the existing accounting societies that they could fulfil the role. In other countries with less developed private accounting organizations, statutory auditors played a more significant role.

22   The United Kingdom went through a similar evolution moving from the ICAEW and ICAS to the UK Accounting Standards Board. In continental Europe and Japan the accounting practices were based on more formal commercial laws, including European 4th and 7th Directives. More recently, the International Accounting Standards Board, organized along the lines of the FASB, has been given authority to establish standards for listed European companies beginning in 2005.

23   Typical of this view is an article by then SEC Commissioner Steven Wallman, 'Accounting and financial reporting are linchpins to the success of our capital formation process and accountants...are the gatekeepers of our financial markets' (Wallman, 1996, p. 77).

24   Mansi *et al.* (2003) use firm-level bond price data and find that use of a Big 6 auditor reduces the rate of return required by investors and that this effect is almost three times larger for non-investment grade issuers. The value of the audit opinion is difficult to measure empirically because by the time an auditor discovers problems and gives a qualified opinion, the market may already have absorbed much of the negative information in the stock price (Healy and Palepu, 2001). Furthermore, qualified opinions, do not have a standardized measure, and it is also a rare event when a qualified opinion expresses a serious difference between the auditors and the company's management, as each will work hard to avoid such qualifications.

25   Prior to the 4th Directive practices differed in each country. For example, in Germany the audit opinion was basically one sentence indicating whether the financial statements complied with the law.

26   Simunic (1984) noted that 'any situation which alters incentives such that a self-interested auditor is more likely to ignore, conceal, or misrepresent his findings is described as decreasing the auditor's independence' (p. 679).

27 Former SEC Commissioner Wallman states: 'I recognize and agree with the view that auditors can provide advisory services well in part because of the knowledge gained during the course of an audit...however, knowledge about a business that would further the audit function is imparted to accountants through the performance of advisory services. The two positions, far from being mutually exclusive, are complementary and consistent' (Wallman, 1996, p. 81).

28 Andersen Consulting had to give up the Andersen name as part of the court settlement and was renamed Accenture, which had an initial public offering in 2001.

29 Many of the largest accounting firms have similar examples. We focus on Arthur Andersen because of its unique role as auditor of Enron, Worldcom, Qwest, Sunbeam and Waste Management, and its spectacular demise.

30 For a detailed description of Enron's problems and demise see Healy and Palepu (2003).

31 Antle *et al.*'s (2002) findings are robust to preliminary tests with US data.

32 They also found that audit risk associated with litigation risk cannot be efficiently priced. See also O'Keefe *et al.* (1994).

33 For example, see *Wall Street Journal* (1996). See also Toffler and Reingold (2003).

34 In addition to the Andersen clients, recent cases of Adelphia and Healthsouth are likely examples of office-level fee dependence for other firms.

35 Reynolds and Francis (2001) have attempted to analyse the influence of large clients on office-level auditor reporting decisions. Looking at differences by client size, they find no evidence of dependence on large clients influencing accruals and argue that the evidence is consistent with Big 5 auditors reporting more conservatively for larger clients because these clients pose greater litigation risk and hence more reputational risk. DeFond *et al.* (2002) draw a similar conclusion.

36 Several studies, notably Dye (1993), Palmrose (1998, 1991) and Carcello and Palmrose (1994), discuss the rise of litigation risk and its impact on the practice and cost of auditing.

37 Trading by banks was also recorded on this basis.

38 This is a manifestation of the Akerlof (1970) lemons problem.

39 In early 2003, the SEC recognized a fourth firm, Dominion Ratings, as an NRSRO.

40 For example, see Hand *et al.* (1992).

41 Equity prices move in the opposite direction, which Kliger and Sarig interpret as evidence that a ratings upgrade does not change the market's overall assessment of the value of the firm, but affects the division of value between debt-holders and equity interests.

42 We do not discuss here the even more extreme possibility of publicly provided or funded ratings. This remedy has not been seriously suggested as a remedy for potential conflicts and would have, in our opinion, obvious drawbacks.

43 The term universal banking is used here to refer to financial services conglomerates. Sometimes universal banking is defined to include when a financial intermediary may hold equity positions in firms.

44 Moody's Manual of Industrial and Miscellaneous Securities was first published in 1900; analysis of security values began in 1909. For a brief history see www.moodys.com.

45 Fama (1985), Diamond (1991), and Berlin and Mester (1992).

46 Unfortunately, while there is a general belief in the existence of economies of scope there is little empirical evidence. Few studies have produced empirical evidence that substantial economies of scale exist, much less economies of scope. There are significant problems in testing for these effects given limitations of data, but they may also be elusive because the standard approach to estimate production or cost functions failed to account for risk and the endogeneity of risk. Hughes *et al.* (2001) argue that risk-taking may mask scale economies that result from better diversification.

47 The Act permits 'well-capitalized and well-managed' national banks, with a satisfactory or better Community Reinvestment Act rating, to conduct most financial activities through an operating subsidiary. The aggregate consolidated

total assets of all financial subsidiaries of the national bank, however, cannot exceed 45% of the parent bank's total consolidated assets, or $50 billion, whichever is greater. An operating subsidiary cannot engage in insurance underwriting, real estate development, merchant banking, or insurance company portfolio investing. The Act empowers the Federal Reserve Board to define additional activities as 'financial in nature, or incidental or complementary to' financial activities. All insurance, banking and securities activities will be functionally regulated. The Act significantly narrows the broad exemptions from broker-dealer registration that banks enjoyed. The authority of the Board is limited to regulate, examine and require reports from functionally regulated subsidiaries, establishing a streamlined supervisory system for FHCs.

48   Commercial banks were the predominant intermediaries, holding two-thirds of the financial system's assets (White, 2000).

49   The Mutual and the New York Life were mutual companies while the Equitable was a stock company.

50   Although linked to specific investment banks, insurance companies often participated in other firms' syndicates. In addition, there were close ties with banks, trust companies and title insurance companies through ownership, large deposits or other affiliations. This group of institutions assisted with syndicate operations by providing collateral loans.

51   Affiliates or subsidiaries were a new and untested corporate form. The earliest trust affiliate was established in 1903 and the first known securities affiliate in 1908 (see Peach, 1941).

52   Henry Clews quoted in Carosso (1970 p. 113).

53   Markets were pummelled by an even more severe crisis in 1907 when sliding stock prices were joined by a banking crisis and sharp recession. Over the course of the 1907 crisis, stock prices, as measured by the Dow Jones index, plummeted 40%.

54   This structure was similar to the arrangement in German universal banks where investment and commercial banking activities are in separate departments within the bank.

55   This organizational form is similar to Section 20 securities subsidiaries permitted under the Glass-Steagall Act. See Macey and Miller (1992).

56   It should be noted that the new issue bond market shrank from $5.9 billion in 1927 to $4.2 billion in 1928 and finally $2.9 billion in 1929. At the same time, new equity issues were booming. Unfortunately, there appears to be no data on the underwriting institutions for stocks, although securities affiliates garnered a large share of the business.

57   One of the most prominent security affiliates, the First National Old Colony Corporation of Boston (the affiliate of the First National Old Colony Bank) had an investment supervision department with over $1 billion of funds for clients that included 600 banks and many manufacturing and insurance companies. It was highly respected by state bank regulators, for the investment advice it gave its client banks. It won the grudging respect of Senator Glass in the 1932 hearings, as a 'virtuous affiliate' (US Senate, Committee on Banking and Currency, 1932).

58   See Peach (1941) for a detailed list of 'abuses and defects'.

59   For example, the Metropolitan Securities Corporation, a wholly owned subsidiary of Chase Securities Corporation operated several pools in Chase National Bank stock between 1927 and 1931. Drawing in other investment companies, the pool bought and sold Chase stock, turning large profits until the market collapsed. One purpose claimed by the banks for these affiliates was to gain a wider distribution of the stock.

60   The three largest netted a profit of $10 million, while the bank affiliates' pools had profits of only $159,000. Wiggin argued that his family corporations gave sub-participations to officers of the affiliate because they were valuable employees and they should make money in additional to their salaries. Wiggin's successor, Winthrop W Aldrich denounced the pools and vowed that Chase would no longer engage in such activities.

61   Huertas and Silverman (1986) have argued that this fund was an appropriately designed incentive-compatible scheme, helping to solve the problem of the divorce

of ownership from management.

62   Similarly, Representative Henry B Steagall insisted that the New Deal legislation include deposit insurance even though the White House, the Federal Reserve and the larger banks were firmly opposed (Calomiris and White, 1994).

63   Banks that had affiliates were larger and more diversified, with the combined earnings from commercial and investment banking smoothing total fluctuations.

64   Banks were permitted to underwrite and deal in US state and local bonds.

65   The Bank Holding Company Act of 1956 closed a loophole in the Banking Act of 1933 by prohibiting bank holding companies from owning shares in subsidiaries that were not engaged in approved banking-related activities (see Santos, 1998).

66   As National City Company and Chase Securities Corporation were singled out by the Pecora hearings for their conflicts of interest, it is possible that they alone exploited the conflicts. Ang and Richardson (1994) discovered, however, that while the bonds issued by these affiliates were lower quality than the average for affiliates, they were no worse than those for investment banks.

67   In a study of pre-World War II Japan, before commercial and investment banking were separated, Konishi (2002) found that there was no significant difference in the initial yields in bonds underwritten by commercial banks, trust firms, the Industrial Bank of Japan or investment houses. Although the market did not price the bonds to indicate an apprehension of conflicts of interest or certification, issues under-written by commercial bank performed better with lower mortality rates (age-adjusted default rates).

68   Krozner and Rajan (1997) point out that the shift to affiliate form was not driven by the new issue equity boom that surged in 1928. National banks, which had no powers to underwrite stocks in bond departments, created securities affiliates before the surge in equities when bonds were still the dominant new issue.

69   The strict separation of commercial banking, investment banking and insurance made it necessary to define and restrict the activities of each type of intermediary carefully. When banks seemed to find a means to circumvent limitations through bank holding companies, the gap was quickly closed. The 1970 amendments to the Bank Holding Company of 1956 specified the permissible activities for bank holding companies, requiring that they be 'so closely related to banking or managing or controlling banks as to be a proper incident thereto'. The Board of Governors has the power to determine the scope of banking under the 1970 amendments. The test whether an activity was acceptable was whether it could 'reasonably be expected to produce benefits to the public, such as greater convenience, increased competition, or gains in efficiency, that outweigh possible adverse effects, such as undue concentration of resources, decreased or unfair competition, conflicts of interests or unsound banking practices'.

70   In 1984, the FDIC allowed insured non-member banks to offer securities services through subsidiaries (Santos, 1998).

71   Defining a small issue as less than $75 million, 31% of subsidiaries' underwriting is for small issues, while it constitutes only 8% for investment banks.

72   Stefanadis (2003) offers a theoretical treatment of tying and universal banking where universal banks have an advantage *vis-à-vis* independent investment banks when they bundle together services (e.g. tie loans to the provision of investment banking services). He finds that tying may ultimately reduce competition between banks and lower social welfare.

73   There are few studies that examine other potential conflicts of interest for universal banks. Allen *et al.* (2001) look at the potential conflict of interest for banks acting as both lenders and financial advisers, using the cumulative abnormal returns of the target and acquiring firms for a sample of mergers from 1995 to 2000. When a target firm uses its commercial bank as an adviser, the abnormal return is positive, implying that the certification effect dominates the conflict of interest effect. When the acquirer is advised by its bank, however, there is no abnormal return which suggests that the conflict of interest dominates the effect of certification.

74   For lower rated bonds (BBB, BB and unrated), there is no difference in the yields, it exists only for bonds rates AA or A. Thus, unlike the United States, there is no

evidence that information sensitive issues benefit from using a universal bank.

75 The pre-1906 US experience shows that combining insurance and banking through interlocking directorates was an inferior choice, providing unusual opportunities for officers and directors to exploit conflicts of interest.

76 The Federal Deposit Insurance Company's *History of the Eighties – Lessons for the Future* (1997) documents how the severe reductions in bank examiner resources at the federal and state level and decreased frequency of examinations exacerbated the banking crisis.

References

Accounting Today (2003), 'The 2003 Top 100 Firms', 17 March-6 April, www.webcpa.com, pp. 30-40.

Akerlof, G. (1970), 'The Market for Lemons: Quality Uncertainty and the Market Mechanism', *Quarterly Journal of Economics* 84 (3), August, pp. 488-500.

Allen, L., Jagtiani, J., Peristiani S. and Saunders, A. (2001), 'The Role of Bank Advisors in Mergers and Acquisitions', NYU Stern Department of Finance Working Paper No. FIN-01-058, December 2001.

Anderson, J. and Shack, J. (2002), 'Bye-bye, "buy"', *Institutional Investor* 36 (5),May, pp. 27-39.

Ang, J.S. and Richardson, T. (1994), 'The Underwriting Experience of Commercial Bank Affiliates Prior to the Glass-Steagall Act', *Journal of Banking and Finance* 18 (2), March, pp. 351-95.

Antle, R., Gordon, E.A., Narayanamoorthy, G. and Zhou, L. (2002), 'The Joint Determination of Audit Fees, Non-audit Fees, and Abnormal Accruals', Yale ICP Working Paper, Yale University, No. 02-21.

Bank for International Settlements (1988), 'International Coverage of Capital Measurement', Basel Committee on Banking Supervision, July.

Bank for International Settlements (1999), 'Supervisory Lessons to be Drawn from the Asian Crisis', Basel Committee on Banking Supervision Working Papers, No. 2, June.

Bank for International Settlements (2000),'Credit Ratings and Complementary Sources of Credit Quality Information', Basel Committee Basel Committee on Banking Supervision Working Papers, No. 3, August.

Bank for International Settlements (2001), 'Overview of the New Basel Capital Accord', Basel Committee on Banking Supervision, January.

Bell, T.B., Landsman, W.R. and Shackelford, D.A. (2001), 'Auditors' Perceived Business Risk and Audit Fees: Analysis and Evidence', *Journal of Accounting Research* 39, pp. 35-44.

Benston, G.J. (1990), The Separation of Commercial and Investment Banking: The Glass-Steagall Act Reconsidered, New York, Oxford University Press.

Benston, G.J. (1998), Regulating Financial Markets: A Critique and Some Proposals, London, Institute of Economic Affairs.

Benston, G.J., Eisenbeis, R.A., Horvitz, P.M., Kane, E.J. and Kaufman, G.G. (1986), Perspectives on Safe and Sound Banking: Past, Present and Future, Cambridge MA, The MIT Press and the American Bankers Association.

Ber, H., Yafeh, Y. and Yosha, O. (2000), 'Conflict of Interest in Universal Banking: Bank Lending, Stock Underwriting and Fund Management', CEPR Discussion Paper No. 2359.

Berlin, M. and Mester, L. (1992), 'Debt Covenants and Regotiation', *Journal of Financial Intermediation*, June, pp. 95-133.

Boni, L. and Womack, K.L. (2002), 'Wall Street's Credibility Problem: Misaligned Incentives and Dubious Fixes?' Brookings-Wharton Papers on Financial Services, pp. 93-130.

Boot, A.W.A. (2000), 'Relationship Banking: What Do We Know?', *Journal of Financial Intermediation* 9, pp. 7-25.

Bloch, E. (1986), Inside Investment Banking, Homewood, IL, Dow Jones-Irwin.

Brand, L. and Bahar, R. (1999), 'Ratings Performance, 1998', Standard and Poor's.

Cairns, A.J., Davidson, J.A. and Kisilevitz, M.L. (2002), 'The Limits of Bank Convergence', *McKinsey Quarterly* 2, pp. 41-51.

Calomiris, C.W. (1995), 'The Cost of Rejecting Universal Banking: American Finance in the German Mirror', in N. Lamoreaux and D.M.G. Raff, Coordination and Information: Historical Perspectives on the Organization of Enterprise, Chicago, University of Chicago Press, pp. 257-315.

Calomiris, C.W. and Kahn, C. (1991), 'The Role of Demandable Debt in Structuring Optimal Banking Arrangements', *American Economic Review* 81 (3), June, pp. 497-513.

Calomiris, C.W. and White, E.N. (1994), 'The Origins of Federal Deposit Insurance', in C. Goldin and G.D. Libecap, The Regulated Economy: A Historical Approach to Political Economy, Chicago, University of Chicago Press, pp. 145-88.

Cantor, R. and Packer, F. (1994), 'The Credit Rating Industry', Federal Reserve Bank of New York, *Quarterly Review* 19 (2), Summer-Fall.

Cantor, R. and Packer, F. (1996), 'The Determinants and Impact of Sovereign Credit Ratings', *Federal Reserve Bank of New York Economic Policy Review* 2 (2), October, pp. 37-53.

Carcello, J.V. and Palmrose, Z.V. (1994), 'Auditor Litigation and Modified Reporting on Bankrupt Clients', *Journal of Accounting Research* 32, pp. 1-30.

Carosso, V.P. (1970), Investment Banking in America: A History, Cambridge MA, Harvard University Press.

Cassidy, J. (2003), 'The Investigation: How Eliot Spitzer Humbled Wall Street', *New Yorker*, 7 April, pp. 54-73.

Chan, L.K.C., Karceski, J. and Lakonishok, J. (2003), 'Analysts' Conflict of Interest and Biases in Earnings Forecasts', NBER Working Paper 9544, March.

Chan Y., Greenbaum, S.I. and Thakor, A.V. (1986), 'Information Reusability, Competition and Bank Asset Quality', *Journal of Banking and Finance* 10, pp. 243-53.

Cowles, A. (1933), 'Can Stock Market Forecasters Forecast?' *Econometrica* I.

Davidson, S. and Anderson, G. (1987), 'The Development of Accounting and Auditing Standards', *Journal of Accountancy*, May, pp. 110-35.

D'Avolio G., Gildor, E. and Shleifer, A. (2001), 'Technology, Information Production, and Market Efficiency', Federal Reserve Bank of Kansas City Symposium, Jackson Hole, Wyoming.

DeFond, M., Raghunandan, K. and Subramanyam, K.R. (2002), 'Do Non-Audit Service Fees Impair Auditor Independence? Evidence from Going Concern Audit Opinions', *Journal of Accounting Research* 40, pp. 1247-74.

Diamond, D. (1991), 'Monitoring and Reputation: The Choice between Bank Loans and Directly Placed Debt', *Journal of Political Economy*, August, pp. 689-721.

Diamond, D.W. (1984), 'Financial Intermediation and Delegated Monitoring', *Review of Economic Studies* 51, pp. 393-414.

De Long, J.B. (1991), 'Did J.P. Morgan's Men Add Value? A Historical Perspective on Financial Capitalism', in P. Temin (ed.) Inside the Business Enterprise, Chicago, Chicago University Press, , pp. 205-36.

Dickey, J. (1995), 'The New Entanglement Theory: Securities Analysts Are Sued in Class Action Complaints', *Insights*, p. 9.

Dugar, A. and Nathan, S. (1995), 'The Effect of Investment Banking Relationships on Financial Analysts' Earnings Forecasts and Investment Recommendations', *Contemporary Accounting Research* 12 (1),Fall, pp. 131-60.

Dye, R.A. (1993), 'Auditing Standards, Legal Liability, and Auditor Wealth', *Journal of Public Economy* 101, pp. 887-914.

Economist (2002), 'Capitulate or Die: Investment Banking Under Fire', *The Economist*, 5 October, pp. 67-8.

Economist (1996), 'The Use and Abuse of Reputation', *The Economist*, 6 April, p. 20.

Ederington, L.H. and Goh, J.C. (1998), 'Bond Rating Agencies and Stock Analysts: Who Knows What When', *Journal of Financial and Quantitative Analysis* 33 (4), December, pp. 569-85.

Eichenwald, K. (2002), 'Secret Deal Part of Tangle in Enron Case', *New York Times*, 1 October, pp. C1 and C10.

Ellis, K., Michaely, R. and O'Hara, M. (2000), 'When the Underwriter is the Market Maker: An Examination of Trading in the IPO Aftermarket', *Journal of Finance* 55 (3), June, pp. 1039-74.

Fama, E. (1985), 'What's Different About Banks?', *Journal of Monetary Economics*, January, pp. 29-39.

Federal Deposit Insurance Corporation (1997), History of the Eighties – Lessons for the Future Vol. 1, Federal Deposit Insurance Corporation.

Financial Stability Forum (2002), Press Release, 4 September, fsforum@bis.org.

Financial Times (1999), 'Talking Up the Market', *Financial Times*, 19 July, p. 12.

Fitch (2003), Statement of Stephen W. Joynt, President and CEO, Fitch, Inc. to US House of Representatives, Committee on Financial Services, Subcommittee on Capital Markets, Insurance and Government Sponsored Enterprises, 2 April.

Fohlin, C. (1999), 'Universal Banking in Pre-World War I Germany: Model or Myth?', *Explorations in Economic History* 35 (4), October, pp. 305-43.

Francis, J., Schipper, K. and Vincent, L. (2002), 'Expanded Disclosures and the Increased Usefulness of Earnings Announcements', *The Accounting Review* 77, pp. 515-46.

Frankel, R.M., Johnson, M.F. and Nelson, K.K. (2002), 'The Relation Between Auditors' Fees for Non-audit Services Earnings Management', *The Accounting Review* 77 (Supplement), pp. 71-105.

Galant, D. (1992), 'Going Public', *Institutional Investor* 26 (4) April, p. 127.

Gande A., Puri, M. and Saunders, A. (1999), 'Bank Entry, Competition, and the Market for Corporate Securities Underwriting', *Journal of Financial Economics* 54 (2), October, pp. 165-95.

Gande A., Puri, M., Saunders, A. and Walter, I. (1997), 'Bank Underwriting of Debt Securities: Modern Evidence', *Review of Financial Studies* 10 (4), Winter, pp 1175-202.

Gasparino, C. (2002), 'Salomon Probe Includes Senior Executives', *Wall Street Journal*, 3 September, pp. C1-C2.

Gasparino, C. and Craig, S. (2003), 'Mary Meeker Won't Face Securities Law Charges' *Wall Street Journal,* 2 April.

Glassman, J.K. and Hassett, K.A. (1999), Dow 36,000, New York, Random House.

Gompers, P.A. and Lerner, J. (1999), 'Conflict of Interest in the Issuance of Public Securities: Evidence from Venture Capital', *Journal of Law and Economics* 42 (1), pp. 1-28.

Greenbaum, S.I. and Thakor, A.V. (1995), Contemporary Financial Intermediation, Dryden Press.

Grossman, S. and Stiglitz, J. (1980), 'On the Impossibility of Informationally Efficient Markets', *American Economic Review* 70, pp. 393-408.

Guinnane, T.W. (2002), 'Delegated Monitors, Large and Small: Germany's Banking System, 1800-1914', *Journal of Economic Literature* XL (1),March, pp. 73-124.

Hand, J.R.M., Holthausen, R.W. and Leftwich, R.W. (1992), 'The Effect of Bond Rating Agency Announcements on Bond and Stock Prices', *Journal of Finance* 47 (2), June, pp. 733-52.

Healy, P.M. and Palepu, K.G. (2001), 'Information Asymmetry, Corporate Disclosure, and the Capital Markets: A Review of the Empirical Disclosure Literature', *Journal of Accounting and Economics* 31, Nos. 1-3, September, pp. 405-40.

Healy, P.M., and Palepu, K.G. (2003), 'The Fall of Enron,' *Journal of Economic Perspectives* 17 (2), Spring, pp. 3-26.

Heaton, J. and Lucas, D. (1999), 'Stock Prices and Fundamentals', in B.S. Bernanke and J.J. Rotemberg, NBER Macroeconomics Annual 1999, Cambridge MA, MIT Press, pp. 213-41.

Hebb, G.M., and Fraser, D.R. (2002), 'Conflict of Interest in Commercial Bank Security Underwritings: Canadian Evidence', *Journal of Banking and Finance* 26 (10), October, pp. 1935-49.

Hickman, W.B. (1958), 'Corporate Bond Quality and Investor Experience', New York, National Bureau of Economic Research.

Hong, H. and Kubik, J.D. (2003), 'Analyzing the Analysts: Career Concerns and Biased Earnings Forecasts', *Journal of Finance* 58 (1), Feburary, pp. 313-51.

Huertas, T.F. and Silverman, J.L. (1986), 'Charles E. Mitchell: Scapegoat of the Crash?', *Business History Review* 60 (1), Spring, pp. 81-103.

Hughes, J.P., Mester, L.J. and Moon, C.-G. (2001), 'Are Scale Economies in Banking Elusive or Illusive? Evidence Obtained by Incorporating Capital Structure and Risk-taking into Models of Bank Production', *Journal of Banking and Finance* 25, pp. 2169-208.

Institute of Chartered Accountants in England and Wales (2003a), 'Guidance for Audit Committees: Reviewing Audit Independence', ICAEW.

Institute of Chartered Accountants in England and Wales (2003b), 'Guidance for Audit Committees: Company Reporting and Audit Requirements', ICAEW.

Institute of Chartered Accountants in England and Wales (2003c), 'Additional Guidance on Independence for Auditors', ICAEW.

Institutional Investor's website, www.institutionalinvestor.com.

Kahneman, D. and Lovallo, D. (1993), 'Timid Choices and Bold Forecasts: A Cognitive Perspective on Risk Taking', *Management Science* 29, January, pp. 17-31.

Keenan, S.C. (1999), 'Historical Default Rates of Corporate Bond Borrowers, 1920-1998', Moody's Investors Services, Special Comment.

Kinney, W.R. and Libby, R. (2002), 'The Relation Between Auditors' Fees for Non-audit Services and Earnings Management', *The Accounting Review* 77, pp. 107-14.

Kliger, D. and Sarig, O. (2000), 'The Information Value of Bond Ratings', *Journal of Finance* 55 (6), December, pp. 2879-290.

Konishi, M. (2002), 'Bond Underwriting by Banks and Conflicts of Interest: Evidence from Japan During the Pre-war Period', *Journal of Banking and Finance* 26, pp. 767-93.

Kroszner, R.S. and Rajan, R.G. (1994), 'Is the Glass-Steagall Act Justified? A Study of the US Experience with Universal Banking before 1933', *American Economic Review* 84.

Kroszner, R.S. and Rajan, R.G. (1997), 'Organization Structure and Credibility: Evidence from Commercial Bank Securities Activities before the Glass-Steagall Act', *Journal of Monetary Economics*, 39.

Landon, T. Jr. (2003), 'NASD Files Two Complaints Against Star at First Boston', *New York Times*, 7 March, pp. C1, C6.

Landsman, W.R. and Maydew, E.L. (2002), 'Beaver (1968) Revised: Has the Information Content of Annual Earnings Announcements Declined in the Past Three Decades?', Working Paper, University of North Carolina, Chapel Hill.

Leland, H.E. and D.H. Pyle (1977), 'Informational Asymmetries, Financial Structure, and Financial Intermediation', *Journal of Finance* 32, May, pp. 371-87.

Levitt, A. (2000), 'Renewing the Covenant with Investors.', A speech by SEC Chairman, 10 May, available at www.sec.gov/news/speeches/spch370.htm.

Loughran, T. and Ritter J.R. (2002), 'Why Don't Issuers Get Upset About Leaving Money on the Table in IPOs?', *Review of Financial Studies* 15, pp. 413-43.

Mansi, S.A., Maxwell, W.F. and Miller, D.P. (2003), 'Does Auditor Quality and Tenure Matter to Investors? Evidence from the Bond Market', Working Paper, Virginia Tech, April.

Macey, J.R. and Miller, G.P. (1992), Banking Law and Regulation, Boston, Little Brown.

McDaniel, R. (2003), 'The Role and Function of Rating Agencies: Evolving Perceptions and the Implications for Regulatory Oversight', Speech to the Association of French Treasurers (AFTE), Paris, 5 February.

McDonald, E. (1996), 'Fear of the Costs Could Forestall Andersen Split – Divorce Could Damage Brand and Sacrifice Position, Yet Internal Strife Persists', *The Wall Street Journal Europe*, 23 December 1996.

McEnroe, J.E. and Martens, S.C. (2001), 'Auditors' and Investors' Perceptions of the Expectation Gap', *Accounting Horizons*, December, pp. 345-58.

McLauglin, J. (1994), 'The Changing Role of the Securities Analyst in Initial Public Offerings', *Insights*, pp. 5-14.

McNichols, M., O'Brien, P.C. and Francis, J. (1997), 'Self-selection and Analyst Coverage', *Journal of Accounting Research* 35, pp. 167-208.

Millon, M.H. and Thakor, A.V. (1985), 'Moral Hazard and Information Sharing: A Model of Financial Information Gathering Agencies', *Journal of Finance* 40 (5), December, pp. 1403-22.

Michaely, R. and Womack, K.L. (1999), 'Conflict of Interest and the Credibility of Underwriter Analyst Recommendations', *Review of Financial Studies* 12 (4), Special Issue, pp. 653-86.

Mishkin, F. and White, E.N. (2003), 'US Stock Market Crashes and their Aftermath: Implications for Monetary Policy', in W.C. Hunter, G.G. Kaufman and M. Pomerleano, Asset Price Bubbles: The Implications for Monetary, Regulatory and International Policies, Cambridge MA, MIT Press, pp. 53-80.

Moody's website(2003), www.moodys.com.

Moore, D.A., Loewenstein, G. and Bazerman, M.H. (2002), 'Auditor Independence, Conflict of Interest, and the Unconscious Intrusion of Bias', Harvard NOM Research Paper, No.02-40.

Morgenson, G. (2002), 'Regulators Find More Red Flags in Another Analyst's Optimisim', *New York Times*, 12 September, pp. C5, C12.

Nazareth, A.L. (2003), 'Rating the Rating Agencies: The State of Transparency and Competition', Testimony before the Subcommittee on Capital Markets, Insurance and Government Sponsored Enterprises of the Committee on Financial Services of the US House of Representatives, 2 April.

North, D.C. (1954), 'Life Insurance and Investment Banking at the Time of the

Armstrong Investigation of 1905-1906', *Journal of Economic History* XIV (3), Summer, pp. 209-28.

O'Connor, S.M. (2002), 'The Inevitability of Enron and the Impossibility of "Auditor Independence" Under the Current Audit System', Working Paper, University of Pittsburgh School of Law.

O'Keefe, T.B., Simunic, D.A. and Stein, M.T. (1994), 'The Production of Audit Services: Evidence from a Major Public Accounting Firm', *Journal of Accounting Research* 32, Autumn, pp. 241-61.

Palmrose, Z.-V. (1986), 'The Effect of Non-audit Services on the Pricing of Audit Services: Further Evidence', *Journal of Accounting Research*, Autumn, pp. 405-11.

Palmrose, Z.-V. (1988), 'An Analysis of Auditor Litigation and Audit Service Quality', *The Accounting Review* 63, January, pp. 55-73.

Palmrose, Z.-V. (1991), 'Trials of Legal Disputes Involving Independent Auditors: Some Empirical Evidence', *Journal of Accounting Research* 29, Supplement, pp. 149-85.

Parkash, M. and Venables, C.F. (1993), 'Auditee Incentives for Auditor Independence: The Case of Non-audit Services', *The Accounting Review* 68, pp. 113-33.

Partnoy, F. (1999), 'The Siskel and Ebert of Financial Markets?: Two Thumbs Down for the Credit Rating Agencies', *Washington University Law Quarterly* 77 (2).

Peach, W.N. (1941), The Security Affiliates of National Banks, Baltimore, The Johns Hopkins University Press.

Pratt, T. (1993), 'Wall Street's Four-letter Word', *Institutional Dealers' Digest* 59 (13), 29 March, p. 18.

Puri, M. (1994), 'The Long-Term Default Performance of Bank Underwritten Security Issues', *Journal of Banking and Finance* 18.

Puri, M. (1996), 'Commercial Banks in Investment Banking: Conflict of Interest or Certification Role?', *Journal of Financial Economics* 40.

Rajan, R.G. (1995), 'The Entry of Commercial Banks into the Securities Business: A Selective Survey of Theories and Evidence', Paper prepared for the Conference on Universal Banking, Solomon Center New York University, January 1995.

Rajan, R. and Servaes, H. (1997), 'Analyst Following of Initial Public Offerings', *Journal of Finance* 52 (2), June, pp. 507-9.

Ramakrishnan, R.T.S. and Thakor, A.V. (1984), 'Information Reliability, and a Theory of Financial Intermediation', *Review of Economic Studies* 51 (3), July, pp. 415-32.

Reynolds, J.K. and Francis, J.R. (2001), 'Does Size Matter? The Influence of Large Clients on Office-level Auditor Reporting Decisions', *Journal of Accounting and Economics* 30, pp. 375-400.

Ritter, J.R. and Welch, I. (2002), 'A Review of IPO Activity, Pricing and Allocations', *Journal of Finance* 57 (4), August, pp. 1795-826.

Ryan, S.G., Herz, R.H., Iannaconi, T.E., Maines, L.A., Palepu, K., Schrand, C.M., Skinner, D.J. and Vincent, L. (2001), 'SEC Auditor Independence Requirements', *Accounting Horizons* 15, December, pp. 373-86.

Santos, J.A.C. (1998), 'Banking and Commerce: How Does the United States Compare to Other Countries?', *Federal Reserve Bank of Cleveland Economic Review* 34 (4), pp. 14-26.

Saunders, A. and Walter, I. (1994), Universal Banking in the United States: What Could We Gain? What Could We Lose?, Oxford, Oxford University Press.

Securities and Exchange Commission (SEC) (2000), 'Final Rule: Revision of the Commission's Auditor Independence Requirements', Washington DC,

Government Printing Office.

Securities and Exchange Commission (SEC) (2003a), 'Report on the Role and Function of Credit Rating Agencies in the Operation of the Securities Markets', January 2003, http://www.sec.gov/news/studies/creditratingreportoio3.pdf.

Securities and Exchange Commission (SEC) (2003b), 'Rating Agencies and the Use of Credit Ratings Under the Federal Securities Laws-Concept Release', June, http://www.sec.gov/rules/concept/33-8236.htm.

Securities Industry Association (2001), Best Practices for Research, New York, SIA Monograph.

Shiller, R.J. (2000), Irrational Exuberance, Princeton, Princeton University Press.

Simunic, D.A. (1984), 'Auditing, Consulting and Auditor Independence', *Journal of Accounting Research*, 22, Autumn, pp. 679-702.

Stefanadis, C. (2003a), 'Brokering, Underwriting and Integrated Investment Banks', Federal Reserve Bank of New York, May.

Stefanadis, C. (2003b), 'Tying and Universal Banking', Federal Reserve Bank of New York, March.

Stickel, S.E. (1881), 'Reputation and Performance Among Security Analysts', *Journal of Finance* 47 (5), December, pp. 1881-936.

Subcommittee on Reports, Accounting and Management of the Commission on Government Operations, US Senate (Metcalf Committee) (1977), 'The Accounting Establishment: A Staff Study', Washington DC.

Sutton, M.H. (1997), 'Auditor Independence: The Challenge of Fact and Appearance', *Accounting Horizons*, March, pp. 86-91.

Thomas, L. Jr. (2003), 'U.S. Accuses a Top Banker of Obstruction', *New York Times*, 24 April, pp. C1 and C4.

Toffler, BL. and Reingold, J. (2003), Final Accounting: Ambition, Greed and the Fall of Arthur Andersen, Broadway Books.

US Congress (2002), 'Rating the Raters: Enron and the Credit Rating Agencies', Hearings before the Senate Committee on Governmental Affairs, 107th Congress, 471, 20 March.

Wakeman, L.M. (1984), 'The Real Function of Bond Rating Agencies', in M.C. Jensen and C.W. Smith (eds), The Modern Theory of Corporate Finance, New York, McGraw Hill.

Wallman, S.M.H. (1996), 'The Future of Accounting, Part III: Reliability and Auditor Independence', *Accounting Horizons* 10, pp. 76-97.

White, E.N. (1986), 'Before the Glass-Steagall Act: An Analysis of the Investment Banking Activities of National Banks', *Explorations in Economic History* 23 (1),January, pp. 33-55.

White, E.N. (1990),'The Stock Market Boom and Crash of 1929 Revisited', *Journal of Economic Perspectives* 4 (2), Spring, pp. 67-83.

White, E.N. (2000), 'Banking and Finance in the Twentieth Century,' in S.L. Engerman and R.E. Gallman, The Cambridge Economic History of the United States Vol. III: The Twentieth Century, Cambridge, Cambridge University Press, pp. 743-802.

White, L.J. (2001), The Credit Rating Industry: An Industrial Organisation Analysis', Paper prepared for the conference on 'The Role of Credit Reporting Systems in the International Economy' held at the World Bank, 1-2 March 2001.

Wigmore, B.A. (1985), The Crash and Its Aftermath: A History of Securities Markets in the United States, 1929-1933, Westport, CT, Greenwood Press.

Womack, K.L., 'Do Brokerage Analysts' Recommendations Have Investment Value?', *Journal of Finance* 51 (1), March, pp. 137-67.

Addendum
Conflicts of Interest in the Financial Services Industry: What Should We Do About Them?

Conflicts of Interest in the Mutual Funds Industry

Eugene N. White
Rutgers University and NBER
March 1, 2004
© Eugene N. White 2004

Mutual funds are one of the great innovations of the financial sector in the last half century. By permitting small investors to purchase a liquid, diversified portfolio of securities at low cost, mutual funds have provided a majority of American households with the means to invest in stocks and bonds. Their growth has been prodigious, with mutual funds invested in stocks and bonds, increasing from 2.9 percent of assets of all intermediaries in 1960 to 16.6 percent in 2000.

The Investment Company Act of 1940 set up the structure and regulation of the modern mutual fund industry. Designed with the small investor in mind, mutual funds were provided with a relatively simple and transparent structure of governance and rules. The Act sought to eliminate a variety of abuses that had tainted the industry, including excessive fees, improperly valued portfolios, and misleading accounting and advertising practices.[1] Even with careful restructuring, the loss of reputation after the scandals of the 1930s kept the mutual fund industry small until the last quarter of the twentieth century. The revitalized industry found economies of scale and scope that led to the appearance of both families of mutual funds and funds sponsored by large multi-product financial institutions. These developments provided investors with more investment options and lower cost services.

As markets grew faster and became increasingly sophisticated, opportunities for exploiting the governance structure and liquidity rules appeared. Inherent information asymmetries made it difficult for shareholders to ensure that the directors of the funds were monitoring management. Conflicts of interest arising from incentive structures and the combination of activities induced investment advisors to pay less attention to the interests of mutual fund shareholders, permitting late trading and market timing activities at their expense. The scandals that erupted in 2002 focused attention on long-standing problems that had grown more severe. Carefully designed reforms are needed to improve governance, increase

---

[1] Peter Tufano and Matthew Sevick, "Board Structure and Fee-Setting in the U.S. Mutual Fund Industry," *Journal of Financial Economics* 46 (1996), pp. 321–355.

transparency and supervisory oversight, and set trading rules to reduce arbitrage opportunities that lower the rate of return for the vast majority of investors.

Growth, Governance and Liquidity

In the 1990s, bond and stock mutual funds entered a period of extraordinarily rapid growth. Between 1990 and 2002, the number of these funds climbed from 2,338 to 7,267, while their accounts and net assets rose from 61 million with $1,065 billion to 251 million with $6,392 billion. The ownership of these funds also became more widely diffused. In 1990, 25 percent of all households owned mutual fund shares; by 2002, this number had risen to 50 percent, representing 54.2 million households. An important factor behind this expansion was the use of mutual funds for retirement savings. By 2002, mutual funds accounted for $2.1 trillion or 21 percent of the "retirement" market, with half of the funds in employer-sponsored defined contribution plans. The other half was in IRAs, where mutual funds' share had grown from 22 percent in 1990 to 46 percent in 2002. Overall, mutual funds accounted for 6.7 percent of household financial assets in 1990, rising to 17.8 percent in 2002.[2]

The scandals in the mutual fund industry have direct implications for the majority of American households. These households rode the boom and bust in the stock market in the 1990s primarily in mutual funds. The total assets in equity funds soared from $239 billion in 1990 to $4,042 billion by 1999, only to collapse to $2,667 billion by the end of 2002. Unlike the other financial industry scandals, the mutual funds problems appear to have developed not only in the boom but also in the wake of the bust. Net new cash inflows to equity funds rose steadily from $13 billion in 1990 to $124 billion in 1995 and then to a peak of $309 billion in 2000, shrinking to $32 billion in 2001, with $28 billion of withdrawals in 2002. The potential decline in income to mutual fund investment advisors from this collapse seems to have been a crucial incentive behind some instances of fraud.

The success of the mutual fund industry rests on providing households with a low-cost safe method of investing, where all investors are treated equally and shares in the fund are highly liquid. The individuals and institutions purchase shares issued by mutual funds, which they may buy either directly or through an agent. The shareholders elect a board of directors, which is responsible for overseeing the management of the fund, including the selection of the investment advisor who manages the portfolio of investments and the principal underwriter who sells the fund shares. The board is supposed to look out for the shareholders' interests; and independent directors who should not have any significant relationship with the advisor or underwriter play a key role. Even before the scandal broke, the SEC was concerned about the need for director independence and it changed the rules governing directors in January 2002 to require that the majority of directors be independent.

Liquidity is a key attribute of mutual funds, and the price at which shares may be redeemed is known as the net asset value (NAV). A fund's share price or NAV is defined as equal to the market value of a fund's securities less its liabilities, divided by the number of shares outstanding. In an effort to ensure that all investors have an opportunity to buy at the same price every day, the NAV is set each day using the prices of securities at the close of the NYSE at 4 P.M. EST. Orders may flow in all day but the NAV is the price at which purchases and sales are made. If there are no

---

[2] The data source is the Investment Company Institute, *Mutual Fund Fact Book* 43rd ed. (2002).

available quotes or the quotes do not reflect market value, the directors may use a "fair market" value to set the price, although this approach requiring judgment is rarely used.

To cover the costs of mutual funds, shareholders pay shareholder fees and annual fund operating expenses. Shareholder fees may include sales charges, redemption fees, exchange fees (for moving money from one fund to another in a family of funds), and an annual account maintenance fee. While shareholder fees are charged directly to the investor, the operating expenses are deducted from fund assets before earnings are distributed to shareholders. These expenses include the management fee to the investment advisor, distribution (12b-1) fees to investment professional and other services, and other expenses.

The scandals in the mutual fund industry have largely arisen out of the failure of the governance structure. The structure of mutual funds governance has shareholders delegate monitoring of the investment advisors to the directors. Given the large number of investors, there is a free rider effect because it is very costly for any individual shareholder to monitor the advisors. Thus, directors should take the central role in overcoming the information asymmetry between shareholders and the fund managers who, given the incentive structure of compensation, have interests that can diverge from those of investors. The advisors' role in the operation of the mutual fund is crucial as they select the diversified portfolio that would be too costly and difficult for the investors to individually assemble. Problems arose because the directors have not adequately monitored investment advisors to ensure that they were acting in the best interests of the shareholders. The interests of managers were not closely aligned with those of shareholders, and conflicts of interest were exacerbated by the fact that many mutual funds are sponsored by multi-product financial institutions that have divergent client interests. While there were some personal conflicts of interest for advisors who personally profited at the expense of the shareholders, other conflicts of interests were rooted in the multiple interests of investment advisors.

Stern and Canary Capital

On September 3, 2003, New York State Attorney General Eliot Spitzer again trumped federal and state securities regulators when he announced that his office had uncovered a new major scandal.[3] Before much of Wall Street fell under Spitzer's scourge in 2001 and 2002, Terry Glenn, head of the mutual fund industry's Investment Company Institute (ICI), was still able to characterize the industry as being "untainted by major scandal for more than 60 years."[4] Spitzer's initial target was Edward J. Stern and his hedge fund Canary Capital Partners LLC.[5] Canary had engineered an arrangement with Bank of America's mutual fund group, Nations Funds, permitting it to engage in "late trading" and "market timing." The Attorney General learned of late trading when a former employee of Stern Asset Management, Noreen Harrington, reported that she had heard traders bragging about the practice. She confronted Mr. Stern and said that she did not think it was legal. She hoped that regulators would discover the problem but after a year, she contacted Spitzer.[6]

---

[3] The SEC was only notified of Spitzer's settlement two days beforehand. (Thomas, "Big Fine," *New York Times* (September 4, 2003), p. C8.

[4] Quoted in Karen Damato, "Mutual Funds' Relatively Untainted Image May Be Lost," *Wall Street Journal* (September 4, 2003), p. C1.

[5] Scion of Leonard Stern, the billionaire chairman of Hartz Mountain Industries, Edward Stern was formerly a reporter for *Spy* magazine and a manager of the *Village Voice*.

[6] Riva D. Atlas, "Fund Inquiry Informant Discloses Her Identity," *New York Times* (December 9, 2003) p. C1 and C4.

"Late trading" and "market timing" take advantage of the design of open-end mutual funds, which provide daily liquidity by permitting investors to convert their portfolios into cash by the sale of shares to the mutual fund company at the calculated daily NAV, with all transactions supposedly delivered to intermediaries by 4 P.M.[7] "Late trading" occurs if a trader is able to buy and sell shares at the 4 P.M. NAV price after the close of the market at 4 P.M. when other investors would have to pay the next day's net asset value or price. Any news late in the day that altered the value of stocks in the funds would change the value of the fund. A "late" trader could trade at the stale 4 P.M. price and buy or sell the funds the next day at a profit. Profiting at the expense of the other investors in the mutual fund by late trading is illegal under New York State's Martin Act and the SEC's regulations.

Market timing, on the other hand, is not illegal, but it is considered unethical. This practice takes advantage of the fact that the most recent transaction prices at 4 P.M. may not always fully reflect the available market information when the NAV is set. The problem is greatest when there are time zone differences for U.S. mutual funds that invest in foreign securities. If a U.S. fund invests in Japanese stocks, it typically takes the last prices available to it at 4 P.M. EST, using the yen closing prices from the Tokyo Stock Exchange and the prevailing Yen-dollar 4 P.M. exchange rate. However, the Tokyo exchange closes 9 hours earlier, and given the time difference, the prices are 15 hours old. These prices may be "stale" if news since the closing in Tokyo moves prices the next day. Traders may thus be able to profit by buying at the stale prices embedded in the funds' NAVs. Similarly, there are arbitrage opportunities in funds for domestic small-cap equities and high-yield convertible bonds that trade infrequently and have large bid-ask spreads. The last trades in these markets may be "old" and not mirror current information. If traders engaging in arbitrage based on these opportunities can quickly move in and out of a fund, the value of the fund will be for long-term investors who will also bear the costs from the additional transactions. Most funds have policies that are supposed to discourage this type of activity.

Comparing late trading to "betting on a horse race after the horses have crossed the finish line,"[8] Spitzer's complaint alleged that Canary not only engaged in late trading and market timing with Bank of America-sponsored mutual funds, but Bank of America also provided it with a state-of-the-art electronic trading platform and an up-to-date list of the funds' holdings so that derivatives could be designed for short sales. To facilitate late trading, before 4 P.M., Canary faxed the bank a list of trades that could be canceled or confirmed with a pre-close time stamp. This arrangement was spawned by a conflict of interest within the bank. The door to this illegal activity was opened by the private client division of Bank of America, which had cultivated Edward Stern in the hopes of establishing a close business relationship with the wealthy Stern family. By cooperating with Canary, Bank of America received commissions from the trades as well as fees from other investments that were made in Bank of America.[9] Although funds often assess penalties for frequent traders, Stern did not pay any penalties; in fact, he received $300 million in financing from Bank of America to

---

[7] The practice of investors directly trading with the mutual fund contrasts trading in closed-end and exchange traded funds, whose investors trade with each other on equity exchanges.

[8] Ian McDonald, "Questions, Answer on the Spitzer Case," *Wall Street Journal* (September 4, 2003) p. C 9.

[9] The broker for Bank of America, Theodore C. Sihpol III, was charged with larceny and securities fraud on September 16 for arranging for the hedge fund to buy shares after 4 P.M. Riva D. Atlas, "Ex-Broker Charged in Criminal Fraud Case," *New York Times* (September 17, 2003), p. C1.

engage in short-term trading strategies.[10] This privileged insider arrangement benefited Canary funds, which rose by 28.5 percent in 2001 and 15 percent in 2002 when the S&P 500 declined by 13 percent and 23 percent, respectively.[11] Settling civil charges that Stern had violated New York law against fraud, false statements, and deception and concealment in securities trading, no wrongdoing was admitted; Stern and Canary paid $10 million in fines and $30 million in restitution, reflecting the estimated $40 million that they had earned from the two activities. Stern also agreed not to trade in mutual funds or manage public investment funds for ten years. Following this settlement, Bank of America fired three of its officials and agreed to make restitution to shareholders for assisting in Canary's activities.

In Stern's scheme, Canary Capital was assisted in its late trading by Security Trust Company of Phoenix. This bank was an important player as a mutual fund intermediary. Only 10 percent of American households purchase mutual fund shares directly; the remainder is bought for them through intermediaries. Security Trust serviced 401(k) plan administrators, brokers, financial advisors, trust companies, banks and others, gathering their orders and matching them with buy and sell orders, sorting and processing the net orders to different mutual fund families at the end of each business day. Security Trust had disguised Canary's orders as pension plan purchases, permitting late day trading, with orders as tardy as 9 P.M. According to the SEC, Stern's hedge fund made $85 million from these trades and paid Security $8.5 million. In addition, Stern's Samaritan Asset Management funds engaged in market timing through Security Trust where the trades were disguised by multiple accounts in Security Trust's name and sub-accounts within accounts for pension funds. When this assisted fraud was revealed, the Comptroller of the Currency, the primary regulator of Security Trust, ordered it closed on November 25, 2003. Three executives—the founder and CEO, the president, and the officer in charge of trading—resigned and faced charges of grand larceny and fraud brought by the New York Attorney General.[12]

The Widening Scandal

"It's like we tapped on the edifice and it crumbled."[13]

The practices of late trading and market timing were far more widespread than anyone had anticipated, although they were apparently known to insiders. Many managers condoned or even encouraged these practices in clear contravention of their public policies. For example, MFS Investment Management, the oldest mutual fund company in the U.S., with $134 billion of funds, permitted market timing while publicly insisting that it did not. The MFS fund prospectuses of January 25, 2001 stated: "MFS Funds do not permit market timing or other excessive trading

---

[10] Both Bank of America and the Canadian Imperial Bank of Commerce have been accused of extensively financing hedge funds to engage in late trading with "total return swaps." Riva D. Atlas, "Trades Backed by Big Banks Draw Interest of Regulators," *New York Times* (January 9, 2004), p. C1 and C4.

[11] Canary started trading in 1998. In 1999, the fund earned a return of 110 percent. This success attracted outside money from wealthy individuals, swelling the size of the fund. Investors were charged a fee of 1.5 percent of the funds, while management took 25 percent of the profits, placing it at the high end of the hedge fund business. Robert Frank, "Now Mutual Funds Under Fire," *Wall Street Journal* (September 4, 2003), p. C1 and C9.

[12] Diana Henriques and Riva Atlas, "Trust Company Is Said to Be Facing Charges in Fund Inquiry," *New York Times* (November 25, 2003), p. C1 and C3 and Diana Henriques and Riva Atlas, "U.S. Closes Mutual Fund Intermediary," *New York Times* (November 26, 2003), p. C1 and C4.

[13] David D. Brown IV, head of the Investment Protection Bureau of the N.Y. Attorney General's office, quoted in Riva D. Atlas, "He's the Other Force in the Fund Investigation," *New York Times* (December 27, 2003), p. C1 and C2.

practices. Excessive, short-term (market timing) trading practices may disrupt portfolio management strategies and harm fund performance. MFS Funds will reject or restrict an investor's purchase orders if there is a history of market timing." But at the same time it sent a memo to wholesale brokers who sold their funds, informing them that MFS Funds: "plan to continue to allow future exchanges even if a pattern of excessive trading has been detected." Ordinary investors were left in the dark about the opportunities for market timing allowed to some traders.[14]

It seemed puzzling that the SEC had missed this problem; thus Spitzer's inquiry created a firestorm. The day after the attorney general's announcement, the SEC sent a letter to all large mutual fund companies, requesting all documents on company policies regarding late trading and market timing. Companies were given until September 15 to comply. In addition, class-action lawyers began to file suits against the companies named by the New York Attorney General.[15]

In his complaint against Stern, Spitzer had cited but not charged Janus Capital Corporation, Strong Management Inc., and Bank One Corporation.[16] The motivation behind these firms' participation in illegal or unethical behavior is unclear, but some had been under pressure in the bear market. Bank One behaved similarly to Bank of America. With low-performing mutual funds, it launched its own hedge fund in 2001, creating a new potential for conflicts of interest. In 2002, it gave Canary a $15 million loan to pursue market timing in exchange for an investment in its own hedge fund. Janus, which had gained a reputation in the bull market for growth funds, was in the doldrums. The firm had been hemorrhaging funds in 2001 and 2002. In an email cited in Spitzer's complaint, the head of Janus' international business, Richard Garland, gave permission for Canary to engage in market timing and stated that "I have no interest in building a business around market timers, but at the same time I do not want to turn away $10m–20m!"[17] Janus Capital responded to pressure from regulators and shareholders by putting in its prospectuses new language that cleared up its rules on short term trading, strictly enforcing limits on "round trip" trades and doubling its fee to 2 percent for shares redeemed within 90 days of purchase. Furthermore, it agreed to make restitution to shareholders and more frequently disclose its holdings of securities. The head of its international division, Richard Garland, who had supervised funds where Canary Capital had engaged in market timing trading, resigned.

Strong Capital Management managed $43 billion in 66 mutual funds, including those in the Invesco Funds Groups. The founder and chairman of Strong Capital and head of the Invesco funds, Richard S. Strong, is one of the richest men in America, worth approximately $800 million. Strong exerted control over this financial group, in which all the funds had the same board, consisting of Strong and five outsiders.[18] Although Strong and his firm had prospered in the boom, Invesco's mutual funds had a mediocre performance and the firm tried to raise

---

[14] Landon Thomas Jr., "Memo Shows MFS Funds Let Favored Clients Trade When Others Couldn't," *New York Times* (December 9, 2003), p. C1 and C4.

[15] Landon Thomas, Jr., "S.E.C Putting Mutual Funds Under Scrutiny on Late Trading", *New York Times* (September 5, 2003), p. C1.

[16] Landon Thomas, Jr., "Big Fine Over Trader's Mutual-Fund Moves," *New York Times* (September 4, 2003), p. C1 and C8. and Randal Smith and Tom Lauricella, "Spitzer Alleges Mutual Funds Allowed Fraudulent Trading," *Wall Street Journal* (September 4, 2003), p. A1.

[17] Ken Brown, Aaron Lucchetti and Carrick Mollenkamp, "How Canary's Song Charmed Firms," *Wall Street Journal* (September 4, 2003), p. C9.

[18] Karen Damato, "Strong Chairman Pledges to Cover Fund Losses," *Wall Street Journal* (October 31, 2003), p. C 15. The directors were paid between $124,000 to $152,000 in 2002.

money through a hedge fund. In a deal with Canary, Strong permitted Canary's hedge fund to trade in and out of its mutual funds for an investment in its hedge fund. In its complaint against Strong, the New York Attorney General alleged that Strong traded in and out shares of his company's funds for his own account and the accounts of his friends and family in order to profit from market timing. These various market timers' investments constituted as much as $900 million of Invesco's $18 billion of assets by the middle of 2002. However, the prospectuses for Invesco funds stated that the company only permitted four exchanges in and out of funds over a 12-month period, although the company retained the right to modify or terminate the exchange policy if it was in the best interests of the shareholders. News of the investigation led to a flight from Strong's mutual fund group, which lost $226 million by the end of November. As a consequence of this pressure and Spitzer's investigation, Strong gave up control of the mutual fund group on December 4, 2003, and resigned as chairman and chief executive of Strong Financial. Strong pledged to reimburse the funds for any financial losses, and Spitzer sought the return of more than $160 million in management fees earned by executives on funds traded by market timers.[19]

Late trading and market timing induced by conflicts of interest were far more widespread than even the New York Attorney General's office had initially believed. The SEC, other state attorneys general, and even financial firms themselves uncovered many more abuses. Alliance Capital Management suspended two officials for helping Canary engage in market timing, while Prudential Securities dismissed 12 brokers and managers for facilitating market timing. When Steven B. Markovitz, a trader at the Millenium Partners hedge fund, pleaded guilty to late trading, Merrill Lynch followed up by firing three brokers for permitting Millenium Partners to engage in market timing with its funds. At Fred Alger Management, three officers were fired for market timing and late trading and its vice chairman, James Patrick Connelly, Jr., was sentenced to one to three years in prison and fined $400,000 for tampering with evidence sought by the New York Attorney General. Citigroup and Bear Sterns began their own investigations, leading Citigroup to fire five employees and Bear Sterns to fire six.

At Putnam Investments, the fifth largest mutual fund company, two fund managers were fired for making personal trades in funds they managed. The SEC filed suit against Putnam and the managers, arguing that the company knew that they were engaged in this activity, withheld the information from the outside directors, and failed to take actions to stop it.[20] When the SEC settled with Putnam, Spitzer criticized the settlement as feeble; however, the market punished Putnam further. The state treasurer of Massachusetts said it would fire Putnam from the management of its $1.7 billion pension funds, and its action has been followed by other public funds.[21] The huge California Public Employees' Retirement System pulled out $1.2 billion. By mid-November 2003, Putnam's assets had fallen 7.6 percent since October 2002.[22]

---

[19] Riva Atlas and David Barboza, "Funds Scandal Hits Invesco and Founder of Strong," *New York Times* (December 3, 2003), p. C1 and C4. Riva D. Atlas, "Spitzer Vows Legal Action Against Head of Fund Family," *New York Times* (October 30, 2003), p. C1 and C4.

[20] Gretchen Morgenson, "At Putnam, the Buck Stays Put in a Pocket," *New York Times* (November 2, 2003), Section 3, p.1. The CEO of Putnam, Lawrence Lasser, had $100 million in bonuses over the past 5 years, and restricted stock awards worth $22 million, $15 million in deferred compensation, while receiving $200,000 a year as a trustee of the mutual funds.

[21] John Hechinger and David Armstrong, "Putnam Says It Was Subpoenaed," *Wall Street Journal* (October 31, 2003), p. C1 and C2.

[22] Riva D. Atlas, "Janus Tightens Trading Policies; Calpers Pulls Out of Putnam," *New York Times* (November 19, 2003), p. C1 and C8.

In another headline case, two of the founders of Pilgrim Baxter & Associates, which managed PBHG funds—Gary Pilgrim, CEO, and Harold Baxter, President—resigned on November 13, 2003. With his wife and two friends, Pilgrim had created a hedge fund that made money from market timing trade in PBHG funds, including ones for which he served as advisor, earning him $4 million. Baxter also allowed a brokerage firm run by a friend to trade in and out of PBHG's funds and shared non-public information about the portfolio with the brokerage. Seven days later, both the SEC and the New York Attorney General filed fraud charges against Pilgrim and Baxter.[23]

The Costs of Market Timing

Although late trading and market timing were news to the public, these practices were not new, even if the willingness of the management to suborn the interests of their customers may have dramatically increased in the past few years. If market timing traders can move funds rapidly in and out, often not paying the published penalties in fund rules, they dilute the value of the funds and increase the transactions costs for the other fund investors. In addition, if these forms of arbitrage increase, managers will have to keep more cash on hand to handle the frequent payouts. Higher holdings of cash will reduce the amount of funds that can be invested, thus lowering the performance of the fund.

While the practices of market timing and late trading have recently received enormous media attention, there is no data on the actual amount of this arbitrage that has taken place. Instead, our best estimates of these operations are found in academic studies that examine the potential arbitrage opportunities for market timing arising from NAV predictability. Following the conditions of the late 1990s, the most recent study by Zitzewitz estimated the potential excess returns from market timing, assuming that arbitrageurs acted on the expected next day fund returns arising from NAV predictability and traded up to 4 P.M. and made the maximum transactions.[24] Predictability arises because, for example, American economic news affects both American and Japanese equities, making movements in the S&P500 a potential predictor of Japanese stocks, given the time difference in the opening of markets. Generally, foreign stocks respond to common news that affects U.S. stock prices contemporaneously or with a one-day lag. Out-of-sample predictions for NAVs were made using the Chicago Mercantile Exchange Nikkei 225 to capture information after the close of the Tokyo market for Japanese funds, the S&P500 after 11 A.M. to obtain information after the close of European markets for European funds, and the post-2 P.M. S&P500 change and the Russell 2000 24–hour change for information on domestic small cap funds. Zitzewitz found very high returns. The annualized excess returns for international funds was 58 percent for Japanese funds, 39 percent for European funds, 20 percent for domestic mid- and small-cap equity funds, and 8 percent for equity-debt hybrid funds. The increased recent market volatility, amplifying arbitrage opportunities, more than doubled the returns.

Using these estimates, Zitzewitz calculated the dilution or losses to long-term shareholders from market timing arbitrage. For 1998–2001, he found that regional international equity funds lost 1.6 percent of assets per year, general equity

---

[23] Floyd Norris, "Manager Prospered as Investors Suffered," *New York Times* (November 14, 2003).p. C1. Reed Abelson and Riva Atlas, "Founds of Fund Group Accused of Fraud," *New York Times* (November 21, 2003), p. C1 and C8.

[24] Eric Zitzewitz, "Who Cares About Shareholders? Arbitrage-Proofing Mutual Funds," *Journal of Law, Economics & Organization* 19:2 (2003), pp. 245–280.

international funds 81 basis points, specialty equity funds 33 points, and mid- and small-cap U.S. equity funds 12 basis points. Scaling his sample to represent all funds, total dilution for 2001 was revealed to be $4.9 billion, of which $4.3 billion was accounted for by international funds.

These results are similar to earlier estimates by Greene and Hodges who found a dilution of 50 basis points from February 1998 to June 1999.[25] Goetzmann, Ivkovic, and Rouwenhorst also examined the daily returns from a simple market timing strategy against 391 U.S.-based international open-end equity funds from 1990 to 1998. They compared a simple strategy buying and selling funds based on the movement of the S&P500. Using closing prices from foreign exchanges at the end of the U.S. trading day induced a substantial amount of predictability in the fund returns and yielded very large excess returns. They calculated that over 1990–1998, this opportunity would magnify returns from a buy and hold strategy by 20 percent per year while having only 70 percent of the funds volatility. The net wealth transfer from this potential market timing was estimated to be $1.1 billion or 0.44 percent of funds in a 17-month period ending June 1998.[26]

These studies, covering only market timing, reveal that potential losses to long-term investors are extremely high. Zitzewitz and Goetzmann, Ivkovic, and Rouwenhorst point out that current redemption fees are not sufficient to block this activity. Even if market timing is limited to a few "round trips" between cash and funds, the excess returns remain quite high. Designing the appropriate solutions to constrain these forms of costly arbitrage requires an understanding of the incentive and governance problems that have allowed them to persist and grow.

The Agency Problems of Mutual Fund Directors and Managers

Mutual funds face an important agency problem. Investors want their mutual funds to maximize risk-adjusted returns, while mutual fund managers seek to maximize their profits. The free rider problem created by many thousands of shareholders exacerbates the difficulty of adequately monitoring mutual fund management. Thus, the task has been delegated to the boards of directors of mutual funds, which in turn poses a new agency problem between investors and their directors. Mutual fund boards consist of either inside directors who are affiliated with the firm sponsoring the fund or the investment advisor and outside directors who are supposed to be independent. The failure of directors to discover and control the spiraling problems of market timing has suggested a broad failure of governance.

Although the crisis is recent, there are some long-standing critics of mutual fund governance. One of the most outspoken critics is John C. Bogle, founder of the Vanguard Group of mutual funds. He blamed the recent problems on the funds' boards: "The Investment Company Act says that the interests of fund shareholders must be placed ahead of all others, but the interests of managers have taken precedence."[27] Bogle claimed that when funds do poorly, there are rarely any management changes or fee reductions, only fee increases. The complaint that the interests of the investment managers or advisors often supersede those of shareholders is a common one. One securities law expert, Lewis Lowenfels, argues that "Under existing law, the investment advisor is able to exercise a pervasive

---

[25] Jason T. Greene and Charles W. Hodges, "The Dilution Impact of Daily Fund Flows on Open-End Mutual Funds," *Journal of Financial Economics* 65 (2002), pp. 131–158.

[26] William N. Goetzmann, Zoran Ivkovic and K. Geert Rouwenhorst, "Day Trading International Mutual Funds: Evidence and Policy Solutions," *Journal of Financial and Quantitative Analysis* Vol 36, No. 3 (September 2001), pp. 287-309.

[27] Gretchen Morgenson, "Who's Watching Your Fund Manager" *New York Times* (September 14, 2003), Section 3, p. l.

influence over the board."[28] Lowenfels believes that directors are spread too thinly and claims that "mutual fund directors sit on too many boards, and they are paid too much money for the time they can devote to each individual portfolio." [29]

If mutual fund managers can pursue their interests rather than secure those of shareholders, it is because management fees do not align investors and management interests. The management companies or advisors are usually compensated by a fee that is a fixed percentage of assets, creating an incentive to increase total assets rather than maximize investors' risk-adjusted returns. The ability of managers to pursue higher compensation via asset growth is facilitated by the behavior of mutual fund investors. Examining the determinants of mutual fund choice, Sirri and Tufano concluded that "mutual fund consumers chase returns, flocking to funds with the highest recent returns, though failing to flee poor performers."[30] Studies of the mutual fund industry have shown that investors focus on limited information and strongly respond to mutual fund rankings by such publications as Morningstar Mutual Fund Services, Lipper Analytical Services, *Business Week, Barron's,* and *Forbes* that measure annual performances at the end of the calendar year. These studies have documented that the response of investors to rankings produces a strongly non-linear relationship between past performance and inflows to funds.[31] Higher performance relative to industry benchmarks produces significant fund inflows. As differential performance increases, these responses weaken, as "sophisticated" investors have already entered, but then there is an even greater inflow at returns exceeding 15 percent of the benchmark as "uninformed" investors respond. Competition in the mutual fund industry thus becomes a tournament where managers focus on rankings.[32]

In this tournament, the strong performance-flow relationship enables managers to manipulate the riskiness of their portfolios to adjust performance and hence inflows, total assets and compensation. Chevalier and Ellison found empirical evidence for 1982–1992 that if firms were below the benchmark by the end of September, the riskiness of a fund's portfolio was raised to seek a higher return, while if the fund was ahead, firms tended to lock in the gains by indexing the market. The risk of a portfolio could be raised by changing the fund's security holdings or altering it synthetically with derivative positions. Examining the period 1980–1991, Brown, Harlow, and Starks provided additional evidence that tournament "losers" increase portfolio risk relative to "winners," with an even stronger response in the last five years of their sample. In addition, Chevalier and Ellison discovered that the non-linear relationship between fund performance and fund flows was stronger for younger firms. Given the flood of new mutual funds in the past ten years, these findings imply that there were greater incentives for manipulation within the industry.

These studies on management behavior have implications for the willingness of managers to countenance market timing and even late trading activities. To the degree that market timing activities swell the size of a fund's total assets, as they apparently did in the headline cases, managers with compensation based on the

---

[28] Morgensen, (September 14, 2003), Section 3, p. 8.

[29] Morgensen, (September 14, 2003), Section 3, p. 10.

[30] Erik R. Sirri and Peter Tufano, "Costly Search and Mutual Fund Flows," *Journal of Finance* 53 (1998), pp. 1589–1622.

[31] See Sirri and Tufano, Richard A. Ippolito, "Consumer Reaction to Measures of Poor Quality: Evidence from the Mutual Fund Industry," *Journal of Law and Economics* 35 (April 1992), pp. 45-70, and Judith Chevalier and Glenn Ellison, "Risk Taking by Mutual Funds as a Response to Incentives," *Journal of Political Economy* 105:6 (December 1997), pp. 1167–1200.

[32] Keith C. Brown, W.V. Harlow, and Laura T. Starks, "Of Tournaments and Temptations: An Analysis of Managerial Incentives in the Mutual Fund Industry," *Journal of Finance* 51:1 (March 1996), pp. 85–110.

fund's total assets had a strong temptation to condone these unethical and illegal activities. When the market declined and there was no growth or contraction of assets, managerial income would decline unless management could find a means to expand assets. The expansion of the industry in the late 1990s created more young funds with an even greater predisposition to manipulate performance. Given the increased incentives for managers to slight shareholder interest, directors needed to redouble their efforts to monitor and restrain them.

To better align the incentives between shareholders and managers, a growing number of mutual funds have begun to use incentive fees to compensate management. Although they accounted for only 108 funds in 1999, mutual funds using incentive fees held 10.5 percent of assets and were the fastest growing group. As regulated by the Investment Company Act of 1940, these incentive fees must be "fulcrum" fees, centered on an index (most often the S&P500) where there are increased fees for superior performance. These schemes include a base fixed fee and upper limits on the variable component. Encouraging managers to focus on returns rather than asset growth seems to enhance performance and lower expenses. Like non-incentive funds, these mutual funds take more risk when they under perform and decrease risk when they do well to lock in their success. Where incentive fees are used, Elton, Gruber, and Blake found that managers who are principals or long-term employees of the management company have more generous incentives than external mangers, most likely reflecting the greater ability of internal managers to set their own compensation.[33] Internal managers are less likely to be replaced when they have poor fund performance and thus take higher risk. Elton, Gruber, and Blake concluded that investors are better off with internal managers in incentive funds because even though expenses are higher, they produce higher returns. However, incentive-fee funds do take more risk than other funds and they increase risk after a period of poor performance. The flow of funds into this type of fund indicates that the market accepts the combination of risk and return. Altogether, these results suggest the mutual fund boards of directors may find incentive fees to be a superior form of contract to align shareholder and manager interests.

The most important legal obligation of a mutual fund's board of directors is to negotiate and approve of contracts with the management, setting managers' compensation and shareholders' fees. The independent directors have a special role as a majority of the independent directors must approve of all advisory and distribution contracts and the fees. While boards have the right to terminate a contract with management, this decision is very rare, and boards have never removed a sponsoring firm.[34] The fund sponsors, whom independent directors are supposed to monitor and with whom they negotiate fees, usually select the initial independent board members for a new fund. High compensation and selection by sponsors are blamed for inhibiting boards from exercising independence in setting fees and policies. Furthermore, directors have little contact with shareholders and board elections are almost never publicly contested.

The Investment Company Act originally required that each mutual fund have a board with at least 40 percent independent directors who could not be affiliated with the sponsor, underwriter, or broker. The SEC's decision to increase the independent share to 50 percent in 2001, before the outbreak of the mutual fund scandals, represented a major change, reflecting its concern about insider control.

---

[33] Edwin J. Elson, Martin J. Gruber, and Christopher R. Blake, "Incentive Fees and Mutual Funds," *Journal of Finance* 58:2 (April 2003), pp. 779–804.

[34] Tufano and Sevick, p. 325.

Critics have asked that there be more disclosure of directors' backgrounds, attendance, and what committees they head. Some contend that the definition of independence is not tight enough, as they currently allow, for example, a former investment advisor to become a director after only two years.

Boards vary considerably in structure; typically they have a dozen or fewer members and usually meet four times a year. Given the infrequency of the meetings, outside directors may be at a disadvantage relative to inside directors who work for the sponsoring firm or investment advisor. Critics also complain that directors cannot adequately monitor a large number of funds. It is common for individuals to serve on the boards of many funds sponsored by one group, such as Fidelity or Merrill Lynch, thus increasing their compensation. For the 50 largest fund sponsors in 1992, there were 635 persons filling 10,162 independent seats, with independents occupying 71 percent of all seats. For example, in 2003, the directors of Fidelity oversaw 270 funds and directors at Putnam oversaw 119 portfolios. At the Bank of America, all its funds had as their chairman A. Max Walker, who was 81 and had overseen the funds for more than 30 years. Seven of the 11 trustees were independent, including Walker.[35]

Compensation for directors may also tend to align their interests with those of the advisors rather than the shareholders. Compensation appears to have increased with asset growth, which has led to charges that directors look favorably upon managers engaged in riskier strategies. The highest compensation in the mutual fund industry was paid to the trustees of Putnam Funds, followed by those at Merrill Lynch Asset Management, Morgan Stanley, and Dreyfus Funds. It has been alleged that many boards have kept their high levels of pay or even increased them while the performance of the funds declined in the bear market. One study by Morningstar found that higher fund costs were associated with higher directors' salaries.[36] Although no study has examined whether these higher costs are possibly associated with better monitoring or more complex portfolios, it is noteworthy that Putnam had the highest compensation and failed to identify the conflict of interest problems.

While critics of mutual fund directors claim that they cannot adequately discipline management, there is empirical evidence that supports the view that stronger, more independent boards do, in fact, help to control the behavior of managers. Tufano and Sevick found that shareholder fees are lower when boards are smaller, have a larger share of independent directors, and have directors who sit on a large fraction of the mutual fund groups' other boards.[37] However, Tufano and Sevick also uncovered some limited evidence that independent directors who are paid higher fees approve of higher shareholder fees. They cautioned that while this empirical evidence generally supports the idea that the greater the independence of a board, the more it will act in the interest of investors, they cannot rule out that sponsors with certain fee targets may select specific board structures.

In another study, Zitzewitz found econometric evidence that funds with a larger proportion of outside directors and lower expense ratios were more likely to impose short-term trading fees or fair-value pricing.[38] Thus, managers facing more outside directors and with smaller expense funds available had more pressure to act on behalf of fund investors and limit costly arbitrage. As an example,

---

[35] Patrick McGeehan, "Reform Knocks. Will Funds Answer?" *New York Times* (September 7, 2003), p. C1.

[36] Morgenson, p. 8.

[37] Tufano and Sevick, p. 321–322.

[38] Zitzewitz, p. 275–276.

Zitzewitz pointed out that Vanguard, a low-expense-ratio fund family, was among the first fund groups to implement redemption fees and fair-value pricing. Before the scandals erupted, some limited attempts were adopted by funds to control arbitrage, with about 30 percent of international funds having some short-term trading fees by the end of 2001, and some very limited fair-value pricing. This evidence on mutual funds' boards is generally in line with conclusions from empirical studies of traditional corporate boards that more independent boards show a greater disposition and ability to manage the conflicts of interest between managers and investors.

Solutions?
Market Discipline and Governance

When the market became aware that conflicts of interest were being exploited, there were rapid withdrawals of funds by individuals and institutional investors. The problem with market discipline by investors is that the information needed to monitor investment managers is difficult for them to unearth. Waiting for prosecutors to uncover problems is not an efficient means for generally solving the informational asymmetry between shareholders and fund managers. Monitoring of managers should be the task of directors, and the scandals revealed a failure of governance.

While critics have often alleged that boards of directors are nearly powerless to induce management to act in the interest of shareholders, the empirical evidence reveals that boards do respond and that greater independence increases both discipline of management and moves to limit costly arbitrage. Reconciling this evidence with the headline cases where directors appear to have completely failed suggests that boards are best at making gradual adjustments, but that events in the industry beginning in the late 1990s moved very rapidly, outpacing board responses. These circumstances emphasize the importance of a responsive legal and regulatory system to identify and prosecute exceptional cases while enhancing the powers and independence of mutual fund boards.

The number and independence of directors thus remains a prime concern. In Senate hearings on November 18, 2003, William H. Donaldson, chairman of the SEC, told Congress that the SEC had formulated new proposals to be considered on January 14, 2004, to raise the share of independent directors for mutual funds from 50 to 75 percent. The mutual fund board chairman would be required to be independent and portfolio managers would be ordered to report their personal trading in funds they manage. Directors would also be obligated to perform annual evaluations with their own independent staff (with a chief compliance officer reporting directly to the board), and funds would have to offer more details about their fees.[39]

These changes would force a major shift in the compensation of some mutual fund boards, and the proposals have been widely criticized in the industry. The Investment Company Institute (ICI) pointed out that many of the funds already had some of the proposed features and some troubled funds already had independent chairmen.[40] Yet, the empirical evidence available emphasizes that

---

[39] There appears to be some hostility toward even these modest market-oriented reforms. Senator Richard Shelby, head of the Senate banking committee, said he is not convinced of the need for new laws. Furthermore, Secretary of the Treasury John Snow and Fed Chairman Alan Greenspan have tried to discourage new regulations, cautioning that any new requirements should not damage the market and or increase costs.

[40] Stephen Labaton, "SEC Outlines Plan for Tighter Control of Mutual Funds," *New York Times* (November 19, 2003), p. C1 and C8.

greater board independence should promote shareholder interest. However, these reforms need to be complemented with changes in some of the basic rules governing the design of mutual funds to control the basic opportunities for arbitrage.

Deadlines, Redemption Fees, and Fair Value

The design of mutual funds, where shares are traded at one time—4 P.M. EST—each day, probably guaranteed equal treatment of all investors fifty years ago. But the much more rapid transmission of information and the capacity to execute trades has created opportunities for exploitation of this rule. There are three possible solutions for ensuring that all investors are treated equally: hardening the 4 P.M. rule, raising the costs of redemption, and using "fair-value" measures to set prices.

After the first disclosures of late trading, the Investment Company Institute responded on October 30, 2003, by recommending a hardening of the 4 P.M. rule to eliminate late trading. Until the scandal broke, funds had accepted delivery of orders until as late as midnight from banks, brokers, and retirement account administrators who claimed to have stopped accepting orders from customers at 4 P.M. The scandals proved that these intermediaries were not abiding by their promises. Consequently, the ICI proposed that 4 P.M. be the deadline, not for orders to be in the hands of brokerages and 401(k) programs, but for orders to be delivered to the fund companies.[41] The SEC essentially took up this recommendation when it voted unanimously to propose a rule that sets a strict 4 P.M. cutoff for trades. Any trade received by a fund, its transfer agent, or clearing agency after 4 P.M. EST would receive the price set on the next trading day. This proposed rule will go into effect early in 2004 after a brief comment period.

The proposal was endorsed by the Secretary of the Treasury John W. Snow and William J. McDonough, chairman of PCAOB, but it was attacked by West Coast firms and employee benefits advisers as well as some individuals on Wall Street. The American Benefits Council complained that the strict rule would mean that 401(k) plan participants would be forced to trade a day late because of the administrative work that is required to process a trade. These investors and those served by brokers would be at a disadvantage, as they would be unable to trade at the same price as investors who place orders directly with mutual funds. Whether a one-day delay is a serious problem for most individuals who are long-term investors is open to question; and the SEC argued that the benefits outweighed the costs.

In response to the proposal of a hard 4 P.M. deadline for customer orders, Fidelity Investments and the National Securities Clearing Corporation have explored the possibility of creating a clearing house for trades where all orders would be delivered by 4 P.M. A clearing house would be a neutral party that would handle the time stamps to verify that all orders arrived promptly at 4 P.M..[42] Hardening the 4 P.M. deadline and establishing a clearing house, coupled with improved monitoring by directors and the SEC, would help to reduce the ability of the unscrupulous to conduct late trading, although there would be some as yet unmeasured costs placed on investors.

To address the problem of market timing, the ICI suggested further changes in its October 30th report. The ICI called for all funds to impose a minimum 2 percent redemption fee on shares sold within five days of purchase. Until now, firms

---

[41] Karen Damato and Tom Lauricella, "Mutual Funds Vow to Fix Their Clocks," *Wall Street Journal* (October 31, 2003), p. C1 and C15.

[42] Diana B. Henriques, "Fidelity Seeks a Clearinghouse for Trades," *New York Times* (December 26, 2003), p. C1 and C3.

have had discretionary authority to charge such fees when shares are sold within 60 or 90 days of purchase. As market timers hold a fund for at most a few days, the ICI believed this would discourage many forms of market timing.[43] The recommendation was followed by an announcement on February 11, 2004, that the SEC would consider mandatory redemption fees on investors who quickly trade in and out of a fund.[44]

The problem of raising redemption fees is that higher fees reduce the attractiveness of mutual funds to investors, weakening their advantages or investment in individual stocks or exchanged traded funds. According to the estimates of Zitzewitz, the 2 percent redemption fee would not eliminate market timing.[45] For the most profitable arbitrage against Asia/Pacific funds, a zero redemption fee permits 56 "round trips" with an annualized excess return of 54.7 percent. A 2 percent redemption fee would lower expected round trips to 6 with annualized excess return of 15.7 percent. Given expected market volatility, to cut the trips to 1 per year with a return of 4.7 percent, a redemption fee of 3.5 percent would be required. For other mutual funds subject to market timing, a 2 percent redemption fee would eliminate virtually all arbitrage. An alternative solution, sometimes employed by funds, is to restrict the annual number of redemptions, but even a limit of three allows for profitable arbitrage. Redemption fees can work, but they are a costly instrument for investors. If the dilution caused by market timing is annually equal to 1 to 2 percent of the market value of funds, redemption fees of 2 percent appear high especially if they are applied to funds not susceptible to market timing.

Both "hard" deadlines and high redemption fees do not directly tackle the real problem, the short-term mis-pricing of mutual funds that creates the illegal or unethical arbitrage opportunities. A direct method to prevent market timing from using stale prices is "fair-value" pricing. Among its proposals, the SEC is considering requiring mutual funds to adopt "fair value," correcting stale prices from closed Japanese markets with updated information.[46] This practice is sometimes employed by Fidelity and Vanguard, which appear to be less vulnerable to market timing.

Fair pricing may move toward setting the right price, but given that it is judgmental and requires adequate monitoring, it may be subject to abuse as well. Some proposals suggested simple partial fair value methods, using fair-value pricing only on days when there are extreme movements or marking foreign assets to similar American ones (mark-to-ADR pricing). In several examples, Zitzewitz shows that these would still leave ample arbitrage opportunities. In general, he believes that even with 24-hour trading, it is unlikely for arbitrage opportunities via market timing to disappear because current after-hours trading on foreign exchanges has much less liquidity and hence some staleness to prices. Goetzmann, Ivkovic and Rouwenhorst find that fair pricing to improve NAV prices, by using close substitutes such as the information in the Nikkei 225 futures contract traded in Chicago, would be helpful but point out that a complete solution would require fully taking the predictable portion of the next day's NAV and including it in the current day's NAV. The ideal solution would be to ensure that the prices at which shareholders trade embody all the available information, but given that NAV prices are constructed out of market prices, they may always be imperfect to some degree.

[43] Karen Damato and Tom Lauricella, "Mutual Funds Vow to Fix Their Clocks," *Wall Street Journal* (October 31, 2003), p. C1 and C15.

[44] Stephen Labaton, "SEC Proposes Rules to End Late Trading In Mutual Funds," *New York Times* (December 4, 2003), p. C1 and C10.

[45] Zitzewitz, pp. 265-268.

[46] "The scandal spreads," *The Economist* (October 11, 2003), p.75.

Late trading may be virtually eliminated by harder deadlines, a clearing house, and improved monitoring of management. A major reduction in market timing is more difficult to accomplish, as high redemption fees or limited trading potentially impose high penalties on all investors, while failing to eliminate the practice that dilutes shareholder value. The direct approach of fair-value pricing can help to eliminate the problem at a lower cost. It is most effective for extreme values and where there are suitable markets to obtain information on NAV predictability, but there is no method for preventing some staleness in NAV prices. Before raising redemption fees higher, reform of governance and broader adoption of fair-value pricing are needed to limit market timing arbitrage.

Transparency and Fees

While the price of many financial products—a fee or an interest rate—is easy to observe, it is claimed by many critics that pricing of mutual funds is clouded by an asymmetry of information between the funds and their customers. Based on the empirical studies, it is argued that most investors do not pay attention to costs when selecting funds, but instead choose funds on the basis of their recent performance. If customers have a hard time assessing the true cost of investing in mutual funds, it would provide an opportunity for managers to exploit conflicts of interests to their own benefit or that of other customers at the expense of the mutual fund investors.

The fee schedules of mutual funds are based on the three types of shares, Classes A, B, and C. Originally in the postwar period, most funds were sold by brokers. Brokers were paid an upfront charge or a "load" for their services. Until the 1970s, the typical "front-end load" was 8.5 percent of the money invested. The shares of funds where fees are paid as "front-end loads" are termed Class A shares. Today, most front-end loads are 4 to 5 percent with a 0.25 percent annual fee. Investors may instead pay a "deferred load" if they buy Class B shares. B shares charge no initial commission, but have an annual marketing fee called a 12b-1 fee. When a B share is redeemed, there is a fee starting at 5 percent of assets and declining at 1 percent a year until it converts to an A share. The 12b-1 fee originated in the 1970s when assets of mutual funds were contracting in the bear market. The SEC had opposed the idea of using investors' money in the funds to pay for sales and distribution costs after they had paid their loads, but it was argued that additional marketing efforts could spawn fund growth and lower costs by economies of scale. The SEC was convinced and in 1980 permitted these 12b-1 fees to pay for distribution and advertising costs. They rose from 0.25 percent of assets per year to as high as 1 percent. Although some of this increase may be explained by a decline in the up-front loads paid, there is considerable concern that management may have been able to exploit these rising fees.[47] Beginning in the 1980s, Class C shares appeared. These shares are issued by "no-load" funds, which have only a 0.25 percent of assets a year fee to cover the 12b-1 service costs.

These fees are intended not simply to cover the costs of operating the mutual fund but also to manage redemptions. If there are fewer redemptions, mutual fund returns will be higher because managers will be able to reduce their cash holdings needed to pay out redemptions. Load fees and redemption fees operate differently to deter redemptions. Front-end loads are used to induce investors to self select into funds where there are few redemptions. In general, redemption fees are more

---

[47] Christopher Oster, "Critic of Fund Fess Was Once Their Advocate," *Wall Street Journal* (January 9, 2004), p. C1 and C15.

successful at dissuading redemptions than front-end fees are at discriminating between different investors.[48]

In addition to fees, costs to customers include expenses. Expenses include management fees paid to the fund company for picking securities, administration fees paid to lawyers, accountants, and board members, and insurance premiums. Expense charges as a percentage of assets range from a high among the 25 largest funds of 1.69 percent for Alliance to Vanguard's .28 percent. Vanguard's costs are low because the fund management company is owned by the funds and provides its service at cost, while the publicly held asset management companies like Alliance are not. The ICI claims that costs of owning stock funds fell from 2.26 percent in 1980 to 1.28 percent in 2001, but the structure of fees is sufficiently complex that many are skeptical as trading costs from commissions are not included. Bogle of Vanguard claims the current cost is actually 2.7 percent.[49]

Recent revelations suggest that there has been considerable exploitation of the information asymmetry. Many brokers apparently failed to give appropriate fee discounts to customers. After the SEC and NASD began investigation of Merrill Lynch, the company began its own study of purchases of Class A shares of mutual funds made since January 1, 2001. Merrill Lynch found that customers did not receive appropriate discounts in 70,000 cases when their purchases were large enough to exceed break points for reduced charges and agreed to reimburse $11 million to fund buyers.[50]

Investors also appear to have been largely unaware of another cost, "shelf space" payments made by mutual funds to brokerage firms to push their funds. These revenue-sharing payments are legal if they are properly disclosed. Although this information should appear in prospectuses, it is argued that the language is opaque.[51] The Edward D. Jones & Co., which has the largest brokerage network in the U.S., received an estimated $100 million a year from Putnam and six other fund companies. Jones gave these funds huge attention; its brokers were provided with information almost exclusively about these funds. The seven fund companies accounted for 90 to 95 percent of Jones' sales.[52] The practice is thought to have become more common in the 1990s, and the largest fifty mutual funds annually pay $1.5 billion in revenue-sharing payments to brokers.

In a similar case, the SEC charged that Morgan Stanley's customers did not know about shelf space payments or that they were coming out of their funds. On November 17, 2003, Morgan Stanley agreed to pay $50 million to settle civil charges by the SEC that it paid its brokers more when they sold its own mutual funds. In addition, Morgan Stanley was accused of steering customers to funds that gave Morgan stock trading business.[53]

The discovery at Morgan Stanley led the SEC to open an investigation into this practice in 15 firms. The SEC discovered that mutual funds commonly steered the trading of securities in their portfolios to brokerage houses that promoted their funds in exchange for their trading business. It should be cautioned that given the

[48] Tarun Chordia, "The Structure of Mutual Fund Charges," *Journal of Financial Economics* 41 (1996), pp. 3–39.

[49] Christopher Oster and Karen Damato, "Expenses Become Burning Issue But Increased Disclosure Alone May Not Be Enough for Investors," *Wall Street Journal* (December 11, 2003), C1 and C9.

[50] Patrick McGeehan, "Merrill Will Reimburse Fund Buyers $11 Million," *New York Times* (December 4, 2003), p. C10.

[51] The language used by Putnam in its prospectuses mentions that it may "pay concessions to dealers that satisfy certain criteria established from time to time by Putnam Retail Management relating to increasing net sales of shares of the Putnam funds over prior periods, and certain other factors." Quoted in Laura Johannes and John Hechinger, "Why a Brokerage Giant Pushes Some Mediocre Mutual Funds," *Wall Street Journal* (January 9, 2004), p. A1 and A5.

[52] Johannes and Hechinger, (January 9, 2004), p. A1 and A5.

[53] Floyd Norris, "Is the Mutual Fund Issue Abuses, or Is It Fees?" *New York Times* (November 19, 2003), p. C1 and C8.

huge number of mutual funds, some of which are similar in character, salesmen would naturally provide selected information to customers. Sirri and Tufano pointed out that customers may prefer to purchase funds within groups like Merrill Lynch Asset Management or Fidelity because it lowers search costs.[54] However, in many cases, it appears that investors were not adequately informed of conflicts of interest. The SEC study found that 14 of 15 Wall Street brokerage houses had received cash payments from the funds for promotion of their shares, and 10 of 15 had revenue-sharing payments in the form of commissions for trading stocks for the funds. Typical payments for "shelf space" at the brokerage were payments from 0.05 to 0.40 percent of the sales and up to 0.25 percent of the value of the investors' assets managed by the broker. Thus, for every $100,000 of new sales, a broker would receive a payment of $50 to $400 plus $250 every year for which the investment remained in the funds. According to the SEC, only half of the brokers disclosed their revenue-sharing arrangements, and those that did frequently did not provide adequate disclosure.[55]

Several solutions have been proposed to solve the information asymmetry between investors and mutual fund salesmen. Increased disclosure/greater transparency have been favored by many critics. In Senate testimony, William Donaldson, chairman of the SEC, said that his agency would promote more transparency on funds' expenses and commissions. The SEC thus continued its traditional emphasis on disclosure with enhanced rules for ensuring that investors are fully aware of any possible conflict of interest, leaving the market to discipline any firms that seek to exploit any conflicts of interest.

An alternative solution is to regulate or control the fees, that is, the imposition of a form a price controls. Opposed by the SEC, New York Attorney General Spitzer has sought to introduce a fee reduction solution in settlements with individual firms.[56] The first of Spitzer's targets for this approach was Alliance. When extensive market timing was discovered, the head of Alliance's mutual fund sales group, a portfolio manager, and the head of hedge-fund sales were asked to resign. Then, Spitzer turned his attention to Alliance's fees, which were the highest among the top 25 firms. Alliance was accused of charging its shareholders' advisory fees that were six times what it charged its institutional clients for essentially the same service. On December 16, 2003, Alliance agreed, as part of a settlement with the New York Attorney General's office, to cut its management fees by an average of 20 percent for the next five years and pay $250 million to reimburse investors. Spitzer promised to push for further fee reductions at other firms and viewed this forced reduction as an inducement to other firms to match the cuts.[57] The Attorney General's office argued that the fee reduction was necessary to prevent fund managers from recouping the fines from shareholders, emphasizing that the cost of cleaning up the industry would not be borne by the investing public.[58]

Spitzer's fee initiative provoked criticism that he was interfering with the free market and that disclosure was the appropriate remedy. Coerced fee reductions set a dangerous precedent. Ad hoc, firm by firm settlements would create a highly uneven playing field for the mutual fund industry. Given the great diversity of

---

[54] Sirri and Tufano, p. 33.

[55] Stephen Labaton, "S.E.C. Has Found Payoffs in Sales of Mutual Funds," *New York Times* (January 14, 2004), p. A1 and C2.

[56] Tom Lauricella, Monica Langley and Susan Pulliam, "Alliance Capital Offers Fee Cut As Part of Proposed Settlement: Terms of Deal Split SEC, Spitzer," *Wall Street Journal* (December 11, 2003), pp. C1.

[57] Riva D. Atlas, "In Settlement, Alliance Agrees to Cut Fees," *New York Times* (December 17, 2003), p. C1 and C2.

[58] Christopher Oster, "Fund Investors Face Higher Post-Scandal Costs," *Wall Street Journal* (December 31, 2003), p. A1 and A2.

mutual funds, no one fee structure would be appropriate; and, as elsewhere, price controls would be a very poor policy tool for the problems of the mutual funds.

Regulatory Oversight and Enforcement

One of the astonishing aspects of the mutual fund scandal was that regulators seemed to have either overlooked or ignored the festering problems. This failure allowed Spitzer to charge in, and as he bluntly put it: "The regulators who were supposed to have been watching this industry were asleep at the switch. And I'm going to pull that switch."[59] While the SEC may have overlooked problems in the mutual funds business while pursuing more high profile problems, many former officials were astonished. Arthur Levitt, former chairman of the SEC during the Clinton administration, admitted: "I probably worried about funds less than insider trading, accounting issues and fair disclosure to investors," but conceded "I believe this is the worst scandal we've seen in 50 years and I can't say that I saw it coming."[60]

Critics from Lynn Turner, former chief accountant of the SEC, to John Bogle, founder of Vanguard, have argued that the SEC was captured by the Investment Company Institute, which has been able to exert its influence over writing the rules governing mutual funds. In many ways, the ICI had more expertise and influence with a budget of $30 million and a staff of 170, with over 20 who worked on regulatory issues and 10 on legislative issues. Levitt tried to double the size of his examination unit overseeing the industry, but Congress repeatedly refused; and more recently, the industry beat back efforts to have executives disclose their mutual fund holdings and the compensation of top officers. In the Sarbanes-Oxley Act of 2002, the ICI mutual funds were exempt from many of the rules imposed on the rest of the financial industry.[61]

Prior to the scandals, the SEC did not pressure the mutual funds to adopt counter-arbitrage strategies. In a 2001 letter to the Investment Company Institute, the SEC had emphasized that fair valuation was a requirement if it was determined that a significant event had altered the price of a foreign security after the market had closed, but it left funds considerable latitude to determine whether significant events had occurred and what was the appropriate method of fair valuation.[62] However, this power was rarely exercised by mutual funds. Zitzewitz found that most international funds did not have a single fair valuation from May 2001 to September 2002 even though it was a period of considerably market volatility. The implication is that enough managers were content to condone market timing because it furthered their interests, in spite of the general awareness of NAV predictability and the effects of dilution. Zitzewitz suggested that the SEC was restrained from more vigorously tackling market timing because it was the subject of political pressure from the mutual funds industry, a large political donor.

Even when the SEC received a budget increase in 2002, there was no specific request to increase the inspections office. It is widely believed that the SEC was chronically understaffed. Fund inspections typically occurred every five years. Because of limited resources, they were not comprehensive, and none of the trading abuses at the heart of the scandal were found in these examinations. In 2002,

[59] Tom Lauricella, Deborah Solomon, and Gregory Zuckerman, "Mutual Funds Face Overhaul As Spitzer and SEC Fight for Turf," *Wall Street Journal* (October 31, 2003), p. A1 and A7.

[60] Stephen Labaton, "SEC's Oversight of Mutual Funds Is Said to be Lax," *New York Times* (November 16, 2003), p. A1.

[61] Labaton, p.A1 and A32.

[62] Zitzewitz, p. 273.

responding to the other scandals, the SEC had its budget increased and it hired more employees, many of whom were scheduled to work on mutual funds. The scandals and consequent pursuit of criminal and civil charges by state attorneys general and the SEC against errant managers has helped to reinvigorate SEC oversight, improved by a large budget increase. Combined with changes in governance and trading rules, these developments will help to limit late trading and market timing and the loss of mutual fund holder wealth.

Conclusion

The scandals of the mutual fund industry have arisen from the exploitation of conflicts of interest by mutual fund managers and sponsoring institutions. The industry has been enormously successful in providing a vehicle that has permitted a majority of American households to invest in securities, and caution needs to be exercised when introducing remedies.

There is no single remedy that will reduce or eliminate the dilution of shareholder value from late trading and market timing arbitrage that exploit stale pricing of mutual funds. Central to controlling these types of arbitrage is the reform of mutual fund governance. Although critics have been skeptical about the ability of boards of directors to protect investors' interests, empirical evidence shows that more independent boards have taken the initiative and have applied remedies to limit costly arbitrage. The proposed SEC reforms to increase board independence are a step in the right direction. To more closely align managers' incentive with shareholders, the newly invigorated boards may consider the replacement of management contracts that set compensation as a percentage of total assets with contracts that reward the achievement of high risk-adjusted returns. These are relatively new types of contracts and experimentation will help develop optimal contracts. Efforts to increase transparency and investor awareness of expenses and other features of mutual funds should improve investors' ability to select funds, although the tournament feature of mutual funds' competition is unlikely to disappear.

Given that the fundamental character of mutual fund trading at 4 P.M. at fixed NAV prices will remain unchanged, hardening the 4 P.M. deadline—backed by more careful monitoring by management and directors—should eliminate most late trading. A clearing house should help to mitigate the costs imposed on investors of earlier delivery of orders. The problem of market timing is more intractable given the nature of mutual fund pricing. The ideal would be to employ fair-value pricing when the true value of securities is not mirrored in the available 4 P.M. prices; however, precise fair-value pricing is difficult to put into effect because its application requires some discretion in the choice of method and when to intervene. The most likely outcome will be more widespread use of partial fair-value pricing to limit the greatest arbitrage opportunities. Redemption fees or limits on redemptions would not be a first choice if fair-value pricing were easy to employ, as they impose costs on all mutual fund investors and reduce the attractiveness of mutual funds. The 2 percent redemption fee may become a standard, in spite of its costs, but higher fees should be resisted; and if readily applicable fair-value pricing methods can be developed, fees could be reduced. Taken together, these reforms can provide better protection of investors from the predations of late trading and market timing.